AN
IMPROBABLE
LIFE

PRAISE FOR *AN IMPROBABLE LIFE*

"A must-read for any leader with a vision for exponential growth. Sankar Sewnauth takes you on his journey from immigrant to employee to CEO. What begins as a one-dimensional business failing financially, under Sankar's leadership, becomes a multifaceted powerhouse creating new businesses, innovative models of service, and never-before-achieved successes. If you want to learn how to grow your business tenfold or even a hundredfold without ever losing sight of the vision, then read *Improbable Journey*. This could be the most important book you read this year."

— Mark S. Peterson
President, Center for Serving Leadership

"Reading this biography has been nothing short of transformative. Sankar gives us a front-row seat as he tells his incredibly authentic story, beginning in a humble and challenging environment of a third-world country, to achieving amazing success in the United States. His life is a beacon of hope, a testament to the power of resilience and determination. Through his remarkable experiences, Sankar imparts profound wisdom that resonates deeply with readers from all walks of life. His story is not just one of personal triumph, but a reflection of the values that shaped him—perseverance, humility, and integrity. As a family man, his unwavering commitment to those he loves serves as a powerful reminder of the importance of roots and the bonds that guide us forward, even in the face of challenges. What stands out most is his talent for leadership. From his early years to becoming a guiding force in his community, Sankar is an intrepid leader whose decisions have inspired countless individuals. His accounting of his life story conveys the essence of what it is to overcome and succeed, making him a role model for anyone striving to leave a lasting impact on the world."

— Andy Lopez-Williams, PhD, ABPP
Clinical and Forensic Neuropsychologist
President and CEO, ADHD & Autism Psychological Services
and Advocacy

"Many years ago, I had the privilege of working for Governor Hugh Carey, who committed New York to fundamentally transform the way it cared for people with intellectual and developmental disabilities. Now, 50 years later, the state's large, highly problematic institutions have been replaced by an extensive network of voluntary, nonprofit home- and community-based service organizations that evolved due to the extraordinary leadership of a small number of talented individuals who dedicated their lives to helping others. There is no better example of that leadership than Sankar Sewnauth.

"With the support of parents, family members, and volunteers, Sankar led CDS Monarch's transition from a small advocacy agency into one of the state's premier nonprofit organizations, making sure that everyone, regardless of their disabling conditions, has opportunities to achieve their fullest potential. Sankar's story of his journey from immigrant to CEO is inspiring, offering a meaningful philosophy of life and practical lessons for managerial success."

— James Introne
Sachs Policy Group

"There is a time in later life for self-reflection. As I proceed through my seventh decade of life, the most valuable of these recollections are about the people we have shared our lives with. For me, one of the most special of these people is Sankar Sewnauth. We are an unlikely pair. He is from South America and of Indian heritage. Me, from a Polish Ghetto in a small town in upstate New York. We met later in life, and we were both devoted to making a difference in life for people who are especially challenged by what are labeled as 'developmental disabilities.' For many years, I was CEO of one of the nation's largest regional systems for service to such individuals, and Sankar was CEO of a large nonprofit organization founded by parents to develop real opportunities for their children to live in community with everyone else rather than in isolated, huge, and not-so-nice institutions. He and I worked closely together as colleagues and close friends on this mission. I have never known anyone with more commitment, steadfastness, and personal zeal than Sankar. He has beaten the odds throughout the years and will continue to do so with the success of publication of his personal story!"

— Sylvester "Sy" Zielinski
Director of OMRDD's DDSO, Retired

"Sankar's story is a compelling read that defines the word, 'American.' His is an uplifting American story about hard work, faith, and family. *An Improbable Life: An Immigrant's Journey to CEO and the American Dream* is about remarkable leadership, perseverance, and enormous resilience. At every step of his incredible life's journey, regardless of his situation, he consistently demonstrated the charisma to build teams in the pursuit of opportunity. He always maintained a positive outlook on the future—always looking forward to the next challenge and objective, whether that involved his family's well-being and growth, business opportunities, or community initiatives. Sankar Sewnauth's story reveals a confident leader and patriot who achieved the 'American Dream' in every sense of the word. His life is a testament to freedom, opportunity, and the country he loves dearly—America!"

— Robert Dail
US Army Lieutenant General, Retired

"Everyone has dreams. That said, many dreams remain unfulfilled because the dreamer doesn't have the determination and persistence to make their dreams come true. Sankar Sewnauth is *not* one of those people. His journey is the story of making a dream come true—living the 'American Dream.' Throughout his quest, he encountered obstacles and challenges that would have defeated those without true courage and fierce determination. Sankar refused to be deterred by the risks of immigration, discrimination, and bias against people of color. Instead, he triumphed over adversity, uplifting others along the way. He is an inspiration to become what we all dream to be–a caring person of character who sets the example by deeds, not words. His life is about personhood at its best, and all who have known Sankar Sewnauth are better people for it."

— Robert Mixon
US Army Major General, Retired

"As I look at the extraordinary life Sankar Sewnauth has lived, two quotes come to mind: Margaret Mead said, 'Never doubt that a small group of thoughtful, committed citizens can change the world.' And Robert F. Kennedy remarked, 'Some people see things as they are and ask "Why?" I dream things that never were and ask "Why not?"' Not trapped by the limits of the ways things were done in the past, Sankar has transformed how providers partner with individuals with intellectual and developmental challenges, as well as how these providers operate. He instills individual dignity and choice at the center of everything he touches and has impacted countless lives in both large and small ways—the true measure of what is profound. Sankar has changed me—both deepening and widening my sense of what is necessary and what is possible. His story will touch you as it has touched me."

— Edward Myers Hayes
President and CEO, Cayuga Centers

"Sankar's leadership and vision were a driving force in the expansion of CDS Life Transitions and its mission of helping persons with disabilities to lead fulfilling and independent lives. When hazards blocked the way, Sankar persevered and never strayed from the course. Thousands have benefited from his leadership. They are not only the individuals served by the organization, but also those like myself who, as a director, served alongside him and saw him in action."

— Greg Gribben
Woods Oviatt Gilman, LLP

"I first met Sankar in 2009, and over the years, I've had the privilege of witnessing his journey of building a life centered on a remarkable family and a transformative career at CDS. His story, from arriving in the United States at a young age to leading CDS Life Transitions, centered in Rochester, New York, into becoming a significant health care brand on the East Coast, is nothing short of inspiring. His deep commitment to both his family and loved ones and his professional mission to improve the lives of others is evident in everything he does. He demonstrates true leadership and a unique ability to pave the way for meaningful change in the health care industry. Sankar is a testament to the power of perseverance, vision, and heart, and I am honored to call him both a friend and colleague."

— Jennifer Carlson, MPA
President and CEO, Finger Lakes Area Counseling & Recovery Agency

"I've had the pleasure of knowing and working with Sankar Sewnauth as outside legal counsel, board member, and corporate officer for almost 30 years. Under his leadership, CDS transformed from an organization with about a dozen group homes into a multifaceted organization. Yet, as milestones were reached, he always highlighted contributions of the CDS staff and never mentioned his pivotal contribution. Sankar's humility as a CEO models President Harry S. Truman's observation that: 'It is amazing what you can accomplish if you do not care who gets the credit.'

"The exponential growth of CDS was a result of Sankar's unwavering commitment that all the individuals served by CDS have their needs met. When he noticed many older individuals served by CDS lacked parents or guardians, the CDS Guardianship Program was created to ensure them court-appointed guardians. Demand for affordable housing and long-term care for senior citizens appeared, and he spearheaded programs to address those needs. Responding to a backlog of demand for veteran services, he established the Warrior Salute Veteran Services program to provide comprehensive support to these heroes. I also know Sankar on a personal level. He is caring, compassionate, and empathetic, and exhibits the highest integrity."

— Rich Yarmel, Esq.
Harter Secrest & Emery LLP

AN IMPROBABLE LIFE

An Immigrant's Journey to
CEO and the American Dream

SANKAR SEWNAUTH

Copyright © 2025, Sankar Sewnauth

All rights reserved. No part of this book may be used or reproduced by any means, graphic, electronic, or mechanical (including any information storage retrieval system) without the express written permission from the author, except in the case of brief quotations for use in articles and reviews wherein appropriate attribution of the source is made.

Publishing support provided by
Ignite Press
55 Shaw Ave. Suite 204
Clovis, CA 93612
www.IgnitePress.us

ISBN: 979-8-9928389-0-9
ISBN: 979-8-9928389-1-6 (E-book)

For bulk purchases and for booking, contact:

Sankar Sewnauth
sdsmgmtllc.com
sdsconsultingservices.com

Because of the dynamic nature of the internet, web addresses or links contained in this book may have been changed since publication and may no longer be valid. The content of this book and all expressed opinions are those of the author and do not reflect the publisher or the publishing team. The author is solely responsible for all content included herein.

Library of Congress Control Number: 2025903958

Cover design by Usman Tariq
Edited by Cathy Cruise
Interior design by Jetlaunch

FIRST EDITION

DEDICATION

There are so many people who joined me in this improbable life, but the one who has stood by me through "thick and thin" has been my wife, Yvonne. When I go to bed every night I thank God for her love, strength, patience, and caring. My life has been made so much more fulfilling and richer having her beside me. Yvonne has been with me every step of the way as I dealt with the most serious medical issues and the many challenges that came with the CEO position at CDS. She stood by me during those decision points that changed our lives forever. I am forever grateful for her love and friendship.

To my children, Abigayle and Andrew, I want to let you know that you mean the world to me. You have both grown up to be good citizens, caring about others and finding ways to participate in our community. Your mom and I could not ask for more. We are very proud of you.

To our precious grandchildren, David, Caleb, Lily, and Hayley, this book is dedicated to you. I am forever changed by your unbounded love for you "Papa." Your "Gamma" and I treasure our time with you.

To my parents, Sewnauth and Shiela Mangar, I pay homage to you for providing the means for your children to have a great education growing up in Guyana. You sacrificed your personal happiness for us. Then, when our father died, it was our mother who continued to take care of her children and provided the means for all of us to leave Guyana. To my sister Indro, who is no longer with us, for sponsoring us to emigrate to America, and to my brother, Devo, who made all the flight arrangements and provided for us in the early days, I say "thank you." I must mention Sabita for her care and support. I am forever grateful for her keeping a keen eye on her siblings throughout our lives. We all have done all we can throughout our lives to make our parents proud.

My life was forever transformed when I was introduced to people with intellectual and developmental disabilities. For 33 years, helping them achieve their personal American dreams has been a most fulfilling journey for me. I am grateful for them allowing me to play a part in their lives. I will always remember their trust, kindness, and love. Serving them has been the honor of my life. To our veterans who sacrificed for us and suffer from PTSD and related illness, providing the Nucor House and the support you need to regain your lives was the least I could do. Thank you for your sacrifice and service. To people with chronic illnesses and families who need affordable housing, it was my privilege to help you get what you need. And to the Board members and employees, past and current, who dedicated yourselves to the CDS mission, thank you.

This book is dedicated to all of you.

TABLE OF CONTENTS

Foreword by Cenette Burdine xvii
Introduction xxi

Part I: Matters of the Heart 1
   Chapter 1: *Why Are You Here?* 3
   Chapter 2: *Medical Crisis* 12
   Chapter 3: *Improbable Birth* 17
   Chapter 4: *Grief and Redemption* 21
   Chapter 5: *Coming to America—The Pay Stub* 29
   Chapter 6: *Never Giving Up—Yvonne and I on Our
                      Journey Together* 37
   Chapter 7: *Proud to Be an American* 42

Part II: Hard Work and the American Dream 49
   Chapter 8: *A New Start at Arc Residence* 51
   Chapter 9: *Building a Career* 56
   Chapter 10: *Capacity Meets Opportunity* 59
   Chapter 11: *Moving Up—Coming to CDS* 63
   Chapter 12: *CDS Takes Another Risk Without Preparation* . . . 73
   Chapter 13: *Making a Difference* 78
   Chapter 14: *Self-Improvement* 81
   Chapter 15: *Company in Crisis* 85

Chapter 16: *New and Brief Beginnings*................89

Chapter 17: *Good Luck*.............................95

Chapter 18: *Becoming CEO*........................101

Chapter 19: *The Rumor Mill* 112

Chapter 20: *Second Chances*......................118

Chapter 21: *Light at the End of the Tunnel* 121

Chapter 22: *The Turnaround*......................125

Part III: Momentous Decisions.....................129

Chapter 23: *A New Beginning*.....................131

Chapter 24: *Strategy and Innovation—Unistel's Rebirth* 134

Chapter 25: *The Right Hire at the Right Time*....138

Chapter 26: *Rebuilding at the Top*...............140

Chapter 27: *Giving My Children Opportunity*......145

Chapter 28: *An Error Provides an Opening* 148

Chapter 29: *Grand Opening*.......................155

Chapter 30: *CDS Monarch vs. Newsletter* 160

Chapter 31: *Innovation in Housing*...............165

Chapter 32: *I Will Find a Way* 171

Chapter 33: *CDS Managed Care Comes to Upstate New York* ..174

Chapter 34: *Getting into the Insurance Business* 177

Chapter 35: *Protecting the Spice Business Long Term*......183

Chapter 36: *Warrior Salute Veterans Services Comes to CDS* ..187

Chapter 37: *Spice Business Pivots to Asia* 198

Chapter 38: *Having Fun: Wanting a Fair Deal*.....208

Chapter 39: *In and Out of Consolidation* 211

Chapter 40: *An Education in Business Dealings* ..218

Chapter 41: *A Great Opportunity*.................222

Chapter 42: *Going off Course* 224

Part IV: Collateral Arteries 227

Chapter 43: *How I Turned Down a Once-in-a-Lifetime Offer—Overseeing an $8 Billion Budget* 229

Chapter 44: *Determination* 234

Chapter 45: *Collateral Arteries* 238

Chapter 46: *CDS Intervenes* 242

Chapter 47: *The Right Place at the Right Time* 245

Chapter 48: *COVID Response* 248

Chapter 49: *Hard Decisions* 252

Conclusion 259

Review Inquiry 265

Will You Share the Love? 267

Would You Like Sankar Sewnauth to Speak to Your Organization? 269

Acknowledgments 271

Coda: Never Give Up 275

About the Author 279

FOREWORD

I first met Sankar Sewnauth in 2012 when I was hired as a consultant by an organized collaborative of more than 50 regional health care and nonprofit service providers. CDS Monarch was among these organizations, and Sankar was its CEO. Not one to wait and follow, as you will soon discover in the reading, Sankar invited me to work with him, his leadership team, and the board of directors to develop business strategies for CDS Monarch. And so began a long, lasting, and rewarding relationship.

My time with Sankar has spanned more than a decade of contemplating and strategizing, launching new initiatives, having thoughtful conversations, and planning for his retirement succession. These engagements have often culminated in high points of honor for me, such as this one, reflecting on my friend and the account of his remarkable journey.

In Sankar's words, you will glimpse his humble beginnings, growing up in a small village in the South American country of Guyana, further educated in the island country of Trinidad, and making his way along an uncertain path to the United States. Once in America, Sankar found employment and worked in many entry-level jobs, from New York City to Boston and, eventually, to Overland Park, Kansas, where he landed a full-time position as a production worker in a Coca-Cola plant. He eagerly traveled back to Guyana to marry his betrothed, Yvonne. Once she was granted entry into the US, they would soon begin building a life together, starting a family, and raising their two children, Abigayle and Andrew. The future was promising for a motivated young immigrant determined to prosper and provide for his family in this new land of opportunity.

Sankar would not squander a minute of his rise from the frontlines of direct care to the executive helm of what is now known as CDS Life Transitions—a formidable $300 million enterprise committed to enriching the lives of some of our most vulnerable citizens. His success is emblazoned with mission-driven purpose, pushing forward with high expectations of himself and everyone around him. Expect directness and authentic praise from Sankar, always knowing where you stand with him . . . like it or not. He appreciates recognition, but would rather have the focus on the team. And he is quick to give thanks and credit where credit is due. He is collegial, social, and the consummate host. He enjoys group celebrations and gatherings and prefers making others feel special for their earnest contributions.

In my observation and experience, Sankar has a strong inclination toward influence and action. He understands and aptly utilizes people's strengths, and values the insights, energy, and resourcefulness they bring to prudent decision-making and getting things done. He holds competence and initiative, loyalty and commitment, and excellence and hard work in high regard.

He is shrewd in his business dealings and in managing important relationships; his strategic thinking is matched only by his notable intuition . . . I am convinced he can see around corners! He will also, without much hesitation, make the tough and necessary decisions even when knowing the outcomes may be difficult to bear.

The above are characteristics that have earned Sankar respect and admiration from myriad others. He is perfect by no means, making his share of mistakes, but as once stated by the CDS Life Transitions board chair, "Sankar is a once-in-a-lifetime leader." Finally, you may not be surprised to learn that Sankar was once asked by New York State officials to run the Office for People with Developmental Disabilities (OPWDD) and its $8 billlion bureaucracy. What a befitting career capstone, if only the timing had been right.

Having sat with Sankar on many occasions to read, review, and discuss the content and writing of his book, I would summarize its core message and sentiment in the following ways: If not for the grace of God, luck and serendipity, pivotal and defining moments, bold asks and big decisions, guardian angels and forsaken demons—as Sankar once pointed out with his impressive self-awareness in its paradoxical complex simplicity—events could have gone another way . . .

Instead, in the pages ahead, you will find this book to be a story of stories that will entertain, inspire faith and courage, promote taking chances and pushing boundaries, and encourage pursuit of dreams undeterred by disappointments and frustrations, fears and insecurities, conflicts and challenges, and mistakes and setbacks. My favorite passages depict the innate ability of Sankar to reframe what appears to be an insurmountable obstacle or unattainable remedy. He demonstrates over and over again that longshots are possible with the right question at the right time, with unassailable resilience and persistence, and by not taking an unconditional no for the final answer.

Sankar is not one to steep in self-indulgence, self-pity, or regrets (at least not for long); he seeks to forgive, be better, and do better, and have others do the same. This is articulated in his lessons learned and revealed in the telling of an unpredictable odyssey of personal and professional triumphs.

As you reach the final page of this book, rest assured this is not the end of the story. Count on Sankar to be forever driven by a yearning for more—more in his love of God, family, and friends; in his quest for a purpose to fruition; and in his improbable life well-lived. I, personally, am blessed to have met Sankar many years ago, to have worked and journeyed with him for more than a decade, and to continue calling him an admired colleague and trusted friend for the years ahead. With a proverbial glass raised high, I hope you will join me in saying . . . here's to you, Sankar. Bravo!

Happy reading to all,
Cenette Burdine
President and Founder, Burdine and Company, LLC

INTRODUCTION

While writing this book, I read *Elon Musk,* Walter Isaacson's biography of Elon Musk. His relentless work ethic, troubled childhood, and triumphant immigrant story felt familiar to me. I related to how Musk was often misunderstood because of his apparent gruffness. For many years, my bluntness and tendency to be strictly business, which are strengths from my Indian and Guyanese cultural heritage, have been misinterpreted as a lack of heart. Mostly, I noticed Musk's drive to push humanity to be better. This book chronicles my more modest attempts to do so as CEO of a not-for-profit that supports individuals with intellectual and developmental disabilities and other vulnerable individuals—maintaining standards of excellence in a sustainable, systemic manner.

When people ask me how I grew CDS Life Transitions from a $16 million annual budget to $300 million, I relate the journey to my collateral arteries, a fairly recent revelation, where my heart healed itself just when I thought I was at the end of the road. Just as my heart grew new arteries around those with blockages to form new connections, as CDS' CEO, I too grew my alliances and my resilience by consistently taking risks, working hard, and refusing to take no for an answer. I discovered the news of my collateral arteries as I faced what seemed like imminent open-heart surgery. Then the most providential events changed the course of my life, as they so often had before.

This book contains many such stories when I beat improbable odds, both professionally and personally. Being an immigrant to the

US from the third world, I've always considered myself an underdog. But in writing this book, my close friend and confidante, Dr. Joel Haas, provided another perspective. He said, "Sankar, there was so much suffering in your life journey." I had never thought of it that way. To me, suffering was a part of life. Then again, nothing worth having in this life comes easy. I recalled a study of executives of major US corporations I came across many years ago. One of the key takeaways was that they all endured personal suffering.

Looking back in history to people who were significantly accomplished and attained worldwide recognition and honor, they all had a thread of some personal suffering and growth; names that come to mind are Mahatma Gandhi, Mother Teresa, Nelson Mandela, and Martin Luther King Jr. They sacrificed so much more. I could never compare my life or my difficulties to theirs. Yet sacrifices must be made, and one's journey is enriched by suffering. In every religion, people's closeness to God is defined by the level of suffering.

From personal experience, I believe that everyone has an obligation to do their very best despite their circumstances. Further, I believe that God put all of us on the earth for a purpose. Everyone makes mistakes, and you'll discover plenty of mine in the coming chapters. You'll read about my personal challenges and the challenges we faced at CDS when I became the CEO. I've never tried to portray either myself or CDS as a victim, so the word "suffering" never occurred to me. *How could it when providence is so evident in my life story?*

Tomorrow brings opportunities for more mistakes and successes. I have faced obstacles and challenges but, in the end, I had to decide my future. I believe you define who you are—and the quality of your life—by the choices you make moment to moment. I often say: "You can only deal with what's in front of you." When life breaks your heart, you may become a victim and feel sorry for yourself, or you may "take the bull by the horns" and forge a new path. I think of it as new collateral arteries.

Hopefully, this book will appeal to people interested in an immigrant story. Mine is another version of what immigrants experience when they arrive in the United States. For anyone struggling to recognize how good life can be, this book shows you how—with courage, purpose, determination and know-how—you can rise above your personal difficulties and achieve success. To those who aspire to positions of higher authority and responsibility, I impart to you much of what I learned throughout my life and in my leadership at CDS Life Transitions. With hard work and a big heart, you can achieve anything, no matter how improbable it seems.

The book is full of stories about my life, within which are life and leadership lessons. By engaging the reader on a personal level, I hope you will walk with me as I tell my story. Along the way, you'll discover examples of persistence, dedication, perseverance, courage, determination, initiative, and faith, which have defined my life.

An Improbable Life: An Immigrant's Journey to CEO and the American Dream is written in four parts. "PART I: Matters of the Heart" opens with three near-death experiences: a frightening heart angiogram in 2019; open-heart surgery in 2002; and grave illness as an infant. Then I recount my years growing up in Guyana, my time in Trinidad attending college, and my arrival to the United States. "PART II: Hard Work and the American Dream" describes my uphill journey to find myself and to discover what America had to offer me. I enter the intellectual and developmental disabilities (IDD) field at the ground level and work my way to CEO of CDS—then an organization in crisis, the stress of which leads to my medical crisis in 2002. "PART III: Momentous Decisions" begins with my new lease on life following heart bypass surgery. I gain influential allies at the State level and the Rochester business community. These alliances help me innovate and exponentially grow CDS amidst daily challenges, an unexpected lawsuit, changing federal and state regulations, and local objections to CDS's expansion of mission. "PART IV: Collateral Arteries" chronicles a providential "curveball" to my heart health concerns and my biggest feat.

Part I

MATTERS OF THE HEART

The first three chapters of Part I chronicle three near-death experiences: my frightening heart angiogram in 2019; open-heart surgery in 2002; and grave illness as an infant. Then you read about my years growing up in Guyana, my time in Trinidad attending college, and my arrival in the United States with my family. *How far we had come*. I look back at my journey from the third world with its ups and downs, and within them, all the good things that happened. Part I ends with relocating my wife and two small children from Olathe, Kansas, to Rochester, New York, where I struggle to find employment for months. In a series of improbable events, within weeks of resorting to food stamps to feed my family, I find my first job in the IDD field as a residence manager making $5.25 an hour.

1
WHY ARE YOU HERE?

"WHY ARE YOU here?" Dr. Ling Ong asked. The heart surgeon towered over me, his face perplexed, as if to say, *I know you have some serious issues, but I don't know why you're on my operating table.* To me, the question had broader philosophical implications.

It was the year 2019. I laid on the operating table in Rochester General Hospital where Dr. Ong was performing an angiogram of my heart. Seventeen years earlier, at age 46, I underwent open heart bypass surgery, where a vein from my left leg was repurposed to bypass five blocked arteries. In 2015, I developed more blockages, and Dr. Ong inserted stents in two arteries. The likelihood I needed more stents was high. Thoughts of my mortality were inescapable.

A couple of months earlier, I noticed some tightness in my chest. This became pronounced when my wife, Yvonne, and I were on holiday in Boothbay Harbor, Maine, a quaint little fishing village about an hour's drive from Portland, Maine. We usually stayed at Ocean Point Inn, our favorite ocean-front resort where we'd vacationed for the last nine years. Rustic and beautiful, the resort spread along the coast. This was the perfect place to take walks and sit by the ocean and read, one of my favorite pastimes—a relaxing getaway from my demanding and stressful job as CEO of CDS Life Transitions.

By 2019, CDS Life Transitions was the largest nonprofit organization, next to the hospitals, in upstate New York. Its annual budget had grown over my tenure from $16 million in 1998 to about $300 million in 2019. Together, CDS Life Transitions and its affiliate organizations had 1,200 employees serving about 15,000 people across upstate New York.

Until my heart bypass surgery in 2002, I had neglected my health as I worked nonstop to build the organization and support my family. Following the surgery, I was determined to keep my heart conditioned and my overall health in good shape. I exercised at least five days a week, augmenting my exercise regime by watching my diet, taking supplements in addition to my routine medications, and doing everything I could to maintain good health. What helped the most was making key adjustments to my approach to my job. For example, I spent more time on community outreach and cultivating donors, and allowed my staff to take care of the day-to-day operations. This relieved me of the day to day stresses and allowed me to focus on the big picture issues.

I paid attention to what the doctors advised; as a disciplined person with a bit of undiagnosed obsessive-compulsive disorder, I thrived under a strict regimen. One piece of advice to reduce stress was taking time off. The nine-hour drive each way from Rochester to Boothbay Harbor and back was worth it to me. We'd arrive in a place that made me feel like nothing else in the world mattered. There, I felt totally isolated and free from the day-to-day stresses of my job.

As the time to commit to our latest trip to Boothbay Harbor approached, I felt under the weather. I just didn't have enough energy and felt lethargic. I feared the stress of the nine-hour drive, particularly since I was recovering from a neck fusion surgery, which I had in January that year. Yvonne, who loved Boothbay Harbor as much as I did, thought differently. Although I wasn't feeling well, she urged me to make the trip. I was not convinced. One night, as we were sitting in our family room watching television, she turned to me and said, "I know you don't want to go. But why don't we make the trip to Boothbay Harbor? It might get your mind off things.

Who knows? You might feel better." I loved Boothbay Harbor, and Yvonne's nudging was all I needed to change my mind. So we made the arrangements and drove to Maine.

On the way, we stopped at Red's Eats, a little food shack on the side of the road in Wiscasset, the last town before entering the Boothbay Harbor area. I'd seen the eatery featured on an episode of *Bizarre Foods* with Andrew Zimmerman. Red's Eats specialized in world-famous lobster rolls; every roll included about a pound and a quarter of lobster meat overstuffed in an open toasted bun. One had to be careful not to pick up the roll right away because it was impossible to fit it in your mouth. I found it best to use a fork and slowly pick off the excess meat, dunk it in warm melted butter, and devour it until I could pick the roll up and stuff it in my mouth. This yearly experience attracted visitors from all over the world.

We all felt the same. Every time, we'd wait in line for about an hour before reaching the counter to place an order with the owner, Debbie. It was so amazing to talk to total strangers in the line as if we were best friends and neighbors, all because we had one thing in common, Lobster Rolls. As always, Debbie greeted us warmly like old friends, saying, "Thank you for coming to visit us *again*. What are you having today?" Over the years, Debbie remembered us as her loyal customers and would always throw in something extra in our order. This time she gave us an order of fried jumbo scallops "on the house," along with our four lobster rolls, a bucket of fried clams, two crab cakes, and one orange soda with ice cream for Yvonne. With all that food, we enjoyed a delicious late lunch, with leftovers for dinner that night in our room at Ocean Point Inn. We couldn't wait to visit our favorite spots along the rocky coast.

The next morning, Yvonne and I had a very nice breakfast of pancakes, french toast, bacon and eggs, and fresh aromatic coffee. Then we decided to go for a walk, which we usually did every morning on these trips. We took off at a brisk pace, enjoying the blue sky and the ocean's hypnotic cadence. About a quarter of a mile out, I felt a tightening in my chest. I stopped to take a breath and then I slowed my pace down a little. I didn't mention it to Yvonne until after the half-hour walk, once the tightness went away. Back at the resort, we discussed the episode, recognizing it was probably the cause of my lethargy. We agreed that I wouldn't overexert myself, and we would enjoy our time at Ocean Point Inn. However, I called the office of my cardiologist, Dr. Matthews, and scheduled an appointment soon after we returned to Rochester. The rest of the trip was very enjoyable. We felt rested and finally it was time to face the nine hour drive back home. Anxiety crept as I thought of the upcoming appointment with Dr. Matthews.

On the day of the appointment, I had a cardiac ultrasound test in Dr. Matthews's office. Then we sat together and reviewed the images. He was of East Indian descent, short in stature, like me, and we were around the same age; but unlike me, he appeared physically fit. He spoke with a forceful and authoritative voice, yet it was with clarity and care, putting me at ease, as he had over the 17 years since my heart bypass surgery.

Unfortunately, the ultrasound didn't show whether my arteries were blocked or not. Dr. Matthews strongly recommended that I undergo a nuclear stress test which would show how blood flowed to the heart at rest and during exercise, often detecting areas of poor blood flow or damage in the heart. This made sense, not that I had room to argue. The test was promptly scheduled for the following Monday morning.

I completed the stress test without incident, which involved walking 15 minutes on a treadmill. Afterward, the technician suggested that I sit in the waiting room to allow my heart to slow down. Meanwhile, the images from the test were reviewed. Expecting the stress test to show blockages, I was on edge. I anticipated the doctors telling me that I needed to undergo another bypass surgery. However, I kept reminding myself that I had to remain calm and rely on my doctors to provide their best clinical judgment.

Fifteen minutes later, the technician joined me in the waiting room to explain that there was an escalated review of the test because the test showed abnormalities which required further consultation. I was impatient, wanting to get back to work. I needed information, so I pushed forward to inquire about my heart's ejection fraction. The cardiac ejection fraction refers to how much blood the heart pumps out of the left ventricle with each beat. The average ejection fraction for a normal heart is between 55 and 70 percent. From my limited understanding, this would tell me if my heart was functioning well or not. The technician, who had been evasive up to this point, took a deep breath, and then shared that it was 35 percent. I was alarmed. I knew that at that rate, my heart was failing. It was a lot to digest. I needed time to absorb what was shared with me.

To give me the space to think through the ejection fraction news, without even knowing the complete test results, I felt I needed time away from the hospital. So I told the technician I was leaving and asked him to call me after consultation with Dr. Matthews.

As I returned to my car, I thought about the neck fusion surgery I'd had in January. I started to process what just happened. *Am I feeling chest pain because of my heart, or is the heart under stress because of neck fusion surgery earlier that year?* A part of me wanted to believe my chest pain was caused by the neck surgery, which placed severe stress on my heart. I've always thought of it as the "surgery from hell." Dr. Girgis, who performed both my back and neck surgeries, had warned me the pain from the neck fusion surgery would be excruciating immediately following the surgery and the recovery period would be long. He was not kidding. For four days the pain was unbearable. Thankfully, Dr. Joel Haas, the Chief Medical Officer at CDS' Health Plan, iCircle, who had become a close friend, stood by Yvonne and I, providing support night and day.

For months following that surgery, I experienced a very difficult start every morning. Out of bed, I walked around as if I was drunk, stumbling and bouncing along the walls. Unable to lift my feet, I forced myself to drag them. The constant pain in my left hand and weakness in my feet and legs made it very frustrating to maintain balance. I was always reaching for something to hold on to prevent me from falling. I was concerned that with the damage to my spine, the way I moved might not improve. Walking down steps was most difficult. My feet wouldn't cooperate. Once I lifted them up, I felt like I was falling face-forward. It was terrifying.

With my ejection fraction news, I acknowledged that in short order I might be facing my mortality. I reflected on my life. Yvonne and I had a beautiful family—two wonderful children, Abigayle and Andrew, a beautiful daughter-in-law, Emy, and four grandchildren, David, Caleb, Lily, and Hayley, who brought a special joy to our lives. I was enjoying a fulfilling career at CDS. Yvonne and I vacationed regularly, traveling to far-off exotic places, just the two of us, and every year we took time to vacation as a family. At Oak Hill Country Club where I was a member, I enjoyed the company of friends who were dear to me. The prospect of being in a dire health situation put all that into jeopardy. I wondered, *How much time do I have left?* I committed to focus on the great life we had in Penfield.

Finally, a week after the stress test, the appointment with Dr. Matthews arrived. His staff conducted another cardiac ultrasound test, after which we reviewed the results. He told me that the ultrasound showed that my heart's ejection fraction was between 40 to 50 percent of normal. This was good news, even though Dr. Matthews could not explain why my heart had shown a 35 percent ejection fraction only a week prior. He advised me to stop worrying that I might be in imminent danger. I was relieved, taking a deep breath—then it caught in my throat. Dr. Matthews recommended an angiogram, which would show any blockages that could possibly be stented. I could tell that he remained concerned. And that's how I came to be lying on the operating table, hoping Dr. Ong could help.

The night before the angiogram, I tossed and turned. The average length of survival after bypass surgery is 18 years. Seventeen years had passed since the operation, and something new and serious was going on with my heart. I told myself that this might, indeed, be the end of the road. That morning, I got up and read

Psalm 23, recalling every verse and reminding myself of God's steadfastness, as I focused on: "Yea, though I walk through the valley of the shadow of death, I will fear no evil: for thou art with me," followed by Psalm 46:1, "God is our refuge and strength, an ever-present help in trouble." I reminded myself that I wasn't in charge of the situation. I had done the hard work to stay healthy. Now I must trust God and the health professionals. My mind was consumed with what was to come. I felt somewhat subdued and reflective as I went about my morning routine. As I brushed my teeth, took my shower, and changed my clothes, and was ready to make the trip to the hospital, I remained hopeful, telling myself that worry solved nothing.

I asked Yvonne to do the honor and drive me to the hospital. We rode mostly in silence, talking briefly about our life. I reassured her that, regardless of whatever happened, I loved her and I loved our family. There's reassurance that, as human beings, in times of distress our minds resort to what's most important: faith and family.

In the hospital's waiting room, I felt a heightened awareness that I was with others in similar situations. The room was full of children, young people, middle-aged people, and old people, and everyone was there because of pressing medical issues. I couldn't help but empathize and feel a surprising sense of kinship with them. Then I thought perhaps I was on my last visit.

Yvonne and I spent the next two hours talking about everything but the impending angiogram with Dr. Ong. I was overwhelmingly preoccupied by what I expected to come; I just wanted to get the procedure over with and was resigned to what would happen. Beneath the surface, I was restless. As a type A personality, I felt a need to do something, but there was nothing to do. I had to put my care in the hands of the professionals. After my lower back surgery in 2016, followed by neck fusion surgery in early 2019, I needed no explanation that my complex medical issues might likely not be resolved. As I was preoccupied with these thoughts, temporary relief came when the curtain to my waiting room opened, and I was informed that Dr. Ong was ready for the procedure.

After I was wheeled into the operating room, Dr. Ong and I reviewed my medical history. I'd had open-heart surgery in 2002 at the age of 46. At that time, the doctors told me that the vein harvested from my left leg and used to repair my heart was estimated to last 15 to 20 years, and that sure seemed to be the case.

Dr. Ong seemed comfortable with our review and proceeded with the catheterization. He consulted with his assistants; meanwhile, I was lying on the operating table very awake and alert, with the catheter in my left arm. This was my third angiogram. The first was prior to my bypass surgery, and the second was in 2016 when Dr. Ong inserted two stents. Both times I was given an intravenous sedative. Now, with a lower dose of sedative, I was clear-headed as I watched the staff study the monitors, and assumed they were finding blockages and putting in stents. That was not the case.

A few minutes into the procedure, Dr. Ong stopped. He turned to me and said, "We're trying to find a place to put a stent, but I can't find one. Every time I think I have a spot, the stent won't take."

Time seemed to stand still. I laid there just wanting the procedure to be over. They kept saying, "Let's try this" or "Let's try that," and I knew they were doing their best. In the short time I was on the operating table I developed a rapport with one of Dr. Ong's assistants, Julie. She asked about my work and recognized the name of our company. I was very pleased to hear Julie say that she was very familiar with CDS. She told me that everything she heard about CDS was great. She expressed further that CDS took care of Rochester's most vulnerable citizens and it was noble work. I was very pleased to hear that. Julie became my advocate, emphasizing to Dr. Ong that I held a significant position in the community as the CEO of CDS. Dr. Ong seemed sympathetic. He tried for nearly an hour to put a stent in my heart. Then everyone stopped what they were doing. The room grew quiet.

Dr. Ong looked at me with the most disappointed expression. He said, "Sankar, I'm sorry. We couldn't put any stents anywhere. None of the stents would take."

This seemed like the end of the road. I was not prepared to hear these words, which had a tone of finality. Dejected, I said, "OK, Doc, what else can we do?"

"There's nothing to do," he said. "You really need to go talk to your cardiologist."

My mind was in a tailspin, unable to process his reply.

Then he leaned over and asked that most profound question: "Why are you here?"

Why, indeed. *Why was I on his operating table? Why was I, an Indian and Guyanese man, in America—much less in upstate New York—at all?*

2
MEDICAL CRISIS

I FIRST LEARNED of my heart condition in 1989 soon after I joined CDS. I was diagnosed with high blood pressure that I controlled with medication. But it was a struggle. Fueled by the desire and determination to excel, I found life incredibly stressful. I set high demands on myself and those around me. Success meant everything to me. That's how I had gone from a $10,000 annual salary in 1987 to making $100,000 by 1998. While excited about the opportunity to lead an organization, I felt a tenfold rise in stress along with the tenfold increase in pay. In hindsight I could have taken better care of myself, but at the time, with a profound sense of responsibility amidst many crises, I wasn't taking care of my health at all.

Then in March of 2002, everything came to a head. I wasn't feeling well. My blood pressure was extremely high, despite taking medications. I had an upset stomach every night before I went to bed. I was constantly taking antacid tablets. One day I decided not to go to work, which was highly unusual for me. Yvonne went to her part-time job at a grocery store, and I asked her to bring home a rotisserie chicken. Even though I didn't have much of an appetite, as soon as she arrived I cut myself a piece of chicken and brought it to my recliner in the family room. After a few bites, my jaws tightened and pain radiated down both arms. Something was happening that I couldn't control.

I stood and began pacing around the room. The pain in my arms and tightness in my jaws persisted for about 15 minutes. During that time, I called my primary care physician's office. He wasn't immediately available, but soon he returned my call. I explained what happened, although the pain and tightness in my jaw had subsided. He told me to come to his office the very next morning. Clearly, the episode foreshadowed what was to come.

An ECG was performed shortly after arriving at his office. Upon its review, the doctor looked at the nurse and said, "He needs a stress test today. Please find a location where that can be done." After a few minutes, the nurse came back to tell the doctor that she had made several calls, and nothing was available. He was undeterred. He repeated to her, "He needs to have the stress test done today." I felt very fatigued but was relieved that I could find answers to my health situation. Little did I know then that I had suffered a mild heart attack the day before.

Thankfully, the nurse found a same-day opening with a cardiologist at Rochester General Hospital. I drove there by myself, even though there were moments of lightheadedness. I considered calling Yvonne, but didn't want to bother her at work. Upon my arrival at the cardiologist's office, I was quickly hooked up to a monitor and put on the treadmill to do the stress test. I felt a lot of pressure in my chest as the speed and grade on the treadmill increased incrementally. After 15 minutes, the technician stopped the machine and guided me to a table where I could lie down while she did another cardiac ultrasound test. Then I sat with Dr. Matthews to review the results.

He didn't mince words, telling me that the ultrasound test showed that my heart was not functioning properly. He explained further that it was likely that at least two arteries that were blocked needed to be opened with stents via a catheterization procedure. Further, with an urgent tone, he insisted that the procedure be performed immediately. The consultation shifted to me being admitted to the hospital, something I had not thought through. It was very sobering.

Something clearly wasn't right with my heart. Dr. Matthews asked me to contact Yvonne so that she could be there with me for the procedure. Soon she joined me, and I was admitted. But the procedure would have to be performed the next morning. Yvonne couldn't stay with me. She had two kids to look after.

The next morning, Yvonne returned to my side. In preparation for the surgery, I was satisfied with the surgeon's explanation of how he would perform the angiogram. He intended to examine the health of the blood vessels and the flow of blood through them, and then he would place the stents where needed. I declined the option of being awake during the procedure. I was not a fan of watching the catheter travel from a vein in my groin to my heart. The procedure began. I was under general anesthesia for 45 minutes.

I awoke with Yvonne at my side and the surgeon leaning over me with a very sober and concerned facial expression. He explained very apologetically that he was unable to put any stents into my heart because of significant blockages. Stents weren't the answer. He recommended a heart bypass operation. My eyes widened and my mouth went dry as he explained that my chest would be split open and a vein from my foot would be harvested and used to replace the blocked arteries.

"I'm disappointed," I said, at a complete loss of what else to say. My mouth felt like it was full of sand.

The surgeon was resolute in his decision, even though he was sympathetic to what I said. After he left the room, Yvonne and I discussed the situation. I was furious. I had read about heart bypass surgery, and what stood out to me was the life expectancy of the harvested veins. I was 46 years old. In 15 to 20 years I would still be in the prime of my life. I was looking ahead and seeing only the finality of bypass surgery. Yet I knew I could not ignore my current situation. Yvonne offered her opinion. "You should trust the surgeon," she said. Throughout our marriage, like a child, I tended to do the opposite of what she told me to do. That moment was not one of them. It seemed surgery was the only rational decision.

I moaned, "From the looks of it, I'm not leaving the hospital." By late evening, I was admitted to a semiprivate room. There were no available private rooms, something I desperately wanted. Yvonne brought me some items from home and settled into the chair by my bedside. Shortly thereafter, Dr. Matthews's nurse practitioner, Terri, visited me to convey his message that he agreed with the surgeon. As she was speaking, a doctor knocked on the door and entered. Terri greeted him warmly. He introduced himself as Dr. David Cheerin. He was a renowned and gifted cardiovascular surgeon at Rochester General Hospital who worked closely with Dr. Matthews. Dr. Cheerin explained that he would likely need to bypass at least four blocked arteries—*a quadruple bypass.*

I was still having difficulty accepting the prospect of having a procedure where my chest was cut open, my heart was stopped, and new arteries were attached. It was a terrifying prospect. Taking it all in, I asked when this procedure could be done. He said that, at the earliest, he could do it sometime the following week. It was Tuesday, and I'd have to wait until the following week? Impatience kicked in. I thought I was already approaching the deep end of the pool. It was time to sink or swim. *If I need this surgery, I won't wait.* Everyone could see my frustration.

Terri left the room. Soon she returned and handed her cell phone to Dr. Cheerin. She said, "Dr. Matthews would like to speak with you."

After the call, Dr. Cheerin turned to me and said that his schedule had changed and he could move up the surgery to Thursday, two days away. Nice guy. It did put me at ease. By then I just wanted to get the surgery over with.

Yvonne and I had a long and heart-wrenching discussion. We had surely had a challenging journey so far. Life was not easy, but we kept our heads down and did our part. We had two beautiful children. We had a beautiful home in Penfield. Through determination and perseverance I had made my way to the top of CDS as its CEO. Life was good. Now our future together as husband and wife, as well as our family's future, was suddenly at risk. But there was no other option. We both accepted that I needed to have the surgery.

We then decided to inform our family. Yvonne contacted her parents and siblings. I shared the news with my four siblings. I was moved that they wanted to come and be with me for the surgery. My brother-in-law, Rick, who was husband to Shelly, Yvonne's younger sister, and lived in Tampa, immediately made plans to be with me as well. When my only person left to call was my mother (Mama), I was overcome with emotion. I was surprised that I wanted Mama's assurance that everything would be OK. With every fiber of my being, I didn't want to die. I wanted to live.

3
IMPROBABLE BIRTH

MY FAMILY ARRIVED over the next 48 hours before the heart surgery. They rallied to my side and reminded me that I had beaten improbable odds since my birth. To cheer me up, Sabita, my eldest sister, recited the events surrounding my birth, which included a mysterious illness and the probability that I would die.

About two weeks before I was born, my mother, who we affectionately referred to as Mama, had terrible back pains and contractions; she couldn't sleep and was very fatigued. Her condition was taking a toll on her and the family. Our father, Papa, came home one day and saw Mama completely exhausted. Right then, he decided to grab her suitcase and take her to the hospital. Sabita was left in charge of her two younger siblings. After a difficult labor, I was born on December 14, 1956, to my parents, Sewnauth and Shiela Mangar.

Sabita was charged with caring for her newborn brother when Mama soon returned to work. But within my first few months I developed restlessness and irritability, and became very weak and pale. I stopped eating and cried nonstop night and day for several days. She kept rocking me until I fell asleep, keeping her sleeping schedule with mine. It got so bad that Mama, Papa, and all our relatives who lived close by feared that I would not survive. Everyone was wondering if there was a bad omen. Superstition ran rampant.

For context, the vast majority of East Indians in Guyana are Hindus. Papa was a devout Hindu and taught himself to read and speak Hindi. He was often invited to read scripture from the Ramayan, one of the Hindu holy books, in our neighbors' prayer meetings. Our family attended the Hindu temple to worship until I was around eight years old; that's when Mama's brother-in-law, Isaac, became the pastor of a church in the next village. This church, in Bloomfield, was operated by the Church of the Nazarene. Mama mandated that her children go to that church. But as an infant, when they thought I was near death, Hindu beliefs factored into my family's view of my mysterious condition.

Hindus in our community believed that when people died, if they weren't reincarnated, their souls stayed among the living. As a boy I attended many wakes and was drawn to the old women who sat around in circles and told stories, some of which involved the ghosts of those who died, now "living" amongst their families. The ghost stories were told as if they were facts, and I grew up with a lot of fear of ghosts, even though I never came into contact with one.

The culture I grew up in was steeped in superstition, so my grave illness took on a supernatural quality. The story was told that our area, where Indian families lived adjacent to the sugar cane fields, was previously inhabited by the Dutch people. Allegedly, our home stood on top of the grave of a Dutch person. This was seen as a bad omen that somehow contributed to my illness. Mama ordered my older siblings to clean the house in preparation for my eventual death and funeral.

In difficult and stressful situations, Hindus sought the advice and counsel of the local priests, called "pundits" (not to be confused with pundits in the US political lexicon). It seemed like the right time to take me to see the pundit. In his study, he looked to the scriptures for insights. This practice was referred to as "opening book," whereby the pundit would open the scriptures, read whatever passages were deemed appropriate, and then share his enlightenment with everyone. Upon reviewing the scriptures and gazing at me, the pundit had a message. He looked at my parents and said, "This child's eyes are bright. He is not going to die." My parents had no reason to disbelieve him. And that was that.

Mama and Sabita remained certain there was a moment when I could've died as a newborn and did not. It was as if I cheated death. At inflection points in my life, I've reflected on why I continue to live. There is solace in thinking that God had a purpose for me.

Fast-forward to March 2002, the heart bypass surgery lasted four hours. When I awakened from the anesthesia, I recognized right away that there was a tube down my throat, which prevented me from talking. The nurse noticed I was alert and removed the tube. My first words were, "Where's Yvonne?" I wanted her next to me.

"I'll call her in from the waiting room—*after* I get you out of bed," he said.

Did I hear right? Out of bed?

I immediately protested. I felt a bit foggy, but had my wits about me. *How could he want me on my feet, when my chest was just split open*? I felt like I was run over by a bulldozer. Yet this gentleman was talking about getting up. I was prepared to be very blunt.

"If you don't get up and start moving around, things will not go well with you," he said. There was a firmness about how he said it that made me realize that I needed to listen to him.

I had no choice but to work with him. He leaned over and grabbed my shoulders, held me close in a hug, and pulled me up. Then he twisted me around so that I was sitting on the bed with my feet hanging over. I remember that moment as if it was yesterday. As I sat upright, a sense of peace and hope came over me. I could sit for a while.

My sense of relaxation was premature. The nurse said, "We're not done. You see that recliner in front of you? You need to walk over there."

Now he is really pushing it, I thought.

I blinked at him in disbelief and motioned at the tubes hanging all about me. I had an IV line attached to my hand, an oxygen tube attached to my nose, and a huge tube coming out of my abdomen providing drainage from the surgery. I didn't know what magic he expected. I felt like Captain Gulliver in Lilliput. I asked, "How do you expect me to walk with all of this?"

He smiled and assured me that he would be with me every step of the way.

With great trepidation I wiggled my way out of the bed and my feet landed on the floor. I slowly shuffled to the recliner, turned around and gently lowered myself onto it. As I sat there and looked around me, I smiled with appreciation that I was alive. Again, I thought, *I am going to be OK.*

The nurse later told me that my heart showed a lot of cholesterol, but Dr. Cheerin successfully created five new arteries with the vein he harvested from my left leg. By then, I was warming up to the nurse. He had done his job. With that happy news, my family left Rochester to attend a relative's birthday party in New York. Except for Mama. She decided to stay with me to see me through the first four weeks of my recovery. I was surprised and grateful. That meant so much to Yvonne and I; we could really use the help with two kids in school and Yvonne working full time.

Two days after the surgery, I was sent home. When the time came, I thanked the doctors, nurses, and staff for their care and support. The ride home was memorable for the number of times I said, "Ouch." Yvonne tried her best to avoid the many potholes along the way, and then again, maybe not. The bumps caused my chest, split open and sewed back together, to move ever so slightly, resulting in moments of sharp pain. I couldn't wait to get home.

A wave of relief washed over me when I stepped into our home. Going into the surgery, I didn't know if I would ever see my home again. I felt relief and a huge debt of gratitude. That night I was determined to sleep in my bed upstairs instead of downstairs on the sofa. With Yvonne's encouragement and with her at my side, step-by-step I climbed the 12 stairs. At the very top of the stairway, I paused to breathe. I was going to be OK.

That pundit was right about me again.

4
GRIEF AND REDEMPTION

MAMA BEAMED WITH pride at the steady stream of visitors, mostly CDS board members and staff, who called on her son while on the mend from major surgery. They brought gifts, shared news, and sat with me to visit. That meant a lot to me—and I believed Mama too. She made me herbal tea and tried her best to think of what else would help me. From time to time she massaged my neck, hands, and feet. This reminded me of the long evenings I spent in Guyana by Mama's bedside, massaging her calves right before she went to bed after her long days of standing on her feet and cooking for the nurses at the hospital. She was doing for me what I did for her.

When she first offered to nurse me back to health, I was surprised and yet thankful. I thought of our trips to Florida and Disney World, when we'd stop by to see her and my siblings. Every time, she cooked all our favorite foods and brought all of her children together. We all had great fun. Now here she was doing the same things to help me recuperate after one of the most serious surgeries imaginable.

Two weeks into my recovery, I couldn't stop coughing. A nurse periodically stopped by the house to check my vitals. She kept saying I was progressing, but I didn't feel that way. I still struggled to fully open my lungs, although I was using the incentive spirometer as often as I could. I later realized that I was too focused on opening my lungs and failed to walk every day. My improvement was slow and measured, a stark contrast from my usual nonstop pace.

One evening my cousin's wife, Leela, a nurse practitioner who lived in Florida, called me. I suspected Mama had found time when I wasn't looking to call her. I diligently answered Leela's questions about the surgeon's instructions and how precisely I was following them. "I'm glad that you're using the stairs," Leela said. "And how is your walking going?"

"Umm..." I was so preoccupied with the lung-opening exercises that I had neglected walking.

Leela reiterated the hospital nurse's warning right after I awoke from the surgery, stressing that if I didn't start walking, my recovery would be very difficult. She wanted me to get off the couch and start walking. That was the wake-up call I needed. The very next morning I was on the move. It was still winter, and I could not walk outside. So I did laps inside our house, from the kitchen through the dining room, around the living and family rooms, and through our morning room—100 steps per lap. Soon after, I was walking on the treadmill and increasing my time from 5 minutes to 15 minutes, and eventually to half an hour. I'm forever grateful for Leela's call and for everyone who helped me during my recovery. Most of all, Yvonne and I were especially grateful for Mama, who spent four weeks helping me recuperate.

My relationship with Mama throughout my childhood and early adulthood was difficult. In the intervening years I wrestled with what to do and came to the realization that I needed to fix my relationship with my mother. Thankfully, by the time of the surgery, her relationship with me was in a much better place. My love for her overshadowed any resentment that had simmered over the years. Visitors who met her would've been quite surprised to learn that I had felt very little love and affection from her while growing up. She provided everything I needed—food, clothes, and a nice home—but she was distant.

My memories of my early childhood were clouded by feelings of anxiety and aloneness. I felt neglected, and for that I deeply resented my mother. Without her love and support, I felt lost. How could a child go about his daily life feeling a deep separation between himself and his mother? What resulted was a feeling of deep loneliness. I put in extra efforts to make friends in our neighborhood, and often as a child in elementary school I could be found in a neighborhood game of cricket. At home, my focus was on schoolwork, chores, and reading novels, but I couldn't escape the feeling that I was on my own.

In hindsight, it wasn't all bad. I attribute my attention to neatness, excellence, and appreciating the nice things in life to Mama. In our first house and in the new house, every piece of furniture and all decorations were her selections; they were of high quality and fit perfectly. Mama wanted her house to be aesthetically pleasing, and she expected her children to keep it that way. We all participated in the chores, which were reviewed the night before. Upon returning from school every day, we had to finish our chores and be ready for inspection when Mama returned from her job as a cook at the local hospital. If anything was out of order, there were consequences—including a dressing down and several lashes across our backsides. She was unflinching when it came to discipline, which was so unlike Papa. She was one of the few mothers in our community who went to work. For her, one paycheck was not enough.

Papa and I were very close. He tried his best to shield me and my siblings from Mama's outbursts and whippings as much as he could. Every day, we quietly worked to get the house in order once he arrived from work. His job was to make the dinner meal while we did our chores. Then he would lie in the hammock on the patio and immerse himself in the latest novel, loaned to him by either me or my brother. He was an avid reader. I probably developed my love for reading from him. On weekends Mama took over the cooking, and while I liked Papa's cooking, I couldn't wait to eat whatever she cooked. She was a far better cook than him.

Their co-parenting may appear modern, but their relationship was strained, living next door to Mama's family, who always had watchful eyes. We had no privacy, something Papa, a very quiet and non-confrontational person, desperately wanted but never could achieve. Making matters worse, my mother was very domineering and overruled my father at every turn. Indian families were primarily patriarchal, so fathers were seen as the leaders of their families. This inversion belied long-standing difficulties between them.

Originally from Nepal, Papa's family was brought to Guyana by the British to labor in the sugar cane fields. At age 10, like his brothers, he had to quit school and work in the fields to help support his family. In contrast, Mama's family lived more comfortably. Mama's father was a supervisor in the sugar cane fields. I recall in wonder him trotting into our yard on his tall, elegant horse, which he used to get around in the fields. Mama's mother was a fierce and strict disciplinarian. I think that's where she got some of her outlook on married life and parenthood. To make matters worse, in Indian culture, disciplinary measures were taken by any elder in the family.

For much of his adult life, Papa was an alcoholic and a chain smoker. He had a tight group of friends with whom he spent a lot of time drinking on the weekends. As time went on, he resorted to drinking by himself upon arriving home from work every day. The relationship between Mama and Papa over the years descended into one of mutual tolerance. To avoid confronting their personal difficulties with each other, Papa resorted to drinking and Mama devoted herself to her children's education. I don't think they had any idea of the impact of their broken relationship on their children.

In 1973, my junior year in high school, we built a brand-new, three-bedroom modern house with all the amenities; the upstairs comprised three bedrooms, a living room, and a verandah that ran across the front of the house. Downstairs had a kitchen with a gas stove and refrigerator, a shower and toilet, another bedroom, a dining room, and an open patio area. Mama, an illiterate without any schooling, saved the money, arranged for the construction, kept track of expenses, and put much of her energy into working with the building contractor to ensure the home came out the way she wanted. Then she went about purchasing furniture and all the decorations. It was a beautiful home, yet it was no reflection of our family's internal battles. The conflict between Mama and Papa simmered every day, like a volcano getting ready to erupt. There was no peace.

Papa continued to drink and smoke without any regard for his health. Then we noticed his behavior becoming erratic. The volcano erupted. He escalated the quarrels, yelling and screaming at Mama, something he did mostly when she provoked him. It was unlike Papa to respond to Mama every time, but then he started to do so. We suspected something was wrong. That went on for a few weeks. One day, when he was not thinking rationally, he wanted to engage my elder brother, Devo, and I in a fight. It was very sad. We stood there and watched our father. I could see his pain and felt helpless that I couldn't do anything to help him. He must have felt so alone. A familiar theme.

Then tragedy came. One morning Papa could not go to work. He had a very unsteady gait when he and I were going down the stairs to the kitchen to prepare our lunch. I grabbed his arms to keep him steady and encouraged him to get back to bed. Little did I know that was the last time he and I talked. During that day, he drifted into a comatose state. Soon after I returned home from school, he was taken to the hospital and that would be the last time he was at home. At the hospital he suffered from labored breathing continuously. Devo, my elder brother and I, and one of Papa's brothers, took turns staying with him on the overnights, much of the time wiping away mucus running down his nose, as we tried our best to keep him comfortable. But he continued to struggle breathing. Four days later, news reached me at school that he had passed away. The diagnosis was cirrhosis of the liver. There were no goodbyes. I felt hollow inside.

While I loved my father, when he died I had a mix of emotions. I loved him dearly, yet I was very angry with him for not taking care of himself. At the same time, I felt very guilty for being the person who went to the vendors and purchased his liquor. It was tough carrying these emotions as a young teenager with no one to talk to. I didn't cry when I heard Papa passed away, and I didn't do so until when, as the son assigned to perform the hindu burial rites, I had to walk around the grave as his casket was lowered into it. Among all the men (women were not allowed at the cemeteries) in our community and my friends, I let the tears flow with a part of me feeling like I was falling into the grave with him. That summer, after Papa's death, my perspective on my life changed. I did not care what happened to me.

Without any relationship with Mama and with the loss of Papa, I became reckless and did whatever I wanted. Trips to the bars and returning home drunk became my preoccupation. I paid no attention to my school work even though it was my last year of high school and I was facing the General Certificate of Education examination (the English educational system's equivalent to an Associates degree in the US), the ultimate test to show that a student either passed or failed each of five subjects. I passed two; English and Mathematics (Arithmetic, Algebra and Geometry). This didn't go unnoticed by Sabita. One evening, she and her husband, Zeph, rode in on their motorcycle. They lived about 20 minutes from our home, where Zeph was the pastor of a small church. With Mama at their side, they summoned me to the verandah for an "intervention." Sabita and Zeph shared that they were moving to the college in Trinidad for the fall semester and proposed that I join them. Zeph had accepted the dean of the men's dormitory position. I didn't say a thing for a while, but began processing the proposal. I suspected Mama had something to do with the intervention, but at the time it didn't matter, because I was starting to recognize that I could not sustain trips to the bar every day.

I had forgotten all about the entrance exam I passed that summer for the Caribbean Nazarene Theological College in Trinidad—a favor to my Uncle Isaac, who by then, was pastor at a large church in the city of New Amsterdam. I spent much of my summers at their home adjacent to the church, where the missionaries from the college administered the exam. While I didn't feel called to be a minister, which was the point of the college, I was convinced that I needed to leave Guyana. Mama had already sent my sister, Indro, her husband, Sam, and Devo to America. I had a decision to make, and while no one was sure what I would decide, I already knew. It was an easy decision. I feared I would die if I kept drinking as much as I did. So I agreed, arrangements were made, and I was soon on a flight to Trinidad.

The most memorable feeling I had about leaving Guyana and going to Trinidad was relief, mixed with excitement, that I was on a path forward and had a lot to live for. No longer would I hang out with friends at home during the day and end my days at the bar drinking. No more stewing over my relationship with Mama and feeling no sense of purpose. While Mama and I had a very strained relationship, I was grateful that she made my exit from Guyana possible. She also paid for my ticket home from college the following summer, and I arrived a more confident, refined young man.

Three years in Trinidad was the escape I needed. While I didn't know what I wanted to do with my life, the experience in the very intimate college community of only 40 students was a lifesaver. With Sabita, Zeph, and my cousins, I was able to distract myself from the inner sense of loss and direction. I remained distant from Mama well into my young adulthood.

With years came wisdom. I came to recognize the fact that Mama was in an unhappy marriage—forced to marry my father instead of another man she was in love with—and she struggled to cope. I still can't imagine how they navigated their lives day after day. This insight did little to alleviate the pain and anger I was experiencing until I initiated a phone call to Mama, who was living in New York at the time, soon after Yvonne joined me in Kansas. I decided that for my own emotional health I needed to find a way to let go of the pain and anger. In that emotional, cathartic, and liberating phone call, I laid out my many grievances, but in the end, I said, "Mama, I love you, and I forgive you." She didn't quite enjoy the conversation, but afterward our phone calls had a different, more affectionate tone. Later, when Mama and I discussed my childhood, she acknowledged that expressing love to her children was difficult for her. Indian families didn't do that. Gradually, my relationship with her changed for the better, none too soon. I made peace with the knowledge that my brother, Devo, was Mama's favorite son.

Nevertheless, experiencing Mama's love and openness was like a deep emotional hole that filled up overnight. It was a godsend. All I ever wanted was to be loved by her and make her proud. When she helped me recuperate from major heart surgery, our new bond further strengthened. Indeed, I forgave my mother to save myself.

Despite the emotional stress, I knew it would not be fair to blame Mama for my poor health. I have had to bear responsibility for it and recognize that some of it might have been due to bad genetics. It's fair to say that this little heart of mine has held me up throughout a lifetime of stress, tension, and challenge—and yet through so many accomplishments, enabled me to store so many wonderful memories that I will cherish for the rest of my life.

5
COMING TO AMERICA—
THE PAY STUB

IT WAS MY mother who engineered our emigration to the United States. The turning point came in December of 1976. I was visiting home, on Christmas break from college in Trinidad. Our house, normally very quiet—with only Mama, my youngest sister, Jankie, and I—was full for the holidays. In addition to Sabita and Zeph making the trip from Trinidad, Indro and Sam were visiting from the US, along with their first child, Joseph. We were only missing Devo, who stayed behind in New York.

I was glad when Mama took time off work to be with the family. It was a busy time, but she was organized and in command. There was nothing to worry about, but I was nervous to speak with her about my plans for the spring semester. I still couldn't figure out my life's direction—much to the chagrin of the college administrators. Seated with her on the veranda, where my intervention had taken place three years prior, I told her I wasn't returning to Trinidad to finish my degree. I'd had enough. To my surprise she just nodded in agreement, and I relaxed, enjoying the festivities.

One bright and sunny afternoon, the whole family was gathered on the patio, engaged in conversation and sharing some of the snacks that Indro had brought from the US: Butterfinger candy,

Hershey's chocolate, licorice, apples, and much more. From down the street, the hum of a motorcycle grew louder. As it approached our house, I recognized the rider, a family friend who was married to one of Mama's cousins. He excitedly rode his motorcycle into our yard, waving a large brown envelope and shouting, "Shiela, I brought you an early Christmas present. You won't believe what it is." Jumping off the motorcycle, he reached for Mama and handed the envelope to her. She handed it to me. The return address was the United States Embassy in Georgetown, Guyana. This could only mean one thing.

Two years before, Indro had applied for legal immigration status for Mama, Jankie, and I. The US Embassy in Georgetown was notorious for slowly processing visas, but we were encouraged that visa applications for parents and children under age 21 received priority. Now Indro nervously opened the envelope and looked over the contents. We had a visa interview appointment in three weeks. My heart soared. Then Indro's face dropped. I held my breath as she listed outstanding items she hadn't submitted to the embassy, including proof of employment and an affidavit of support declaring financial support for five years if we couldn't find work. Mama shook her head and put her hands to her face in disappointment.

Sam, Indro's husband, appeared crestfallen. He advised that, with the list of missing documents, it was unlikely that we would obtain the visas at that appointment. He recommended that we go to the appointment with what documents we had, and hope that the embassy would extend a deadline to submit the missing documents and set a new appointment date. Mama felt encouraged. We obtained all the necessary documents: a completely filled out application, updated passports, copies of chest x-rays, updated vaccinations, and all government clearances. We had everything except proof of employment and income. A pay stub would do.

A few days before the visa appointment, Indro burst into the sitting room with a beautiful smile on her face. She triumphantly waved a wet, crumpled paper. "You won't believe it. This is Sam's last pay stub from the check he cashed the day we flew out of New York," she said. She explained how as she washed her family's clothes in a bucket of soapy water she had checked my brother-in-law's pants pockets for change. And she found this soaked piece of paper—his pay stub. Indro wanted to dry off the paper and submit it with our visa application to show proof of employment and the ability to support us. We agreed there was no harm in trying. Sam was skeptical.

On the morning of our appointment, we arrived promptly for the 5:30 a.m. ferry to cross the Berbice River and were soon on the slow, winding road to Georgetown. Perhaps I was naïve, but something within me believed we would have a successful appointment. The US Embassy's waiting room was already packed at 9:00 a.m. when we filed in on time for our appointment. Within a few minutes a young lady called out, "Sewnauth." It was our turn. She took us to a reception area, reviewed the documents, and requested the affidavit of support and proof of employment. Indro produced the crumpled pay stub and explained the miracle of finding it in her husband's pants pocket, pointing out that they were on holiday and hadn't expected the appointment. The young lady grabbed the pay stub and slid it into the folder, shrugging her shoulders. I was hopeful. Maybe something good was about to happen.

After a few minutes we were ushered into the examiner's office. He greeted us warmly and invited us to sit across from his desk. After introductions, he began perusing our file and made some innocuous comments. Then he held up the washed-out pay stub for closer investigation. Indro grinned sheepishly at him. He quickly returned her smile and said, "This will do just fine." My mouth dropped in surprise. He stood and said, "Welcome to the United States, and I wish you all the very best." Just like that, our lives changed forever.

Mama's and my sister's visas were ready later that day. For mine, we had to first produce a police clearance from Trinidad. What were they thinking? Did I, maybe, escape prison in Trinidad? I calmed myself down. It would delay our departure by only another two to three weeks. We had waited so long and now was not the time to argue. I went to a nearby photo studio and had two passport-size photos taken. It so happened that Sabita and Zeph were returning to Trinidad later that day. They were waiting for us outside the embassy. How providential! Zeph promised to secure my police clearance as soon as they arrived in Trinidad. Ten days later, I returned to the embassy with the police clearance and that afternoon I had my visa. And there was a silver lining: My brother, Devo, hadn't come home for the holidays, which made it easier for him to book our flights.

We decided to keep all plans to emigrate to the US very quiet and limited the news to only immediate family. I kept our visas under lock and key. That may sound extreme, but this wasn't a safe time in Guyana or our local community. Our village was changing day by day, with robberies rampant. Villages were plundered by thieves and, in some cases, by the police who came in the night. There was no mercy for anyone. There was no recourse. America was our hope for a better future.

Mama was relieved to leave Guyana, but as the matriarch of the family, her face was etched with worry and sadness. She was leaving behind three brothers and their families, and entrusting our beautiful home to someone else to take care of. We left much of our clothes and belongings to relatives who remained behind. Mama eventually sold the house to one of her nephews, who has kept it up all these years.

Soon Mama, Jankie, and I were on a British West Indian Airways flight with Indro, Sam, and my nephew, Joseph, heading to America. We arrived at JFK airport in New York City one cold evening in January of 1977. Devo met us at the airport and gave us our first winter coats. We were hurried into a vehicle headed to Indro's apartment in the Bronx. I was preoccupied with the realization that I was a legal immigrant in the United States. I barely noticed as our taxi crept through the busy roads lined with tall buildings that rose out of the ground like giant monoliths. As we crossed the

Triboro Bridge before entering the Bronx, Manhattan to the left was blazing with lights, and the Empire State Building stood tall in all its glory. It was a sight to behold. The realization that we had left the third world and made it to America was overwhelming. I couldn't help but feel a deep sense of gratitude to Mama, Indro, and Devo for getting us to a new life in America.

The life we left behind in Guyana and my time in Trinidad flashed before my eyes. During the three years I lived in Trinidad, I had enjoyed a higher standard of living than in Guyana. In Trinidad, the shopping malls were extensive with shops and restaurants of every kind. There, I was introduced to fish and chips. *What an indulgence.* I bought my first shirts and pants, already made, in a department store. In Guyana, you had to take raw materials to a tailor who then measured you and sewed your clothes. Unlike Guyana, there were indoor toilets and showers in all homes in Trinidad. In our village, our home was one of the few exceptions. In Trinidad, every home also had a television. In Guyana, we relied on the radio for news and the local movie theater for entertainment.

I was at a friend's home near the college in Trinidad when I witnessed the most memorable event on television. It was the 1974 "Thrilla in Manila" boxing world heavyweight championship bout between Muhammad Ali and Joe Frazier in the Philippines. How exciting it was to witness something live on television. The fight lasted for a grueling 15 rounds. Ali won what is considered the best boxing match in history.

The evening we arrived at Indro's apartment in the Bronx was my introduction to American food. A Sara Lee pound cake, neatly cut, greeted us on Indro's kitchen counter. We couldn't resist. It tasted very rich and delicious, with an unforgettable velvety texture. Whenever I come across that Sara Lee cake at the grocery store, I recall my first taste of it. From time to time, Yvonne and I indulge ourselves, straying from our diet to enjoy a slice or two.

I was overwhelmed by the abundance and endless variety of food in the supermarkets: fresh and packaged beef, chicken, pork, cereal, soda pop, alcoholic beverages, and a wide variety of fruits and vegetables. Everything was so readily available. When returning to our apartment from my factory job, I couldn't escape the nearby street corner vendor and the mom-and-pop outlets that sold ethnic foods. Then, as I turned the corner onto Gerard Street, it was difficult to pass up our street vendor's hot dogs, complete with a heavy portion of caramelized onions on top.

Oddly, a new technology I discovered caused me much anxiety: getting on and off the escalator. On my first encounter, I was walking through a shopping mall in White Plains, about a half hour's drive from the Bronx, talking and laughing with my cousins. Then they stepped onto this contraption—a moving stair. I was dumbfounded. "How do I get on this thing? What if I trip?" I protested.

Everyone around me thought I was crazy. "Jump on," they said.

Easy for them to say. Then, when I got on it and ascended to the second floor, I was terrified, not knowing how to get off it. I jumped off, fearing that if I didn't I would get caught in the machinery and get ground up. Fortunately, there weren't many opportunities in the Bronx to get on and off escalators. On the occasions that I did, I relived that anxiety. Many years passed before I grew accustomed to escalators; and every time I ride one even now, I think back to my first experience. I can now laugh about it.

In Indro's two bedroom apartment, like other immigrant families, we lived in close quarters—six adults and a baby. The apartment building shook every time the train roared through the above-ground subway about a hundred yards away. But we were rarely there except to sleep. Devo helped me obtain employment at the belt factory where he and our relatives worked. Our lives revolved around work; everyone was expected to help build our new lives in America. It didn't take long for me to realize that factory work, while honest work, was a dead end, so I enrolled in college in Boston. After a year, I returned to New York and continued my studies at the City College of New York while holding down a full-time job at the same factory (thanks, again, to Devo's gracious assistance). We all fell into our daily routines.

Mama could not forget her brothers in Guyana and made yearly trips to visit them. She never lost sight of the fact that they needed to leave Guyana too. To be able to sponsor them and their families to come to the US, at the age of 50, she learned to read and write so that she could take the citizenship exam. She passed it the first time. Then she submitted all the necessary paperwork for her brothers' eventual emigration, bringing all of them and their families to America.

After two restless years in the Bronx, I jumped at the opportunity to relocate to Hardin, Missouri, where Uncle Isaac was the pastor in a farming community. In the fall of 1979, my cousins, Joe and Ruth, and I moved to Olathe, Kansas, where I found work at a Coca-Cola plant and attended the MidAmerica Nazarene College. There I completed my BA in psychology. With thoughts of settling down, a young woman came to my mind. She was from the local congregation in Guyana where I had substituted as pastor during summers off from college in Trinidad. If only she would have me.

My parents, Sewnauth and Shiela Mangar

From left: Mama, Devo, Jankie, me, Sabita, and Indro

6
NEVER GIVING UP—YVONNE AND I ON OUR JOURNEY TOGETHER

IT HAD BEEN six years since I last saw Yvonne. I was unsure how she felt about marrying me. Sabita acted as an intermediary taking a letter from me to Yvonne and her parents, asking for Yvonne's hand in marriage. Lucky for me, she and her parents agreed. Within two months, at a frenetic pace, arrangements were finalized. Then, Mama, my siblings, close relatives and I made the trip to Guyana for the wedding. Upon arrival at our home in Tain Settlement, our priority was to visit Yvonne and her family. Everyone reconnected as old friends. For me, no one existed but Yvonne. We locked eyes on each other. Everything felt right. In a neighboring church, with about 50 friends and family in attendance, Yvonne and I were married by a Justice of the Peace on June 3rd, 1981. We needed to marry quickly to allow time to gather all documents for her US visa application. Our church wedding followed three days later. I had asked the manager of the Coca-Cola plant where I worked to provide me with a support letter stating how important it was for my wife to accompany me back to Kansas. With that letter and our marriage certificate, Yvonne and I went to apply for her visa at the US Embassy in Georgetown, Guyana's capital.

At the embassy, an examiner escorted us to a cubicle to review the application. After reviewing all the documents, he placed the letter of support from the Coca-Cola plant on the desk and cleared his throat. "Sorry," he said. "She won't be able to accompany you because you're a resident alien with a green card. You're not a US citizen. We give priority to citizens." He gave no consideration to the support letter.

"But I live in a very rural area in Kansas," I said. "Having my wife with me would mean so much."

"She must follow the same visa process you did to emigrate to the United States," he answered. "Your wife's visa will probably take two years, so I suggest you make a plan for that."

Yvonne and I stared at each other in stunned silence. *How could this be? How could we live apart that long?* I attempted to ply the officer's sympathy, but he held his position. Finally, I thanked him for his time, and we left the embassy.

Yvonne was distraught. She was willing to change her life to be with me, and now she was stuck in Guyana with her parents, and we would have to endure a long-distance marriage. There was nothing I could do to help her, except apologize repeatedly. This was one of the worst periods of my life. Like the one time later when I would have to buy food for my family with food stamps, I felt utterly powerless.

I couldn't fathom returning to the United States without Yvonne. Instead of anticipating our new life together, we spent every day dreading my return to Kansas. The Coca-Cola plant had generously given me three weeks off for our wedding, and soon I was due back at work. On the flight back to the US, I was consumed with loneliness and sadness. I resolved to do everything in my power to shorten the two-year waiting period for Yvonne's visa. My cousin, Joe, picked me up at the airport and dropped by the liquor store for a six-pack of Miller Lite. I was not a drinker at the time, and after three beers the room was spinning. Interestingly, I became more depressed. Alcohol was not the answer. I needed to focus on the task at hand, clearheaded.

Soon I had a plan of action. I would call the US Embassy in Georgetown as often as necessary to get their attention. In addition, I would write weekly letters to the embassy pleading our case with every reason I could conjure. On that first call to the embassy, only a couple of weeks after Yvonne and I were there, an agent assured me that the application was under consideration and reminded me that the application just entered the queue. I wasn't discouraged. Next I consulted with an attorney in New York City who specialized in immigration cases. He explained that such visa applications had a process that couldn't be short-circuited. But I was persistent. To please me, the attorney made a call to the Embassy in Georgetown. Unfortunately, he reported back what they had told me. Yvonne had to wait in line. As a last resort, I contacted the local legislator and asked if there was a way he could help, to which he said, "No."

Every waking moment, I thought of my wife back in Guyana and how much I missed her. We spoke on the phone weekly, but phone calls were not a substitute for marriage. I continued making calls and writing letters. Time ebbed slowly.

Four months after our disappointing interview at the embassy, every excruciating day passed a slow-moving train. Then, when I least expected it, Yvonne called me with good news: she had received a notice to appear at a visa appointment at the US Embassy in Georgetown. I screamed in joy. I couldn't believe it. Everyone in Guyana expressed surprise too. A rumor began that I somehow had connections at the embassy. I wish that was true. I think they gave Yvonne the visa appointment four months after the application to just get rid of me. My letters were filling up needed space and my phone calls were preventing them from doing their real jobs. I was certainly a pain in the neck. Nevertheless, our happy future was now in our grasp.

I jumped into high gear. I found an apartment in the nearby town of Overland Park and signed a lease. I moved in, with only a few items from my aunt: the bed that I slept on, a few dishes, and a 10-inch black-and-white television. With a quick trip to a local furniture store, I bought a sofa, a dresser, and a small dining set. Meanwhile, I prepared for the trip back to Guyana to accompany Yvonne to her visa appointment. The Coca-Cola Company was, again, very generous in allowing me more time off to bring my wife home.

Soon after I made my way through immigration in Guyana, Yvonne rushed into my arms. I was overcome with relief. She had missed me as much as I missed her. Maybe more. We picked up our relationship where we left off, inseparable. Yvonne's visa was quickly secured, and soon we left Guyana in high spirits with hopes for a bright future.

The apartment in Overland Park became our home. We lived on fried chicken and fried rice. We watched all the comedy shows on the tiny television that sat on the dresser in our bedroom. At the time, the Odd Couple with Jack Klugman and Tony Randall was our favorite. We thoroughly enjoyed listening to vinyl records of Englebert Humperdinck, Jim Reeves, Nat King Cole, Patsy Cline, and other great artists on our new turntable.

I continued to work at the Coca-Cola plant that supported me through college, and Yvonne found a part-time job at a department store. In 1983 Abigayle was born followed by Andrew in 1987. We were blessed. Overall, life was satisfactory, but lonely. We took our family to church on Sundays, and while we met other churchgoers there, it was difficult to blend in and develop close relationships. It was the same at the townhouse complex in Olathe that we moved to in anticipation of Abigayle's birth. We were the only non-white people in the neighborhood. No one was to blame, but a deep sense of aloneness pervaded our lives. This wasn't the life we wanted. So we uprooted our young family and headed back north.

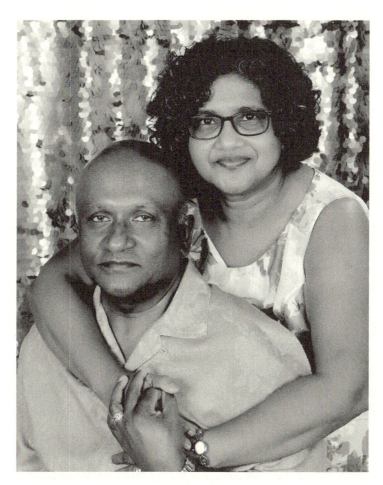
Yvonne and me

7
PROUD TO BE AN AMERICAN

IN AUGUST OF 1987 Yvonne and I arrived in Rochester, New York, by way of Olathe, Kansas. Why Rochester? We made this leap of faith out of desperation to be closer to family. Yvonne's parents and siblings lived in nearby Toronto. We wanted our children to grow up with their cousins and we wanted to live closer to Yvonne's sisters and their husbands. Maybe we could shed the loneliness.

During the 1980s, like other communities, Buffalo's economy was struggling. A person at the job service office recommended that I look at a place called Rochester, about an hour east of Buffalo. It became the *de facto* choice.

My first task after we relocated was to find work. Every Sunday, I walked to the newsstand, got the local newspaper, and quickly circled just about every job opening that related to social and human services, trying to take advantage of my BA degree in psychology. After a few weeks I admitted to myself that to enter the workplace in a new community I had to start with any entry-level position.

I interviewed to be an insurance salesman, but quickly realized that I wasn't the door-to-door salesman type. I even went to the local Coca-Cola bottling plant in the City of Rochester and applied for a position. I hoped to take advantage of my prior experience at the Coca-Cola plant in Kansas. However, they weren't hiring for any positions. So I filled out an application and left it at the front desk.

Then I came to the next advertisement I circled that seemed promising. It was for "management positions." I called the number, and the person on the line said he was expecting me. He had me do a quick math test over the phone, informed me I passed the test, and invited me to a meeting of the top candidates at a local Holiday Inn. I arrived at a room full of people. *So much for "top candidates."* They had invited everyone that responded, it seemed. Another rabbit hole.

The room was organized in rows of chairs facing a table and a television. When it was turned on, people quickly took to their seats, and I joined them. The video began with a stately Hollywood star, John Hausman, describing a product covered by a white cloth, sitting on a table in the front of the meeting room. Once the presentation ended, the cloth was removed, revealing a Kirby Vacuum Cleaner, which had a price tag of several hundred dollars. I laughed. This could not be happening to me. It was another door-to-door sales job. I was taken aback by how much time they took to draw us in with the expectation that by the end of their pitch we would all sign up to sell these vacuum cleaners. Some people around me in that room had good jobs and were openly discussing changing careers to go door to door selling vacuum cleaners. I left the session midway and went home, having discovered one job that I wouldn't do.

I was concerned. I'd had a really good position in Kansas, where my family was taken care of. I had given that up and brought my family to upstate New York. Here I was in a new community of my choice without a job. The knowledge that I was the person responsible for fixing our situation was ever-present. My unemployment dragged on for a couple of months despite my leaving applications at every opportunity.

During the initial weeks in Rochester, we settled into our rented townhouse, taking the time to get acclimated. We sought out the local playgrounds for the kids, visited the shopping mall, the library, and the local grocery stores. To avoid the loneliness we felt in Olathe, I insisted that we travel to spend time with the relatives in Toronto every weekend, just to not feel lonely. I didn't care if people got sick of us or not. We usually returned home on Sundays to prepare for the continued job search.

As we kept busy, I was concerned that none of us had health care coverage. Abigayle, our eldest, suffered frequent ear infections. She was having difficulty uttering her first words, and we fretted that she wasn't hitting this developmental milestone. Yet she was a wonderful child who showed her unbridled love to us and the extended family. We suspected her ear infections might have contributed to her slow speech, and we needed to find her help.

Without a job, I realized that I must file for welfare benefits to obtain health care coverage. I dreaded going to the Department of Social Services to sign up. This was a demoralizing step that I desperately wanted to avoid, but I had no option but to apply. A level of humility was appropriate. Now I had to "face the music" and accept welfare benefits.

We were also eligible for food stamps. How things had changed! In Kansas I had watched people in grocery stores paying with food stamps, and I didn't hold a favorable impression. I couldn't help but look down on these folks. I would say to myself: *Why can't they go find a job? Aren't they embarrassed to use food stamps? How can they act so normally?* Now I was looking in the mirror with those questions and it was uncomfortable.

When we received the first book of food stamps in the mail, I shook my head. I was very hesitant to use them. I'd never asked the government for help before, and although I'd paid taxes since my first paycheck in 1977, I thought the welfare program was meant for other people—not *my* family. Embarrassment was overwhelming and constant. I was ashamed. I considered not using the food stamps, but knew we could use the help.

Finally, Yvonne and I decided to go to the grocery store near closing time with the food stamps. Of all things, I prayed to God that I wouldn't run into anyone I knew. Another rather silly consideration was how I would interact with the cashier. Could I slide the food stamps out of sight when paying for the food? All these considerations swirled in my head. The internal humiliation was inescapable.

The atmosphere of the store felt different as we entered, and I grabbed a cart. It was as if we were going inside to take things that didn't belong to us, like Bonnie and Clyde. I can't quite explain it. We tallied our bill before checking out to be sure that we used up all the stamps. Needless to say, I was very embarrassed when I handed the cashier the food stamps. Afterward, I told Yvonne, "I hope I never have to do that again."

While the food stamps helped stock our pantry, our primary need was health care coverage. We discovered Medicaid health care insurance provided for our family's basic needs, and for that we were most grateful.

During our second month in Rochester, I took Abigayle to have her speech examined. One of Abigayle's teachers advised us that it was best to do so because it would help the school to determine and provide the right support. I made an appointment at the Rochester Hearing & Speech Center located at the Al Sigl Center, which housed many not-for-profit organizations. Everything connected with human services was linked to it. While Abigayle underwent the tests, I roamed the hallways looking at every picture and any posted signs.

I stopped to examine a bulletin board by the Association of Retarded Citizens (ARC), now called the Arc of Monroe. ARC displayed several job postings for "residence manager" positions. On a first look, these seemed like management positions, but as I read more carefully, I realized they were for frontline direct care positions. They involved working with people with intellectual and developmental disabilities (IDD) residing in group homes; no more production work like I did at the Coca-Cola plant in Kansas. I was intrigued.

I went straight to ARC's administrative offices at the end of the hallway and filled out an application. One of the vacant direct care positions was at a residence on Brooks Avenue in the City of

Rochester, about 20 minutes from our townhouse. The former convent housed 14 high-functioning people with IDD. I had no qualms about applying for this entry-level position. The job required only a high school diploma, so I was well qualified with my bachelor's degree in psychology. This was our chance.

As soon as Abigayle and I got through the front door from her speech evaluation, I shared the job possibility with Yvonne. We were hopeful that this was the breakthrough our family needed. I can't express enough how providential it felt to run into that bulletin board and apply for the position. I truly believe that with me taking the initiative, God was doing his part. I've always thought about Abigayle's developmental needs during her early years and how, as we looked for solutions for her, her journey helped our family find our way forward. And the test did show that Abigayle would need support in school. It was better to know earlier rather than later. We were grateful.

A couple of days later, I received a call from the ARC. It was someone in administration who, after some rudimentary questions, invited me to an onsite interview with the house manager. I was on cloud nine. *Just maybe this is the inflection point in our lives and my career*, I thought. Everything felt right.

I overdressed, wearing a tie in hopes of presenting a positive image, and made sure I arrived on time for the interview. It turned out to be a residence that seemed to be about 100 years old. Its exterior looked old and worn out. The house manager, Vicki Sweetheimer, a young lady in her early 30s, received me at the front door. I left the sunny day behind me and stepped into a dark living room. Our walk through the residence further revealed the environment's extensive aging and need of a good sprucing up. Somehow, I knew I would work at that residence.

Vicki thoroughly described the home and the residents. Then she spoke about their staffing challenges. Turnover was very high. The average direct care staff tenure was six months to a year. Then she added, "You know, managers of these group homes don't last very long."

That was surprising, given the current job shortage. I wanted clarification. If she said what I thought she said, this could be life-changing. I asked, "Please say that, again."

"Well, these positions are so tough, there is frequent turnover. I'd be surprised if I'm here in six months," she said with a laugh. "If you work hard, and you want to stay in this field, you'll probably get this job." I contained my excitement. Vicki had just provided me with the answer to my career path. It felt right.

I couldn't help but gain some optimism and hope. At the end of the interview, Vicki offered me the position; within a couple of days the reference checks were completed, and I received the call to start.

Soon after accepting the job, I informed the Department of Social Services that I had found employment. We were immediately cut off from further welfare benefits and, more notably, we instantly lost all health care coverage. We were barely making ends meet. A family living on $12,000 in 1987 could barely afford groceries and rent. I wished the Department of Social Services had shown some flexibility and continued to offer health care coverage for a few more months until we got on our feet. Nevertheless, we had relief when we needed it most. We chose to be grateful. We were looking forward.

PART II

HARD WORK AND THE AMERICAN DREAM

Life in the United States demands sacrifice and hard work; and with it comes the rewards. PART II follows my search for a better life, something excruciatingly painful that I do all by myself. (I'm surely not the first nor the last immigrant to say so). I join Continuing Development Services (CDS) in Chapter 10 and run full steam ahead into a future that seems so far away and elusive. I rise to CEO of CDS in Chapter 19, inheriting an organization in crisis and feeling like an unknown quantity in the field of developmental disabilities. From rumors to cash shortages, I put out fire after fire in a stressful frenzy over the next few years. By 2002, just as there's light at the end of the tunnel for CDS and I'm gaining trust and respect in the industry, I undergo heart bypass surgery.

8
A NEW START AT ARC RESIDENCE

MY DIRECT CARE position at the ARC residence began with a full week of in-depth orientation to the field of developmental disabilities. I faced a steep learning curve, training for a position for which I had no prior knowledge. Like all frontline staff who had only a mere high school diploma, I was required to pass a 32-hour medication administration class, in addition to many other specialty trainings specific to the developmental disabilities field. CPR and first aid training were mandatory. The constant "dumping" of information on us, the new recruits, was overwhelming, but I felt I was entering a field that had meaningful work, and that was all that mattered. I completed all the training by the end of that week and was put to work right away, beginning at 9:00 a.m. that Saturday.

One of my key takeaways during orientation to the field of developmental disabilities was how the services were organized. At that time, services were overseen by the Office of Mental Retardation and Developmental Disabilities (OMRDD), a New York State office under the auspices of the governor of New York. That office was modernized in 2010 and renamed the Office for People with Developmental Disabilities, (OPWDD). OMRDD regulated the care of individuals with IDD, including the environments in which they lived.

As I prepared for my first shift, I recalled an afternoon a few months before. After a long day's demoralizing and disappointing search in Rochester for an apartment, I had faced the reality that no landlord would rent to us because I had no job. At the insistence of my brother-in-law, Rohan, around 4:00 p.m. I made a call to the last advertisement I'd circled on the crumpled section of the Sunday newspaper. Like all the others, when I told the property manager I wasn't employed, he told me he couldn't give us a lease contract. I was about to hang up when he asked, "How do you plan to pay for the year's lease?"

Hope arose in my chest. I said, "Thank you for asking. No one asked me this all day." At $250 per month for rent, we needed to show the property manager that we had $3,000 to cover those payments for a year, plus a one-month deposit. A half hour later, I entered the Twin Beaches two-bedroom townhouse and showed him our bank savings passbook with enough to cover the year's lease. Just before closing time, I signed the contract. And now, thankfully, we wouldn't further dip into our savings to make the payments. Making that last call was like running into the ARC bulletin board. It was another lifesaver. Having a job that paid $5.20 per hour might not seem like much, but it was enough to allow us to make ends meet.

I arrived a few minutes before my first shift and enthusiastically knocked on the front door. Joe, a fellow direct care staff in his 20s, welcomed me. After introductions, Joe walked me through the residence, sharing with me the staff expectations. As a new employee I was charged with "shadowing" Joe, but I couldn't just sit still until he needed me.

This was the start of my career, and I was brimming with excitement. I excused myself and walked around the house, making notations of my observations, especially areas for improvement. I informed Joe that the place needed cleaning, which I offered to do. Then I noticed one of the residents had recently passed away, and his belongings were piled up in a corner in the living room. I asked Joe for his help, and we took everything to the basement. A great start.

Then I introduced myself to the residents and noticed they were all able-bodied. They could certainly participate in the cleanup effort. In my mind, they should accept some responsibility for the conditions at the residence. Keeping the residence clean wasn't just the staff's responsibility. I gathered a few of them and addressed the subject with an impassioned speech. I said, "Hey, guys, I'm Sankar. I'm brand new here, and would love to have you guys join me to help clean the common areas, because as you can see, the house could use cleaning, right?" They all agreed. One individual retrieved a bucket and a mop. I asked him to fill the bucket with water, add some detergent, and mop the floors after the areas were swept. Just like that we became a team. With some hard work we made the place sparkle, and during the process I discovered a sense of accomplishment and an underlying sense of meaning in my work. I was helping people to improve their living conditions. My mother's constant preaching about cleanliness had stayed with me, and now it was my passion.

In the coming days and weeks, I became very attached to the residents. It was well known at the time that people with IDD were stigmatized and segregated from their community. To better support them, I dedicated myself to learning and growing in the field of developmental disabilities. Instead of standing in front of a machine and watching soda pop pass by, as I had when I worked at the Coca-Cola plant in Kansas, now I was guiding, coaching, and helping people who needed me.

As I made my rounds and continued finding ways to improve the home, I was reminded of something the master chemist, Mr. Ken Smith, had said to me the day he retired from the Coca-Cola company in Kansas. He had gone through the facility to say goodbye to everyone, and eventually he made his way to me. He and I rarely talked, though I always respected him. When he shook my hand, I said, "Sir, it's been a pleasure to know you, and I wish you well. Take care of yourself."

I expected that to be the end of the conversation. But Ken wanted a conversation. He said, "Sankar, do you know what you'll do with your career from here?"

My tongue felt covered with peanut butter. It surprised me that he took the time to visit with me, a frontline production worker. I said, "Sir, I don't know what to say. I don't know what I'll do, but hopefully when I finish with my college studies, I will find my area of interest."

He looked me square in the eyes and said, "I need to tell you something. A person who can look at bottles of soda pop on a production line and detect defective products from the good ones just by looking at them is somebody who's going to go places. You're a special young man. I won't worry about you. Good luck." I was rendered speechless.

His notice of me has been one of the building blocks of my self-confidence. Throughout my life, I've returned to that memory, reminding myself that if I applied myself with care and competence, nothing could stop me.

I certainly felt unstoppable when it came to improving the lives of the residents, and this gave my work a sense of purpose that was lacking in my factory jobs. However, the residence's erratic work schedule wasn't especially conducive to a good work/life balance. Our hours were cyclical, which was grueling because there was no set pattern. In a month, every employee worked one week of overnights, one week of evenings, and two weekends. The only difference in the two weekends was that one included the employee going home on Saturday night and returning to work Sunday morning. The other weekend included a sleepover where you showed up to work on Saturday morning at 9:00 a.m. and did not leave for home until Sunday night after 11:30 p.m. During the overnight shifts, we were allowed to sleep when the residents slept, but I couldn't sleep comfortably. Lying on the sofa bed in the living room, I was still in my workplace, responsible for the residents. *Talk about sleep deprivation.*

During my first six months at ARC, we made tremendous strides in the residence. I took the initiative to organize the office and straightened out the residents' individual financial records, especially their savings accounts, educating them on how to use their money to purchase needed personal items. Everyone had savings in excess of the Social Security's Supplemental Security Income (SSI) limit. If we didn't spend enough to get their savings under the limit, SSI checks would be reduced by the equivalent amount until such time as the savings stayed within the limit. So we went on a spending spree.

The residents were surprised that they had a voice in the choices available to them. On one shopping trip, a resident named Mary became quite taken with a bathing suit. Observing her excitement, I said, "Mary, you have money. You can buy that for yourself if you want."

She blinked at me in amazement, with tears in her eyes. "Are you sure I can buy this bathing suit?" she asked.

I said, "Absolutely. You can."

A huge smile spread across her face. She took the bathing suit to the cashier.

By involving the individuals in daily life choices, we were improving their self-esteem and their self-worth. It was wonderful to watch them all grow as human beings. There's a tendency in the field of developmental disabilities to focus more on what the individuals need you to do for them, failing to see them as people, and what they can do for themselves. My interactions with Mary and her peers were always on an even playing field. I showed them respect, and they reciprocated.

9
BUILDING A CAREER

WITHIN SIX MONTHS of my employment at the residence, Vicki Sweetheimer left her position as house manager as she'd predicted. I applied for the job, and with much excitement, I replaced her. I was quickly building a reputation in the ARC organization as someone who took the initiative, and by a force of nature, made a positive difference in people's lives.

With the increased responsibility of managing the house, my heart grew in appreciation for the opportunity to work with these wonderful human beings. Many of them became my friends, like Earl Fishert. He was high-functioning and stood out as a storyteller. He could hold intelligent and mature conversations with anyone. However, he had a medical problem causing him to retain a lot of fluid, so that his abdomen protruded from under his shirt. Whenever he was feeling unwell and couldn't attend his day program, I stayed with him. On these occasions he just wanted to sit with me and talk. We had conversations about everything. As time passed, I gained a lot of affection for Earl.

One morning, as I came into work and relieved the overnight shift, Earl was still in his bedroom. I checked in with him, and he said he was comfortable, but he wasn't feeling well. Later he came down and spent some time with me. I made Earl a turkey sandwich for lunch that he declined to eat, citing stomach complaints. I wasn't so sure he was telling the truth, but I went about my routine doing paperwork, making phone calls to pharmacies and doctor's offices, arranging medication refills, and other routine tasks.

After a while, the house felt very quiet. I couldn't hear Earl moving about. I decided to look for him because he was known to sneak in and out of the house. There was a side entrance right below the stairs going up to the second floor, and the residents used that to exit the house when making trips into the neighborhood. A short stroll away was a restaurant at the corner of Brooks Avenue and Thurston Street. From time to time Earl would sneak out there to buy his preferred foods, which weren't always good for his health. He loved spicy foods, especially chili. We were careful to monitor his activities and ensure that he kept a strict diet on account of the water retention.

On this day, Earl was nowhere to be found. I searched all bedrooms, common areas, the porch, backyard, and the front of the house to no avail. I made one more run upstairs just in case I had missed him somewhere. Then, on my way back down the side stairs, I ran into Earl carrying a Styrofoam cup that smelled of chili. Before I could say anything, Earl jumped in to explain. "I knew you were hungry, Sankar. So I went to the restaurant and purchased this cup of chili for you."

How about that? Earl hadn't missed a step and produced an explanation that seemed reasonable. He even proceeded to hand over the cup of chili to me. What could I say? Was it worth it to tell Earl that I didn't believe him?

I decided to do the right and humane thing. I replied, "Earl, thanks for the chili, but I'm not hungry. You have it."

With a smile on his face, he said, "Are you sure, Sankar?"

I told him I was pretty sure. Even though I knew he shouldn't have spicy chili, I let him have it. I smiled as I walked away, musing that Earl was a human being with a sharp intellect, and he had used it to perfection. He and his fellow residents deserved freedom of self-determination, though maybe they should avoid chili when it's not good for them.

    I committed myself to providing our residents with the best opportunities to strive for their own personal dreams and do so in the best environments. This goal blossomed into my personal vision to ensure that the individuals we served had the opportunity to live their best lives. That guided me every day.

10
CAPACITY MEETS OPPORTUNITY

SIX MONTHS AFTER I assumed the house manager role, I received a meeting request from someone in the ARC residential administration. No details were provided. I felt mildly anxious as I arrived at the meeting. After all, I could be guilty of bending the occasional rule. But any time I let something slip, like Earl enjoying his chili, I did so against a backdrop of a tightly run ship—and not at the expense of our obligations to regulatory bodies.

The administrator quickly put me at ease, saying, "We've been watching you. You're doing a really great job managing one residence. We've never done this before, but we would like to hand you another residence to manage."

My eyes widened with surprise, a feeling that gave way to gratification. She explained that another house manager was leaving, and they thought I could manage two residences. This was a cost-cutting measure on their part, to be sure, but it was also a vote of confidence in my abilities. I saw the opportunity and knew I had the capacity to do it. She disclosed the salary, which was just a small increase. I was making $12,000 as a house manager, yet rising to $15,000 was enough to start lifting my family out of poverty. I felt I had no choice but to take the job.

I was always very organized. My priority was to standardize operations at both sites. The offices at both locations were arranged to mirror each other, avoiding confusion when staff was sent on short notice to fill in at either site. To avoid errors, I prioritized storage of medications. I cut plywood and made cubbies that sat in file drawers, which easily kept the high volume and variety of medications separated.

In filling the vacant positions, we clearly outlined the duties and established an accountability structure. I embraced certain fundamental principles. In leadership one must set priorities, provide clear expectations, and ensure the right staff is in the right position. Goals must be broken down for each employee, and a system of regular performance feedback is necessary. Communication is paramount. That formula has helped me throughout my career as a manager.

I managed the two group homes without difficulty. Yet I was ever so aware that I wasn't part of the American culture, and I brought to the job baggage from my life in the third world. I had a pattern of unreservedly giving my total trust and support to my employees, but I was very tough when they did not meet my expectations. I was very impatient. Staff struggled to relate to me. In all the jobs I held in the field of developmental disabilities, staff and I had to work out our relationships. My guidance, directions, and feedback were reliably blunt and unvarnished. Staff members came to understand that this was not meant as negative feelings toward them and that I truly cared about them. They came to trust and respect me, and as time passed, we developed mutual affection.

After a year at the townhouse, with savings and gifts from my mother and Yvonne's parents, we purchased our first home in the Town of Greece, a suburb on the west side of the City of Rochester. It was a four-bedroom, two-story Cape Cod. As a first-time home buyer with no advisor close by, I was ignorant of the need to have an inspection done prior to the purchase. Soon enough, we discovered the windows were falling apart in decay, the heater was over 40 years old and coughed and rattled like an old steam engine, the roof leaked in several areas, and the kitchen and family room were outdated. We had purchased a "money pit."

Bit by bit I personally made repairs to the kitchen, installed new cabinets and countertops, installed vinyl siding around the outside of the house, and replaced the shingles on the roof. But we did have a professional replace the furnace. These tasks were made easier because Yvonne's family and relatives from Toronto made frequent trips to share the weekends with us. Extra hands made the work so much easier. We never saw these tasks as struggles, but rather as part of life. Andrew and Abigayle were in school, and both were doing well. We felt blessed.

Still we weren't making a lot of money to afford everything we wanted. We had to make choices. For example, driving to Disney World in Florida and visiting family living in that area was all the travel we could afford. The 24-hour trips each way felt endless, and the children were bored out of their minds, but they were troopers. Like Yvonne and I, they couldn't wait to get to Florida but looked forward to the overnight stays at hotels midway. For several years we made these trips two to three times per year. To further save money, I even became Andrew's barber. What would have been a $10 haircut counted. I'm not sure Andrew would say I did a great job, but I tried. This continued until, as a teenager, he started visiting the barber shop.

As we watched every penny, I expanded my handyman capabilities. Without the benefit of YouTube, I watched the Monroe Muffler technician perform the engine oil change on our vehicle once and never went back. I did the greasy job of replacing the engine oil and the oil filter, and began regularly doing these routine maintenance tasks myself. Then, after watching a mechanic performing other repairs, I moved on to replace the brake pads, transmission oil, spark plugs, and wires.

Soon I expanded to doing these repairs for family members. Fixing the cars was a favorite pastime when Yvonne's parents, her sisters, and their husbands visited on the weekends. We would work on the vehicles while consuming a variety of beers or enjoying our favorite scotch whiskey. There were cookouts and parties. Life was good.

11
MOVING UP—COMING TO CDS

AT THE URGING of a close friend on the ARC leadership team, in February of 1989 I joined CDS (Continuing Developmental Services), a nonprofit IDD provider on the East side of Monroe County. I was one of three assistant directors of residential services, overseeing three of CDS's nine residences. I was moving up in the management ranks, which was exciting and equally nerve wracking.

When I was introduced to the staff, everyone was cautious. I was "the new kid on the block." They were feeling me out, and I, them. This job placed me in direct supervisory authority over three residence managers. They were responsible for all the functions at their assigned residences, the same role I had just held at two ARC residences. Systems and processes were different at CDS, and I absorbed information at a frenetic pace, trying to play catch up. At first, feeling like my staff's peer, I had to keep telling myself to remain calm and organized, shifting into my supervisory skills of coaching and mentoring. Over the next six months we fell into a groove as a unified management team.

Like at ARC, CDS's residences were certified by OMRDD. The residences operated seven days per week, 24 hours per day, and always had to be supervised. My team and I had to provide assurance to the CDS management and state regulators of our adherence to regulations, including physical plant code requirements, Americans with Disabilities Act (ADA) compliance, fire drills, staff training requirements, and a lot more.

To maintain certification with OMRDD, the residences were subject to unannounced state audits. These audits coincided with the term of operating certificates that determined the continued operation of each site. While the audits were viewed with a level of wariness, we endured the visits. I was very proud that each residence passed its unannounced audits under my leadership.

Meanwhile, CDS was building a new 70-person day treatment facility in Webster, seven miles from Perinton, where its headquarters and original day programs were located. To facilitate this expansion, OMRDD approved the increase of the Perinton Day Treatment Program's census to accommodate the prospective Webster location's participants. Space became a premium.

One year into my role as assistant residential director, the Webster day program's facility's construction was complete. While 70 participants left the Perinton Day Program to start program at the new facility, the Perinton program's census, which had temporarily included the 70-person Webster census, was permanently expanded by OMRDD, doubling its size. As that happened, the Perinton location's administrator elected to transfer to the new Webster facility, creating a vacancy at the Perinton site. Lucky guy. Soon after the announcement, there was a job posting for the Perinton position. That had nothing to do with me until one afternoon.

I was walking from headquarters to the parking lot when a voice called out from behind me. "Sankar, please hold on for a minute. I'd like to speak with you."

I recognized our executive director's voice, Bob Rosenborg. I turned around, and we exchanged pleasantries. Then he shifted the conversation. "Have you noticed the posting for the administrator of the Perinton Day Program?" he asked.

"No," I said. I explained that I was busy in my current role, having just celebrated my one-year anniversary with CDS. I was content with leading a great team and working with a great leader I respected. As I spoke, Bob's face remained expressionless.

"Well, I've heard good things about you, and I think the day treatment program administrator position would be good for you," he said. "You should think about it."

I replied, "Bob, thank you. However, I feel like I am not ready. I have been with CDS for only a year. I'm still learning."

He was having none of that. Bob continued, "I hear you, but we need you." Then he turned and walked to his car.

In addition to being relatively new at CDS, I knew all was not well at the Perinton program. It was in chaos. It lacked organization and strong leadership. Staff morale was in the basement. The physical plant was worn and dingy. The operation was rudderless. I was unsure why Bob thought I should step in there when I was doing so well as assistant residential director.

Realistically, I only had one option. I had to apply for the administrator position. If I refused, my career at CDS would likely go no further. I couldn't wait to get home to talk about the opportunity with Yvonne. She agreed that it was in our family's best interest for me to take the job.

We spent more time discussing the person who would be my new boss, the supervisor of the intermediate care facilities and the day programs. From what I heard, she was a feckless leader. She had her favorite staff and treated them differently. She was needy and narcissistic. When she returned from vacations, staff were subject to her tales of misery, which became insufferable. No one believed her for a second. Staff who were hard at work while she vacationed had to comfort her upon her return. It was disgraceful.

Nevertheless, I felt I was ready to take on more responsibility at CDS. So I took the job when it was offered to me.

The promotion came with a pay increase and tremendous responsibilities: $5 million budget, 100 employees, 150 people with IDD, operational challenges across the board, compliance issues with the State of New York, and to top it off, an egotistical supervisor over my shoulder. For all of that, my salary increased from $22,000 a year to $30,000, which represented about a 30 percent increase. *Not bad*, I thought . . . until someone in HR told me that my counterpart who took the easy job at the new site was making $38,000—running a site half the size of the Perinton location. This bothered me, but I focused on my career and my family's interests. Racial bias came to my mind, but I ignored it. It was better to be positive.

Preparing for my new responsibilities, I met with the outgoing administrator. He gave me the "lay of the land," lamenting that every day various staff members would come to work and then lined up in front of his office to express every reason in the world as to why they needed to go home. Being a "good guy," he always allowed them to leave, although this created tremendous pressure on everyone who remained on shift, and gradually damaged morale.

To me, there was a simple answer. I thought the problem could be solved if everyone went through the proper channels for time off. Further, I was troubled that staff members were allowed to leave after they showed up to work. I told the administrator, my peer, "Please tell everybody that when I come into work in the morning, I want no one in front of my office. Further, tell them if they show up to work, then I expect them to remain at work." I emphasized that this was a nonnegotiable item to be shared with the employees before I started the job. I realized I was having to clean up the mess that my peer created, aware that he was moving to the new and much smaller site and accepting the fact that he was being paid at least 20 percent more than I was. It seemed like he was being rewarded for doing poor work. But then again, let's remember he was one of my boss's favorites.

On day one, no one was waiting outside my office. I was relieved that the staff came in to work and stayed, although morale was low. Soon, staff saw that they could count on me to provide direction and support. Step by step, we cleaned up the site and its operations.

We established a reliable way of organizing the daily activities, the distribution of staff, and how we dealt with last-minute emergencies. Further, being a "clean freak," I made sure the site looked organized and clean. Walls with holes punched in them were repaired. We replaced handwritten paper signs with more professional printed ones, and waxed and buffed the floors regularly. Emphasizing staff attendance resulted in reliable staffing everyday. It made the world of difference. The future was looking up.

Changes to the physical plant happened more quickly than changes to the work culture. Staff was initially confused by my maxim that "Work comes first, personal relationships come second." I didn't tolerate gossip or cater to personalities because we needed to work as a team for the good of the organization. We were hampered, I observed, because the staff complained about everything. It was the only way to express their frustrations. However, I realized that through listening to their concerns and eliciting their solutions, the morale improved.

Eventually, I gained my employees' trust and respect, and they opened up to me. This took time because I didn't beat around the bush and was rather direct in my communication—very different from my predecessor. We had to work out the nature of my feedback and they came to understand that, while I might not express my feelings toward them, I truly cared about them. Through building relationships with my staff, I began getting a sense of who I was and my leadership style.

Within a short time, we ran a very organized operation. This was vital because our operating certificate was ending within the year, and state auditors were expected to show up at any time to do their audit. I was most concerned about documentation of services provided. The prior administration lacked organization and discipline, so documentation wasn't organized—and was sometimes missing altogether.

In preparation for the audit I coached my staff, based on my experience with state audits in the residential department. Our job was to cooperate and to be transparent and open with the state auditors. But at the same time, I advised that we provide *requested information only*. No one was to volunteer information.

On a Monday morning about six months into the Perinton Day Program administrator role, a team from OMRDD arrived unannounced to do an audit. I alerted all the staff to be ready and welcomed the auditors. After directing them to wait in a conference room, I gathered my staff to execute our game plan.

Right after this, staff members from the new "sister" day program in Webster suddenly arrived to do their own internal audit. This seemed odd, although CDS had a long-standing practice of departments helping each other by conducting quasi-independent internal reviews. There was usually collaboration in planning to avoid surprises. Knowing that there was no planning for this internal audit, I was furious. I met briefly with the Webster team and said, bluntly, " We have state auditors who just arrived for a comprehensive audit of our program. I don't see how you can do your audit today. Please leave."

They stood their ground, saying that they had authority from my supervisor to do the audit. This made me even angrier. I was having none of it. "You are not listening to me. Let me be clear. Go back to work at your location and leave us alone," I demanded. That cleared up any confusion. I recognized that my boss just wanted to put me under pressure. It was malicious and clearly a provocation. She and I had never spoken about doing an internal audit while the state auditors were doing their own audit. I marched to her office only to find out that she would not be at the office for two days. That was new to me. Throughout the state audit, she was unavailable.

As the audit progressed, the auditors and our team collaborated well. They requested documents and allowed sufficient time for us to provide them. Due to the arcane and disorganized record keeping system, we struggled to find needed documents scouring all files from the depths of the filing cabinets and boxes. In some cases, we couldn't locate the requested documentation and admitted so. The auditors also observed staff working with individuals in the classrooms. The situation was high-pressure and tense. However, the frontline staff, supervisors, and clinicians kept their heads down and did their work. The audit seemed like it would last forever, moving very slowly, but we were not detracted. Our priority was to deliver on mission and provide the best services to the participants.

At the end of the third day, the lead auditor informed me that she was concluding the audit and we should prepare for an exit conference at 9:00 a.m. the following morning. Per protocol, I notified my boss's assistant and the executive director's office.

Then I assembled my leadership team and informed them of the exit conference the next morning. Signs of stress were etched across their faces. I said, "Regardless of what they tell us tomorrow, I'm very proud of all of you. We don't run a perfect program, and I don't expect the findings to be perfect. Get some sleep, and let's hope for the best tomorrow."

The next morning, I caught up with the lead auditor just before the exit review and asked her if she could give me an indication of how the audit went. She smiled and said, "I want to thank you for your cooperation during the audit. You made it look seamless. You let us do our job while you did your job. Thank you." These words did not answer my question, but she at least seemed positive. Then to my surprise she added, "You guys are going to shine today."

"Thank you," I whispered to her. The weight lifted off my shoulders. It was the first time in days I relaxed.

At 9:00 am, my supervisor showed up for the auditors' exit conference. She sat at the opposite end of the table from where I sat and avoided looking at me, but I really didn't care if she was there or not. I nodded to the lead auditor to begin. She expressed appreciation for the collaboration between our staff and her team. In reviewing the highlights, she focused on their observations, saying, "We experienced high-quality interactions with you and the individuals you serve. Our time spent with you was very valuable and satisfying. Thank you."

The auditor's recognition of our hard work was gratifying to my team and I. I could see my staff all taking a deep sigh of relief. It was going to be OK.

State auditors had issued a long list of deficiencies following a prior audit. It was their responsibility to ensure safe operations and to reinforce the importance of their work. Surprisingly, our Statement of Deficiencies included only three items, which were limited to policy and procedure. There were no quality-of-care concerns. This was unprecedented. The program had never received such a short statement of deficiencies before. After the auditors left, I thanked my staff and congratulated them on a tremendous audit. They beamed with pride and chattered with excitement as they gathered their coffee mugs and notebooks and emptied into the hallway, eager to get back to work.

I followed them out and ran into my supervisor. "Congratulations," she said. I noted in her voice a lack of sincerity and even a hint of sarcasm. There was also a level of arrogance that I found incredulous. I just did not want to be around her.

"It was a team effort," I replied. I could have addressed her attempt to put pressure on us with an internal audit, but I wasn't going to let her meanness impact my team and me. We were on cloud nine.

She offered to let me take the rest of the day off. I declined and told her I wished to spend the rest of the day with my staff and then I turned and walked to my office down the hall. After all, my staff was still on duty and had held together for three stressful days. Why would I leave them? I was building my team. My boss couldn't stand that I was self-assured and not dependent on her. I had upstaged her. My success had put a spotlight on her lack of leadership, and she was clearly irritated.

My relationship with her never improved. Rather than coming together, I avoided her and she avoided me even more. When we met for periodic supervisory sessions, they were short and to the point. I always brought a written report, if for nothing else than to document my communications with her. This supervisor could have caused me to be bitter. I was bothered by the condescension, bias, rudeness, lack of empathy, and lack of communication from a person in her position. However, my days were busy with meaningful work. Within a couple of years into the administration of the day treatment program, I had a team that was in rhythm with me. They knew what I expected, I knew what they needed, and we worked very well together. I even put aside funds for periodic team get-togethers, unknown to the higher-ups, and we always had a great time. The staff developed affection for me, and I, them.

One day in mid-December, I exited my office, and something seemed off. The hallway, usually bustling with activity, was silent. My supervisor walked toward me, and she didn't say a word as we passed each other. I didn't expect her to be friendly, but to not say anything was surprising; I swear the air temperature dropped a few degrees as she passed by me.

So I popped my head into a meeting room where a few staff members were having a discussion. "What's going on?" I asked. No one said anything. They even seemed to ignore me. A little miffed, I returned to my office. The time passed, as the people we served in our day program left for the day. Then a staff member stopped by and asked me to check on something going on at the Unistel floor a few doors down; Unistel was our employment services division, fulfilling contracts involving light assembly for local businesses. The request wasn't unusual. From time to time there was a call for assistance in that program, and we helped whenever we could. We hurried toward Unistel.

Upon entering the floor, I saw all my staff huddled together as a group. They began clapping in our direction. The staff member who accompanied me said, suggestively, "We have a birthday surprise for you. We came up with something special, and we hope you'll like it."

I was guided to a chair in the middle of the group and a boom box started playing music. I could make out that the genre was Middle Eastern, perhaps from the Arabian Peninsula. Then, to my bewilderment, a beautiful young woman with Levantine features stepped forward and began undulating to the rhythm of the music. She was a belly dancer, and by the looks of it, a professional. I froze. She was dressed provocatively and danced like she was straight out of *One Thousand and One Nights.* As she performed her enchantment, she made her way toward me. She threw her silk scarf around my neck, pulled herself onto my lap, and writhed her body for what seemed like hours, even though it was only a few minutes.

Perhaps it was my dark skin that convinced my staff that my culture occasionally indulged in such pleasures. This was not the case. The predominant emotion that this conjured up in me was one of extreme embarrassment. I felt totally unprepared. The only thing I feared more at that moment was a camera. Thankfully, the dance ended with clapping and cheers from my excited staff.

We followed up the unconventional entertainment with conventional cake and refreshments, everybody sang happy birthday to me, and with that the party was over. I was curious about how they were allowed to hire a belly dancer. It seems they had to ask my supervisor for approval. They said it was a tough battle, but she finally caved to their insistence. It must have nearly killed her, which explains why she walked past me without even acknowledging me in the hallway.

News of the birthday party spread quickly through the entire building. For the next two weeks, I was elevated to celebrity status as colleagues stopped me in the hallways to ask about the party, adding their own salacious comments. I didn't mind. In the end, I appreciated my staff's efforts and creativity. Above all, regardless of the entertainment, it demonstrated that they respected me enough to go to these lengths to provide me with enjoyment. It was a sign of true affection.

12
CDS TAKES ANOTHER RISK WITHOUT PREPARATION

AT THE BEGINNING of 1990, CDS announced that it was opening a new, 12-bed residence dedicated to individuals with autism. It would be built adjacent to the Perinton Day Program. CDS had agreed with New York State that the new home would have residents with severe autism from institutions in New York and surrounding states. Not much was known about autism at that time, and no one at CDS specialized in autism. CDS was entering the unknown without considering the risks. Construction of the residence went smoothly, followed a year later by fanfare with a grand opening.

The new residents moved in over a single weekend; in retrospect it was something we shouldn't have done. The arrivals should have been staggered to allow every resident to orient to the new and foreign environment. The process lacked thorough planning and execution. There were no clear policies and procedures to deliver residential services to people with severe autism. As the saying goes, "They didn't know what they didn't know." From the first day, the new residents acted in very inappropriate and physically aggressive ways as they struggled to acclimate to the new and foreign setting, resulting in injuries to themselves and the staff members, who were scared to go to work. Calls to 911 were a daily occurrence.

I shouldn't have been surprised. Operations at the new residence were led by my supervisor, and I watched as she and the staff struggled to gain control over the chaos. The CDS administration relied on my boss to solve the onslaught of challenges, yet sadly, when faced with this crisis, she placed the responsibility for the criticisms and complaints on her staff, who resented the attacks. Morale started to decline.

One resident in particular, Peter Holt, and his mother consumed our time and energy. While Peter exhibited concerning behaviors every day, Mrs. Holt was unrelenting in her criticisms. That continued throughout the first year of Peter's residency.

He had a reputation for biting people. When he was upset, his eyes would turn red, which the staff quickly learned was a precursor to the biting. His bites broke the skin *every* time. And since his favorite targets were the arms and hands of the staff, we had to purchase special arm guards.

For an entire year, Peter's violent behavior continued. His mother came to our offices several times to sort out his difficulties. She blamed the staff for much of his behavior, expressing suspicion that staff ignored her recommendations. That was patently untrue, but debating with her was futile.

One afternoon, my supervisor called me to her office. When I arrived, she was on the phone and motioned for me to take a seat. I wondered why she called me in. It was rarely for anything good. She frequently dressed me down with the words "You need to understand . . ." I couldn't help but think about how she refused to acknowledge my accomplishments in effectively running the Perinton Day Treatment Program, which annoyed me, but I stayed quiet. *What was on her mind? Please, do tell.*

After she hung up, she narrowed her eyes, and without any pleasantries, said, "Why aren't you involved with Peter Holt's case?"

I bristled. While the residence was in the planning phase, I frequently offered my advice, thinking through operational problems and worst-case scenarios, but she always dismissed me and admonished me to stay in my lane.

Now that she had a problem, she directed her failures at me. "It's your responsibility to provide day program services to our residents," she said. "You need to get at it right away." Internally I was apoplectic, but I concealed my anger; I knew I was the right person to bring the situation under control. It would have been so pleasing if she had just asked for help, but she was not wired that way. She felt asking for help would put a spotlight on her failures.

She proceeded to whine about the new residence, citing all the problems, and not once did she accept that she had failed in executing the startup. Then she turned to me with laser focus, telling me to do my job and fix the problems.

I took a deep breath. There was no use engaging in a debate with her. Rather, I focused on the residents. They came from institutional settings where they had to fight for what they needed, including food, space, and privacy. Upon admission to our residence, CDS naïvely expected that these individuals would suddenly behave like a family, sitting around the dining table to share meals and around the television to watch their favorite shows.

Had CDS done its research, it would have foreseen and prepared for these potential disruptions. Now, faced with this problem, my mind quickly moved into problem-solving mode, and sitting before my supervisor I had already formulated a plan. I smiled reassuringly. "Look, I am aware there's a problem, and everyone's concerned. I'm happy to help if you wish. Would you like to place the individuals in our Perinton Day Program? If so, I will proceed."

She agreed. I knew she was evading responsibility, but I had built good relations and trust with residence staff, and I had faith in our day program staff.

The more I thought about what was happening at the residence, the more I realized that these high-needs individuals with severe autism had spent years in institutions lacking care and oversight. Unwanted behaviors were a result of their frustration when they couldn't communicate their wants and needs, and they perceived they had to protect themselves. Some of them had deep psychiatric issues, but I felt that if we focused on each resident, on their unique personality and perspective, we would find the pathways to helping them. I was certain this was the approach to helping these residents to change the way they interacted with their caregivers and to live meaningful lives. This ethos has always served our individuals well.

Our team established an actionable plan for each individual and then executed it. Our strategy for Peter had to include Mrs. Holt. She was known to insist on meeting everyone who touched Peter's life and demanded a full house for every meeting with her. She would arrive at meetings carrying reams of binders and folders. Staff was on guard around her because she had a habit of "one-upping" everyone. Mrs. Holt was accustomed to everyone doing things her way.

Anticipating her approach, I convened a meeting with her and all staff involved in Peter's care. Her complaints about the residence were centered on the staff not learning how to deal with her son, so I invited her to share her alternative approaches. We left the meeting believing that we needed to consider Mrs. Holt's suggestions, adjust our approach, and hope Peter would respond. Unfortunately, none of Mrs. Holt's suggestions worked.

CDS had no one in-house with expertise in autism, so I reached out to an organization in Ontario, Canada, that specialized in serving individuals with severe autism. Unfortunately, they offered no new ideas. Much of what we had already learned through trial and error was supported by them. They supported how we identified the precursors to outbursts and disruptions, and intervened early when those situations arose. For example, when the staff noticed Peter's eyes turning red, we knew he was getting ready to bite someone and took precautions. For that first year, Peter's biting episodes remained an ongoing challenge. However, during that time several of the other residents' behaviors improved. With fewer calls to 911 and stability in staffing, we all breathed a sigh of relief.

Between biting episodes, staff who worked with Peter enjoyed a very cordial relationship with him. He communicated his wants in writing. One day, a staff member asked him what he wanted to do with his life. Peter wrote: "I want to go home." No one had connected his acting out to a desire to return to his program on Long Island. He missed his surroundings and his routine.

I communicated this revelation to my boss, and to her credit, she agreed to contact Mrs. Holt. She convinced her that Peter should return to Long Island. Mrs. Holt wasn't easily convinced about any suggestion we made, so this was a victory. Two staff members accompanied Peter on the drive back to Long Island. The trip was successful, and we never heard from Mrs. Holt again.

13
MAKING A DIFFERENCE

BY 1993 THE Perinton Day Treatment Program was thriving. My boss left me alone, and we were an autonomous department. Our program built a reputation for accepting individuals with high needs, including people who were turned away from other programs. That was CDS's commitment to families and their loved ones with IDD, and I made sure we never lost sight of it.

Our work culture embodied the reason CDS existed. My team came to work focused on how we could make each day better than the last one for the people with IDD that we served. I was amazed by the staff's resilience and perseverance. Often an individual would have an episode of physical aggression. Invariably, staff would get hurt; bites, black eyes, swollen faces, and back injuries were routine. Yet they came back to work each day committed to each person's care and progress, without regard for their personal safety.

One of those challenging individuals was Kelly Cutpert, a 25-year-old Caucasian woman who had been kicked out of the recent of many day programs in Western New York. Her family resided about an hour from the Perinton Day Program, but despite the long distance, they were open to Kelly attending if we accepted her. She was autistic, and per her record, she had difficulty adjusting to her environment. The situation was complicated by the fact that she was mute and only communicated through sign language. The only written comment said, "She's very difficult and can't be controlled. She will throw things and lash out at staff when she doesn't get her way." That wasn't much on which to base a decision.

To better appreciate Kelly's needs, we invited her parents to visit the day program and tour the different program areas. After the tour we met to discuss Kelly's potential admission. Kelly's parents were desperate for Kelly to be in a day program with others like her, and for her to have a purpose in her life. Kelly's mom was in tears for much of the appointment. She couldn't bear the possibility that her daughter couldn't be further helped.

My team and I were very sympathetic to Kelly's parents' plight, and we agreed to a trial, being mindful of her record. We put our heads together, reviewing all of Kelly's records and her parents' insights, and developed a preliminary plan of care. We would introduce Kelly to a classroom with a group of individuals who were calm and quiet. We wanted her to be in an environment without disruptions and outbursts throughout the day.

In preparation for her first day, we relocated all participants in that room elsewhere and emptied out the furniture, except for a kidney-shaped table. We placed it along one wall, along with a single chair placed in the center facing the table, its back to the wall. This served to "box in" the person sitting in the middle, thus avoiding any sudden movements. The staff was assigned to greet Kelly at the scheduled time of her arrival and accompany her to the room. Along the passageway we posted additional staff, just in case Kelly exhibited any inappropriate behavior.

When she arrived, I was at the entrance along with the staff, but I allowed the staff to do their job. We had anticipated that Kelly needed to get acquainted with her physical environment. The program area was a maze of classrooms and hallways. Luckily, this worked for Kelly. Once she entered the building, she began walking along the hallways, and soon she established a pattern to the order in which she would walk. She stopped a few times to look in the program rooms; she used sign language to ask staff questions. She walked through our halls for about a half an hour. Then Kelly allowed staff to guide her into the room prepared for her. Unprompted, she walked to the table and sat in the chair. I let out a sigh of relief and went back to my office. We slowly brought participants who had been temporarily reassigned back into the room. Kelly seemed unaffected.

At my desk, I remained alert for any distress calls on the intercom. The staff periodically reported to me about Kelly's day; she seemed to be adjusting to her environment. Staff allowed her to take the lead. There were no outbursts or any acts of aggression for the whole day.

The staff met after everyone left for the day and reviewed the experiences with Kelly. There was no inappropriate behavior, and Kelly allowed staff to work with her. Staff universally liked her and felt confident that she would do well in the program. We asked ourselves, "How come no one had figured out who Kelly really was before? Why didn't they learn how to work with her?" The answers never came.

Kelly stayed in our day program for years. Every time I encountered her, she asked me my name and then moved on. I couldn't help but smile and think about how far she had come. I felt privileged to be able to help Kelly and her parents.

14
SELF-IMPROVEMENT

AS I CONTINUED to grow as a professional at CDS, it became clear to me that if I wanted to progress in the organization beyond my day program role, I needed to develop relationships with the CDS executive team. I decided to pick up the game of golf—a sport in which they participated. They always participated in the CDS Foundation's annual golf tournament, and I was determined to join them.

I devoted much time to learning the game of golf. Through watching golf on television, I figured out the basic posture and movement of the golf swing. I had been on the cricket team while attending college in Trinidad, and I easily applied those skills to golf. I bought a used set of golf clubs, and one afternoon I went to a local driving range to try them out. Within a half an hour, I was doing a decent job of hitting the golf ball.

Eventually, I made my way to a golf course and tested my skills. On the first hole, a par 4, I got on the green in two shots. I was excited. Then, without any feel for the putter or the green, I took an additional 8 strokes to get the ball in the hole. This was frustrating, and yet I found the experience thoroughly enjoyable. Over time, my golf game came together, but I never took anything for granted.

As I began my hobby as a golfer, I pondered over the fact that to be considered for higher-level positions I was missing one qualification. I needed a master's degree. I enrolled in the State University of New York (SUNY) Brockport's Master of Public Administration Program. For the next three years, I went to night school three nights per week—rain, shine, or snow. Those years were painfully hard because after a hard day's work at CDS, I would grab a quick dinner and head to school in downtown Rochester. This meant spending little time with my young children or my wife, who was becoming the "rock" of our family.

Higher education for me was mostly tolerable. I realized I was already practicing just about all I was being taught; however, the one course I benefited most from was Financial Administration. I took the course with confidence, since I was always good at math. During the four years at the day program, after the annual budget was published by the chief financial officer and his staff, I mapped out the day program's projected revenues and expenses. Senior management was focused on the bottom line, profit and loss (P&L), and I wanted to hit the financial targets. Unfortunately, no one at CDS ever thought to teach leaders the basics of financial management, including how to build a budget, how to read a P&L statement, how to track expenses, or how to identify the drivers for profits and losses. The Financial Administration course at SUNY Brockport taught me all of that. This course gave me a new sense of empowerment that I had never felt before.

In the spring of 1996, during my last semester before graduation from Brockport, CDS was in trouble. The newly opened Sean Donahue Health Center, a project that CDS launched to offer comprehensive health care services to individuals with IDD and the general population, was hemorrhaging money. There was increased financial scrutiny across the organization and the day programs, the only significant profit center, so I had to devote even more time to managing the program's finances. I literally could not afford the time I spent driving back and forth to classes, yet I still needed six more credit hours to satisfy the course requirements for the MPA degree. I was in a dilemma.

So I did what I always knew how to do in a jam: I changed the situation. I contacted the chair of the MPA Department at SUNY Brockport, Dr. Altmeyer, and proposed to her two independent study projects with a 25-page paper on each, in lieu of attending classes. Fortunately, she was understanding, and valued my education over strict course protocol, so she readily agreed. She didn't have to help me, but she responded to my need. I have never forgotten her kindness.

This made a huge difference. It was no longer necessary for me to leave our home three nights per week. I could focus on work and while at home I could work on my MPA projects. I like to think the solution was not unlike the way Captain Kirk in the *Star Trek* series earned his fame among the other Starfleet captains: he beat the Starfleet Academy's Kobayashi Maru No-Win Training Simulation by hacking and reprogramming the simulation. Of course, the stakes and consequences for me were a little different than for a Starfleet commander. But I changed the conditions of my environment to accomplish a goal: in this case my MPA degree. As I received my diploma that May, I felt like all the pieces were in place for my future in the IDD field and CDS.

Then my peer at the Webster facility decided to resign and accept a senior position at one of CDS's competitors. The story was told that he was handpicked to replace the founder/CEO of that organization. His departure gave the CDS executive director an idea. He wanted to consolidate the leadership of the two sites under one leader. It was just like what had happened to me at the ARC when they wanted me to take on another residence. Now CDS wanted me to take responsibility for the Webster facility in addition to the Perinton facility. There I felt my boss's bias like never before. The Webster administrator was making $38,000. I was making $32,000 for an operation twice the size of the Webster operation. Yet she remained firm that I would take on the responsibility for the second facility, a $4,000,000 budget, 70 individuals with IDD, and 50 employees. Together, the two sites represented a $9,000,000 budget serving 225 participants with 150 employees; all with a $10,000 pay increase. I sucked it up and accepted the new responsibilities. Another person might have been bitter, but I kept myself focused on the positive. My salary increased by almost 25 percent. My family's financial situation was about to get much better and I was just looking ahead. I felt we were moving up in the world.

From left: Me, Robert Mixon, and Sy Zielinski getting ready for a round of golf

15
COMPANY IN CRISIS

THE YEAR 1996 brought many changes to CDS. The organization had invested heavily in the Sean Donahue Health Center, borrowing from the bank and spending more than $3 million. CDS spared no expense. This operation was intended to expand CDS's mission to offer people with IDD comprehensive health care services in a setting that offered the same services to the general population. At the center's opening, CDS Executive Director Bob Rosenborg, instead of being happy, turned to me and said prophetically: "Sankar, I think the opening of this clinic may be the undoing of CDS." Twelve months later, the center closed. Soon after, my supervisor resigned. She was responsible for the debacle and saw the "writing on the wall." Finally, the organization was rid of an employee who was a cancer. Then Bob resigned, having served as executive director for 23 years. He could not escape his leadership failures.

CDS was descending into a financial crisis, and the search had begun for a new executive director. At the time, CDS ran 11 community residences, 2 day treatment facilities, a large case management program, an early intervention program and the Unistel employment services program. Staff turnover was about 40 percent. There were quality issues across the organization, and finances were in crisis. I was committed to keeping the day programs running with as little disruption to our services as possible. All eyes turned to me to cut costs and drive more profits beyond what was forecasted in the day program's budget. We were in a "pressure cooker."

One Saturday morning, CDS Board President Adam Goldstein, with whom I had developed a close relationship, called me to ask if he could stop by my house. He was typically buoyant and optimistic, but on this occasion he appeared worried.

"Something isn't right at the transportation department," he said gravely. "I'd like you to lead an investigation and get to the bottom of this."

Adam did not provide much information, but I could not wait to start my investigation. As the director of the day programs, responsible for transporting more than 400 people to and from their day programs, I saw the crumbling 35 handicap accessible vans which comprised the central transportation fleet. The vehicles were poorly maintained. One of the vans passing through the parking lot had one of its front wheels fall off. Brake pads were completely worn down on many of the vans, exteriors were covered with rust, and the drivers were concerned for their safety and the safety of the individuals they transported. I knew exactly where to begin my investigation: Nationwide Coach Sales (NCS) and its owner, Randy Holden. NCS was set up solely to serve CDS. It was contracted to provide CDS with all its transportation vehicles, including handicap-accessible vans, and to perform all repairs and routine maintenance.

I agreed to do the investigation and to report any findings directly to Adam. This was a complicated and delicate issue because Randy Holden was also a member of the CDS Foundation's Board of Directors. He had somehow squirmed his way into the foundation as a director and later was made the vice president of the foundation, with the full support of Brigitte Goldstein, Adam's wife, who was the foundation's executive director. Holden's company was derelict in its duty to CDS. Adam wanted answers and I couldn't wait to provide them.

I wasted no time. That Monday, I presented myself to the transportation department. Oddly, just prior to my arrival, the transportation manager resigned and vacated his post. The timing of his resignation was suspicious. I wondered about the timing of his sudden departure. Nevertheless, "Good riddance," I said to my team.

Within 24 hours, I discovered that major fraud had been committed by Holden and NCS over a five-year period. Holden swindled CDS out of $400,000 on vehicles we never received. He falsified contracts to purchase 10 vehicles and secured financing for those vehicles, but never delivered them to CDS. I investigated the VIN numbers on the contracted "vehicles" and discovered those vehicles never existed; the VIN numbers were fabricated. I called them "phantom vehicles." Even more egregious, for five years Holden and NCS had billed CDS $120,000 annually for maintenance and repairs that rarely happened.

But his shameless and fraudulent schemes didn't end with automobiles and vans. He expanded into confectioneries, convincing Unistel to purchase an assortment of sexy chocolate molds, including those of golf balls, with the intent that Unistel would get into the business. CDS signed a contract to pay Holden's mother $40,000 for the molds. The venture of course never materialized, even though CDS was making payments to Holden's mother. In total, in the five year period, Holden defrauded CDS out of over $1 million. To divert attention from himself, he cleverly concealed his corruption and piracy by contributing $75,000 in total to the foundation during the five years he was on the board. A bold scheme. His position on the board had been little more than a Trojan Horse to gain trust and access to the CDS treasury.

Since CDS operates under the auspices of the New York State Medicaid program, the findings of the investigation were reported to the NYS Office of the Medical Inspector General (OMIG). Over the next six months, OMIG maintained a presence at CDS while its investigators reviewed all the records and conducted interviews.

As I assisted their investigation, I kept my finger in the wind of CDS's internal politics. Many personalities and interests were involved, and these had to be artfully managed. Holden had been made the vice president of the CDS Foundation and technically still held this position. I maintained regular communication with Adam and Brigitte Goldstein regarding the status of the investigation, and over time Brigitte came to trust my abilities and valued my discretion. Board members wanted the situation resolved with minimum disruption and publicity, something I couldn't promise. Every evening when I returned from work and spent time with my family, I was never fully present; I loved my children and my wife and wanted to be there for them, but my mind was pulled elsewhere.

OMIG eventually confirmed all the incidents of fraud I had uncovered. Without internal controls, CDS was spending money without enough revenue to cover the expenses. It resulted in a very weak balance sheet. This was only the beginning of a devastating time for the organization, internally and in the public.

16
NEW AND BRIEF BEGINNINGS

AMIDST THE FRAUD investigation, an executive search firm based in Boston was engaged to recruit talented candidates and recommend them to the board of directors to replace the executive director. The firm's principal partner came to Rochester to interview the board members and senior staff, including me. As he wrapped up our conversation, I asked him if CDS was considering any internal candidates. He told me no, and I took his response with complacency. My confidence had improved over the years. If I had had the opportunity, perhaps I would have applied. Like everyone else, I trusted that the executive search firm knew what they were doing.

Within four months of searching, CDS hired a new executive director, Xerox Marketing Executive Enrique Brunner. As he introduced himself to staff across the organization, he repeated the same story: "The CDS offer letter arrived on my desk at the same time as a letter of offer from another company." He would pause for dramatic effect, then add, "And without opening the other envelope, I accepted the position at CDS. I have fallen in love with your mission and your people."

I asked myself, *Was he serious? Who wouldn't want to know what was in the other letter?* But I let it go. He was a very charismatic and charming fellow, and we ate it up. All the senior level employees believed the right choice had been made. We were supportive of Enrique. He had an open-door policy and was very communicative and responsive. We had plenty of reasons to be hopeful he would succeed.

Within his first month, Enrique informed us that he had filled the vacant director of human resources position with a new outside hire. Her name was Carol Feltner. It was good timing; CDS was facing a 40 percent turnover in staff and needed help. Carol was nice, but not much was known about her other than that she spent a lot of time with Enrique in her office and they regularly left for lunch together. But she offered no solution to the staffing problem.

About six months into Enrique's tenure, Brigitte Goldstein asked to meet with me. As if in a spy movie, we met in a park on a bench overlooking a duck pond. She pensively talked about a failure of trust. Then she said, "Sankar, I can't say much, but there's a new development that will rock the organization."

'What do you mean?" I asked with concern.

She sighed. "When you can't trust people, life is so much more difficult."

We sat in silence for a while. A woman and two small children approached the pond. They began throwing bits of bread, and instantly the ducks swarmed around them. I smiled, thinking of the times Yvonne and I had taken our kids to the park. It had been so long. *Were they too old for that now?* I wondered. Brigitte finally spoke. She said, "In the coming days, there will be revelations that will shock you. Be prepared."

I left my meeting with Brigitte very unsettled, and I wondered why Adam hadn't said anything about this to me earlier. Answers arrived the following Monday morning when Enrique called an impromptu meeting with us in the conference room. He thanked us for coming and proceeded cryptically by informing us, "I have enjoyed my time here at CDS these last six months. I have come to love the organization, and I want to share something personal with you."

Oh, no. Was this the revelation on the duck pond Brigitte was referring to?

Enrique continued, "My wife and I have had difficulties, and we're getting a divorce. We tried, but we were unable to reconcile our differences. However, the separation and divorce are being handled very amicably." Then he turned and directed his attention to Carol. He said, "There is someone in the room with whom I developed feelings. She reciprocated, and we're in love. Carol and I are moving in together."

Carol sat quietly and smiled. The executive team members exchanged glances. It was disorienting and we were speechless. Enrique scanned the room for a response, but none came. "I hope you are all happy for us," he mumbled. With no response from us, Enrique and Carol exited the room together.

As soon as they left, the discussion that followed centered on loss of trust and violation of ethics. It was reckless and imprudent to hire someone with whom you are having an affair to a senior position in the company.

The irony is that the individual brought in to address the crisis in staff turnover led to turnover of an executive director. The last thing CDS needed during this difficult time was another executive director in only six months. We left the room and returned to our offices. I called Adam to share the news of the meeting, conveying our disappointment and renewed concerns for the future of CDS. Adam ended the call, thanking me but informing me there was even more to come.

We soon learned that Carol was a community volunteer coordinator at a national company based in Rochester prior to being hired by Enrique as HR director at CDS. Our executive director had clearly violated our trust and put his personal life over the good of the organization.

Enrique was gone within the week, and Adam stepped in to fill in as interim executive director. Adam had sprouted his own concerns about Enrique. He had been negligent in most of his responsibilities: returning CDS to financial health, shoring up human resources, rebuilding quality assurance, and nurturing community relations, an area on which he had marketed himself during his interviews. Rather than addressing the issues at CDS he was enjoying extended lunches with Carol and stuffing an expense account with lavish dinners.

My confidence that the search firm knew what it was doing was shaken. CDS's contract with the search firm included a clause that if their candidate didn't last one year in the position, they would conduct another search at no cost. That process began, and soon a candidate was identified. He ran a small not-for-profit organization. He was in his 30s—a decent fellow, but lacking in personality. He showed very little emotion and answered questions without any level of interest or engagement. I was more concerned that his tenure in executive management was limited. CDS's budget was $16 million and it was a more complex organization than his prior company. However, we all wanted to see him succeed, and we were in dire need of an executive director.

Julie Frost was CDS's director of vocational services, with whom I enjoyed a close relationship. She and I met with the new executive director during the transition and advised him on how to deal with Adam as board chair and Brigitte, Adam's wife, as the CDS Foundation's executive director. The foundation's work had come to a halt while Brigitte turned her attention to CDS's affairs. Brigitte had become Adam's eyes and ears at CDS. She had power, and everyone was careful to please her. We strongly advised the incoming executive director to avoid getting in Brigitte's crosshairs. After all, I had a close relationship with Adam, Brigitte's husband and wanted everyone to get along. The executive director did not heed these warnings.

Despite having a new executive director, Adam remained the *de facto* head of the organization and committed himself to steering CDS through the turbulent time. Julie and I began meeting frequently with Adam and Brigitte, and he invited us into board meetings where new members were asking hard questions. They didn't like the organization's unrest and directed their concerns to Adam, questioning his leadership. It was tense, and we, the senior staff, were nervous. *Could CDS withstand more turmoil?*

Adam felt targeted, but showed resolve. After a challenging board meeting, he pulled Julie and I aside and said, "I have never failed at anything. I have sacrificed myself to help CDS, and I'm not going anywhere. You all should stay and join me as we move forward." Julie and I confirmed our support.

That evening, I unloaded my concerns on Yvonne. I feared that CDS was headed for extinction. Our quality of service was substandard, finances were in shambles, and there was a steady exodus of staff. Moreover, we weren't doing right by the people we served. Our reputation in the community, blemished with vehicle fraud and the loss of two executive directors in less than 12 months, was in tatters. The situation at CDS seemed hopeless. I looked to Yvonne for reassurance.

"If all this is true, maybe you should start looking for a new job," she said. "My part-time job at the grocery store can't support our family."

She was right. Our children were in school doing their best, and we wanted them to have the best we could afford.

By now it was early January of 1998. The new CDS executive director was floundering. I took Yvonne's advice, pulled the trigger, and selected an executive search firm to help me find a job. Within a week, I was offered the opportunity to run a 120-bed assisted living community called The Fountains. But it was in Detroit. "Would you be interested in relocating?" they asked.

"Yes," I replied, seeing no other option. In my mind I was jumping from a sinking ship and needed a lifeboat. Treading water was not an option. Within days, I completed a second phone interview with the leadership of The Fountains. I felt good about the interview, and they apparently agreed. Shortly after, the search firm called asking for references. The job was mine if my references checked out.

I put the phone down and reflected deeply on all the opportunities CDS had afforded me. I, a person from the third world, had left that world behind and risen to the senior level of one of the leading not-for-profit organizations in Rochester. I had made friends with the people we served: my direct staff, parents and advocates, board members, senior management leaders, and OMRDD staff at the local and state levels. I pursued and obtained an MPA degree, learned to play golf, and moved my family to a new home in Penfield. Our children had settled into their new schools, and we were settling into our new life. Now I was preparing to abandon the organization that had done so much for me and leave Rochester, a city that had become home. I was suddenly conflicted and irresolute about my decision, but I knew I had to finish the search process. It was a difficult time and I felt unsettled and unsure. The situation at CDS seemed hopeless. I prayed that God would help my family and I find our way forward.

17
GOOD LUCK

WITH THE OFFER in hand, I needed to prepare Adam Goldstein for the reference check call he would receive from The Fountains, so I scheduled lunch with him at a local restaurant. *Hopefully, he will be happy for me,* I tried to convince myself. With the future of CDS uncertain, my departure shouldn't be a great surprise to him.

This lunch began as usual. We both ordered grilled chicken and baked sweet potatoes and engaged in light conversation. Toward the end of our meal, I said, "Adam, you won't like this, but I have decided to leave CDS. I have had a job offer. I'm not sure the organization will make it."

He furrowed his brow and sniffed, but maintained his calm demeanor. "Where's the new job?" he asked casually. I told him about The Fountains, and Detroit, and handed him the search firm's contact information, informing him to anticipate a call from them. Although he expressed disappointment, he agreed to give me a positive reference. I trusted Adam.

As I stood up, preparing to leave, I felt I should share something that was on my mind that I had not stated to anyone. I said "You know, it's a shame you never looked inside to fill the executive director position. What an opportunity missed!" Adam did not respond. I then turned and walked away. I drove back to the office, conflicted with feelings of remorse, and kept my door closed for the rest of the day. My staff sensed something was amiss, but I couldn't say anything.

The very next morning, my phone rang around 7:30 a.m. It was Adam. He said, "Overnight, I did some thinking, and I'd like to stop by your office today to share some ideas." We agreed on a time later that morning. *Could this have anything to do with how I had left our meeting? Was it possible Adam was considering me for the executive director position?* I suddenly experienced a sense of optimism.

When he arrived at my office, we greeted each other in an embrace. The conversation began unremarkably. Then Adam said, "I contacted the search firm working with you rather than waiting for them to reach out to me for your reference. I hope you don't mind."

And? I thought to myself, holding my breath.

"I asked them what they saw in you to recommend you to the leadership position in Detroit," he continued, leaning forward. "I prodded for specific qualities." I exhaled as he summarized how the search firm "sang my praises." They told Adam that during the interview they encountered a seasoned manager. They shared that I was clear and concise with my answers. Adam was very pleased to hear that I had communicated my leadership style, which leaned toward vision, organization, setting priorities and high performance, and transparency. I had admitted that, while I was relatively new to senior leadership and had much to learn, I was a quick study. I would take the initiative to learn everything about the organization and get to know everyone within a short time. I wasn't one to wait for directions. I thrived on independence and empowerment. Adam relayed all of this to me with expressions of pride.

"Of course, I have you to thank as my mentor and coach," I said.

"And it has been an honor," he said. "And Lew and Phyllis Wolf would like to meet with you."

I was stunned. Lew and Phyllis were the founders of CDS. Lew had served as president of the board for 23 years before handing the reins to Adam. During the early years of CDS, Phyllis served as secretary. They truly were invested in the care of their son, Daryl, and all the people with IDD we served. I had gotten to know them very well and there was a mutual feeling of respect and affection. I learned later that, after talking to the executive search firm, Adam had a discussion with Lew about me relative to the continued struggle of the current Executive Director and the need for a new executive director.

A breakfast meeting was arranged, during which Adam, Lew, Phyllis, and I talked about everything but the executive director position. I was confused. Trying to conceal disappointment, I behaved as if it were simply a friendly lunch and avoided the subject. But it is often hard to know what is on the minds of people. Later Adam told me they had decided to remove the current executive director and replace him with me. The meeting with him and Lew was simply for Lew to enjoy breakfast with me. The next day, Adam sent out notice for a meeting of the board of directors, not inviting the new executive director. At this meeting, they would vote to remove the executive director and to appoint me as his replacement.

The evening before that meeting of the board of directors, I spent time thinking about who would be my second in command. Julie Fost, the director of vocational services, and I were very close. We were often on the phone after hours as we discussed staffing and other operational issues. She and I were a team, but I also knew she wouldn't react well if she were taken by surprise by my promotion to executive director. So, while I swore confidentiality to Adam, I called Julie and posed a hypothetical scenario. I asked, "If the board approaches me to take the executive director job, would you serve as my deputy?"

She laughed dryly. "That's too big of a hypothetical scenario. What if they ask *me* to take the job? Would you support *me*?"

"Absolutely," I said. I was sincere, but I also knew fully well that her scenario wasn't "in the cards." It was not how I hoped the conversation would go. Julie was tough when her mind was made up. I thought, *Could she be a potential problem*? I ended the conversation quickly.

The following evening, I waited in Adam's living room with Brigitte for news of the board's deliberations. Finally, the call came. I was invited to the board member's home where the meeting was being held. Each board member welcomed me and asked me a few questions, which I gladly answered. The meeting concluded and I went home without a resolution.

The next morning Adam called me at work to relay the news: the votes to terminate the current executive director's employment and appoint me as the new executive director had passed. I immediately called Yvonne to share the news. We were elated. I had just received a vote of confidence from the board, my career took a leap forward, and we wouldn't have to leave Rochester.

My mind shifted immediately to the organization. Big problems were ahead of me. The following day, I sat at my desk and laid out my priorities in writing: meet with staff across the agency, visit the people we served, meet with the local developmental disabilities services office (DDSO) staff as new executive director of CDS, meet with my staff to identify the driving issues, meet with families and develop plans of action.

Once the outgoing executive director left the organization, Adam officially offered me the position. I accepted, and he advised me to convene a meeting with our senior and mid-level employees in one of the conference rooms. I quickly arranged the meeting. The room was packed. As Adam announced the new changes, stillness fell over the room. Another executive director had fallen, and I could sense the uneasiness. It would now take a lot more to earn their confidence. Staff congratulated me on the appointment. A level of confidence and hope showed in the room. After I returned to my office, a steady flow of staff came in and out, congratulating me. However, Julie, my closest colleague, had stormed out of the conference room when the announcement was made and isolated herself in her office.

Later that day, I stopped by her office as I'd done many times. I said, "Hey, Julie. How are you—" My greeting hung in my throat as she immediately cut me off, visibly angry.

"You and I are the same age, and we've been in management about the same length of time," she shouted. "Why wasn't I considered? What happens to me now? I don't see how I can work for you. I'll just keep my head down and do my job." Then she returned her attention to her computer.

I was shocked. I understood why she would feel slighted, but why did she say she couldn't work for me? That took me by surprise. It occupied my mind for days. I spoke about this with Adam, and he suggested that I give Julie time to get over the shock. My hope was that she would stand beside me and perhaps become my Chief Operating Officer.

The next week, I had my first one-on-one supervisory meeting with Julie. I hoped she'd had time to cool off. However, that was not the case. She refused to provide me with a report, either verbally or in writing. Instead, she verbally assaulted me, reiterating the hurtful comments she said before. But the most hurtful was when she said, "I still don't see how I can report to you. I don't respect you." She meant to hurt me and surely did. I felt sadness and disappointment. Before Julie could say anything else, I turned around and left her office. Afterward, I reached out to board members to express concerns about Julie's unwillingness to cooperate. They recommended patience. I agreed. Maybe with time she would come around.

Three weeks into the job, Adam began to temper our communications. By my 30th day as executive director, Adam's support for me had clearly softened, and with his commitment dropping, I felt I could not continue. Staff came to me to report that Julie was saying disparaging things about me, imperiously broadcasting her lack of respect for me.

One evening I complained to Adam about Julie's lack of respect and blatant insubordination. I gave him an ultimatum: either Julie goes, or I go. My ultimatum was met with silence. I added, "If I don't have the board president's support, I should resign."

"I didn't realize how serious this problem had become. The two of you worked so well together, but I support your decision to let Julie go if you think it is best," he said. I was relieved. Perhaps I was turning the corner back into Adam's good graces.

The next morning, I asked the director of facilities, who was responsible for corporate security, to accompany me to Julie's office. Her door was open, so we walked in and I sat in a chair across from her. She looked at me with a flat expression. It didn't bother me. Any affection I had for her was gone. I said, "Julie, let's get straight to the point. Despite my repeated pleas for you to make peace with my appointment and find a way to work with me, you've done the opposite."

She drew in a sharp breath as if to speak, and I held up my hand to stop her. All the color drained from her face as I continued. "You've said to me and others that you have no respect for me and don't see how you could report to me. Well, that must end." I leaned toward her and paused. *This was it.* I said, "Effective immediately, you are terminated from employment at CDS."

Julie gasped with surprise.

I motioned to the facilities director and said, "Help Julie pack her things up and help her to her vehicle."

"Wait, Sankar. Can we talk about this?" she asked. I could sense the sudden surprise and disbelief in her voice.

I stood to leave and left her with these words. "You had your chance. That time has passed. Sorry. Good luck."

It was my first staff action as executive director. I have always maintained that firing an employee is one of the toughest things a leader must do. This case stayed with me for a long time. I came to terms with the fact that, as the senior staff member on the team, it was my responsibility to build a team that was competent and cohesive. With all the troubles at CDS, I needed all leaders to work together as we tackled the myriad of problems.

18
BECOMING CEO

I WAS THE third executive director within a year, and meetings of the CDS Board of Directors were expectedly tense. The organization was virtually bankrupt, but the board had never paid attention to the organization's finances. No attention was paid to the P&L or the balance sheet. Now there was no choice but to address the financial issues which brought the CDS Foundation under scrutiny. The foundation had been established to raise funds to support the mission, especially funding gaps. After five years of operations, it had cost CDS more than a million dollars just for staff salaries, and our return on that investment was nonexistent. Randy Holden was found guilty of fraud against CDS and New York State, and was heading to jail, but he seemed to be only part of the story. His annual donation of $15,000 had dried up, but so had his fraudulent activities. So why wasn't the CDS Foundation in a stronger position?

Attention quickly turned to Adam's wife, Brigitte. Board members were perplexed as to why she was so involved with CDS operations when her role was to raise money to support our mission. When this topic arose, all heads turned to Adam. I learned from board members that Adam spearheaded the creation of the foundation. Because Brigitte had fundraising experience, he had used his influence to convince the CDS Foundation to hire his wife as its executive director. Now in the spotlight, he became agitated and was unable to produce satisfying answers to the board's questions. The conflict of interest was indisputable and it was a problem. The delicate issue was what to do about it.

Concurrently, the board was getting a handle on its governance role, distancing itself from the day-to-day management of CDS. The members recognized the growing need for a chief executive officer. Until then, the president of the board of directors had served as the CEO. At a board meeting, the directors voted unanimously to change my title from executive director to president and CEO. This position was designed for a senior CDS employee whom the board would hold responsible and accountable. Everyone agreed that they needed to step away from the day-to-day operations and allow the CEO to run the business.

President and CEO. This was music to my ears. I immediately revised my job description to reflect the new title and sent it to the board members for approval. With their approval, I signed it and sent it to be placed in my HR file. Suddenly, I felt free from the need to consult Adam for everything. No more seeking permission from Adam to do what I thought was best for CDS.

One of my first actions as CEO was to contact Sy Zielinski, director of the local office of OMRDD. As director of day programs, I had established good communication with Sy and his staff. He was gracious, but with all the recent hits to CDS's reputation, I also sensed caution. I apprised him of the board's dilemma with Adam and Brigitte in hopes he might provide valuable advice. Sy understood the issue and wanted to help. However, he was mindful that OMRDD would not interfere with the organization's internal affairs. He did offer that OMRDD had the authority to investigate any appearance of conflict of interest and any perceived interfere with the organization's smooth operations.

I believed a transparent, independent review of the conflict of interest with Adam as the board president and Brigitte as the executive director of the foundation was appropriate. At the next executive committee meeting, I shared Sy's insights. Adam flushed.

"There's nothing wrong with me—or my wife—at CDS," he stammered. He squinted at me with malice. "I don't know why this is coming up now." Adam knew there was a risk of exposure, and it revealed itself in his body language. Board members were not deterred. They wanted to see a change. However, to keep matters cordial and nonconfrontational, I agreed to keep any investigation internal.

I knew I did the right thing in bringing attention to the conflict of interest issue between Adam and his wife. However, in doing so, I showed Adam—still the board president—that I was no longer deferential to him and his wife. It was a bold and risky move, and I thought, *Adam will not sit still. He will come after me.* I knew I was exposed. But rather than being intimidated, I became more determined to change the way business was done. The situation might have been different if Brigitte had built up a sizable cache in the CDS Foundation.

After that meeting, I called Lew and Phyllis Wolf and asked if I could visit them at their house. They were wonderful people who carried themselves with class and elegance. I had lost my dad when I was 17, had no male figure I could look up to, and had no regular contact with my mother, so I had come to regard Lew and Phyllis as surrogate parents. Over coffee, I explained what transpired with Adam at the meeting. "He seems very upset with me and he could take action against me," I said in earnest. My pulse quickened, and my mouth was dry as I explained my predicament. I worried that I had come up against a wall at CDS.

Lew and Phyllis were very encouraging and supportive. Phyllis told me not to worry and reassured me that everything would work out. Lewis agreed. He told me to remain strong and emphasized that I wasn't going anywhere. I left their home feeling encouraged that everything, as they said, would work out.

The next day, Adam and I had our regularly scheduled lunch meeting at the Roadhouse Grill. After the tense exchange at the executive committee meeting, I was surprised he didn't cancel.

Instead, he was reserved, and when he did speak, everything he said was with pathos about the future of CDS. "It's not looking good for CDS. It may not make it. Maybe it's time we look for options to hand it over to another nonprofit in the area," he said. There was no allusion to the executive committee meeting. He seemed to have already decided to look beyond me.

Debating him was pointless. Instead, I remained silent and concentrated on cutting my grilled chicken.

"There are too many problems," Adam continued. "Who knows what will happen?" He studied my face, which I tried to keep expressionless. He was in a bad place, and I wasn't going to join him. We left that meeting further apart than ever before. On the drive back to headquarters, I thought, *Yes, he has written me off. He is going to fire me. Oh well, I thought stoically.* I didn't share our conversation with anyone, not even Yvonne.

One morning soon after our frosty lunch meeting, I was at my desk when the phone rang. Adam was on the phone. *This is it, the termination call,* I thought. I took a deep breath and said, "Hi, Adam. How are you?"

He was having none of it—no time for pleasantries. He said, "I'm calling to tell you that you are the captain of a sinking ship. CDS is going down, and you're going down with it." This level of vindictiveness was startling, but not totally unexpected. I remained passive.

He continued, "In a few minutes you'll receive a fax with my letter of resignation from the board. I'm not hanging around for what's coming."

It caught me off guard. This was the last thing I expected him to do. I wasn't being fired. And just like that, he was gone. I hung up the phone and exhaled, knowing things would get better.

About a year later, I learned from Lew that the night before Adam called me with his resignation, he had called Lew and demanded that I be fired. Lew told me that he responded to Adam by saying, "Sankar isn't going anywhere." Lew's confidence and support changed the narrative without me knowing. But I knew I still had two major hurdles: Adams's wife, Brigitte, and the CDS Foundation.

I conducted a deep dive into the CDS Foundation and concluded that it was a woefully ineffective organization. Each year, CDS was on the hook for more than $200,000 to cover staff's salaries at the foundation, totaling over $1 million in its five years of existence. Yet, year after year, the foundation never realized a return on that investment. The annual foundation gala was an extravagant affair, but also a money pit. CDS underwrote the expenses for first-class corporate gala settings, including food and guest speaker fees. The same was true for the golf tournament; the funds it raised were negligible. Despite five years of fundraising activities, the CDS Foundation's savings account held only $34,000. It appeared the focus of the foundation was more to get CDS to pay staff salaries and, deliberately or not, provide a smoke screen for phantom vehicles, a bogus vehicle maintenance shop, and a failed chocolate enterprise.

Shutting down the foundation and starting over seemed to be the only option. I convinced Lew and the CDS Board to send notice to the CDS Foundation that CDS wished for it to be dissolved. Upon receipt of the letter, the foundation's board of directors balked. Brigitte, unabashed, dug in her heels. The response was that CDS was in no position to dictate anything to the foundation's board; after all, the foundation had been created as an independent entity. I was shocked. CDS was paying for all the staff salaries in addition to other expenses, so how could they have no power over the foundation? I remained resolved and determined. One morning, I woke up with the solution.

While Lew and Phyllis were on vacation, with Gene McConnell's signature as the CDS Board's vice president, I sent notice to the foundation clearly stating that CDS would cease paying their staff salaries in 30 days.

This triggered a firestorm, but in the end, the foundation's board of directors voted to dissolve it. Yet they were bitter. The directors allowed Brigitte to drag her feet in transferring the $34,000 to CDS. They only acquiesced after we committed those funds to purchasing needed furniture for CDS residences, something they already had the power and discretion to do.

I had found a way to dissolve the CDS Foundation, even when doing so seemed impossible. This event reminded me of an incident that had occurred in Guyana after my first year of college in Trinidad when I went home for vacation. Upon arriving in Guyana I made the slow trek to our village, and when vacation came to an end I made all preparations to return to college in Trinidad. Everything went according to plan until I was in the taxi from the Rosignol ferry to Georgetown around 5:00 a.m.

We hadn't driven more than a few miles before I started to hear a clunking sound, which continued. *Clunk, clunk, clunk.* The vehicle slowly lost power and came to a stop at the side of the road. I thought we had a mechanical problem, but the driver informed me that he had run out of gas. I was shocked and inquired, "Did you not think that you would run out of gas? Why didn't you fill up your tank last night?"

He turned to me in the back seat and said, "I really thought I had enough gas to take me to the gas station."

My frustration mounted as the time for my flight was ever so present in my mind. "Do you realize what time it is?" I asked in disbelief. "No gas station would open before 6:00 a.m. Were you planning to wait for an hour? How would you get to the station? I need to get to the airport at least by 8:00 a.m. for a 9:00 a.m. flight. What can we do?" There was nothing he could think of.

"I didn't think it through," he muttered. We sat there for a few minutes. He had no plan for getting out of the situation and getting me to the airport.

My mind went into high gear. I searched for a solution, and the only one I found was to get out of the vehicle, grab my suitcase from the trunk, and start flagging vehicles heading to Georgetown, hoping a taxi had compassion and room for me. I soon found myself with my hands in the air, waving at every passing vehicle. I noticed they were all full as they whizzed by. No one was even slowing down.

About 10 minutes later, a public passenger bus was heading my way. I flagged it down and when it slowed, I jumped onto it. As I looked toward the seats, I noticed that the bus was full of people of Afro-Guyanese descent. As a child growing up, I had witnessed how Indians and Afro-Guyanese stayed away from each other. The settlements were established to support the sugarcane factories with the inhabitants, East Indians, working in the fields. Afro-Guyanese lived away from the sugar plantations. Politics solidified the separation of these two major races in Guyana. Indians belonged to the People's Progressive Party aligned with the Soviet Union. Afro-Guyana belonged to the People's National Congress, aligned with the United States. Before Guyana gained its independence from the British in 1966, it had an interest in keeping the Indians and Afro-Guyanese suspicious of each other, with their imperialist motto, "Divide and conquer." Yet in our home, the relationship with Afro-Guyanese was different. Mama had many Afro-Guyanese friends who were her coworkers at the hospital. On weekends, these women would go to each other's homes to cook, enjoy their favorite drinks, and just share their everyday stories. I gained a lot of affection for all of them, just as my siblings did. Yet Guyanese society was separated along racial lines.

As I entered the vehicle, everyone stared at me as if to say, "What are you doing here?" I didn't let that bother me. It was very early in the morning and it looked like everyone was barely awake. I turned to the driver and explained that I was headed to Georgetown and asked him how far he was going. He said he was only transporting people within the village and only had another 15 to 20 miles on his route. He promised to take me as far as he could and would try to get me another ride so that I could make my flight. As it was a public bus, the driver stopped every half mile to pick up passengers. It was agonizingly slow making our way through that community.

After about 10 minutes the driver pulled the bus over to a corner of the road, grabbed his lunch bag and a flask, then left the vehicle, disappearing into a café. "Why is this happening? Did I miss something", I said to myself. Five minutes passed. No one seemed concerned, as if this was completely natural. Every minute I wasn't moving was a minute against me getting on that flight. I built up my courage, exited the bus, and entered the café. The sky was still dark, and when I went inside, I found the café dimly lit. I made out someone sitting at the counter, and upon closer observation I saw that it was the bus driver. He had a cup of coffee in front of him and was just sitting there. He was surprised to see me and looked at me with curiosity.

I somehow found my nerve and said, "Sir, as you know, I am headed to Georgetown, and from there I must make my way to the airport. My flight is at 9:00 a.m. It's already close to 6:00 a.m. I would really appreciate your help. Can you get me back on the road?" At first, he just stared at me, and I didn't know what to expect. To my surprise he said, "OK, let's see what we can do." He stood up six feet tall, towering over me. But he had kindness in his eyes, which melted away the hesitation I had. He discarded the remaining coffee and said, "OK, let's go."

We got back on the road, and as we moved, the driver stretched his hand outside the window, waving at each vehicle passing from behind. Everyone was overtaking and passing him. I had a sinking feeling. Then one vehicle slowed down beside us, at which point the driver shouted, "I have someone in the bus headed to Georgetown. Do you have room for him?"

Relief washed over me as the taxi driver yelled "yes" and the bus pulled over to the side of the road. I paid the bus driver and thanked him for what he did for me, grabbed my suitcase, and ran to the waiting taxi. Soon I was in the backseat, resuming the slow and winding road to the airport. During that time, I reflected on the Indian taxi driver who was supposed to take me to Georgetown and ran out of gas. He was inept in performing his job. He was ill-prepared for the simple task of taking me, his passenger, to my destination. There was no sense of responsibility or remorse. On the other hand, the Afro-Guyanese bus driver went out of his way to be helpful, for which I felt deep gratitude.

Two and a half hours later, our taxi arrived in Georgetown. As the driver was preparing to drop me off at the taxi stand, a taxi driver was standing next to his vehicle waving his hand at us. Our driver told him he had a young man who needed to get to the airport as quickly as possible. Fortunately, the taxi driver was looking for one more passenger to take to the airport.

I grabbed my suitcase, and soon we were on the 30-minute drive to the airport as fast as the taxi driver could take us. My flight was scheduled to depart at 9:00 a.m. The boarding process would have started at 8:00 a.m. By the time we got to the airport it was already 9:15 a.m. I was concerned. At the terminal, with my suitcase in my hand, I ran for the British West Indian Airways flight to Trinidad. In Guyana, flights were infrequent. If I missed my flight, there was a strong possibility that I wouldn't leave Guyana for a while.

The terminal was nearly empty. I assumed the flight had already left. At the counter, with apprehension and yet hope, I asked the attendant if the flight had departed. I felt another rush of relief when she told me it had not. I remember looking up and whispering, "Thank you, Lord!"

Soon I was on the flight heading to Trinidad, and I reflected on the entire morning. I was only 19 years old, but felt like I had aged 10 years. It had been a rollercoaster of frustrations and small victories. Most of all I was proud of myself that I never gave up at any point. Instead of looking at it as a morning full of difficulties, I recognized it as a time full of opportunities—of temporary problems that needed solutions. I just had to find them by working with others and trusting the goodness in people. I took the initiative and the actions necessary to arrive at the airport, and I was not taking no for an answer. I learned that I should always focus my energies on the possibilities instead of the obstacles, never give up, and accomplish what I set out to do no matter what. If obstacles arise, we never know what breaks may come our way to make things happen.

With the foundation in our rearview mirror, I focused on the many problems facing the organization and ceased any organized fundraising activities in the short-term. I would have to address our fundraising plan at some point, but for now I could breathe easier.

I truly believe that working with the CDS Board of Directors and OMRDD to resolve the sensitive governance issues in a way that improved the image of the organization and brought about some level of transparency at the organization were a result of the years of learning and growing in the third world.

Me with CDS residents Kevin Martin, at left, and Kenny Moriarity

Phyllis and Lew Wolf, CDS Founders

19
THE RUMOR MILL

BY 1999, THE problems at the CDS Foundation were behind us, and Lew was back at the helm of the CDS Board of Directors. CDS finally had my singular attention. I had never held the top position at any organization before. As the saying goes, "I didn't know what I didn't know," and there was a lot I didn't know. The budget was a priority. CDS was a multifaceted organization, operating 12 residences, 2 day treatment programs, Unistel, its employment services program, and its budding early intervention program, which provided at-home clinical interventions to preschool kids with special needs. I became knowledgeable about every operation, and I was learning to analyze data and make decisions.

Every day I uncovered a new problem. I toured our homes, which had been neglected for years. They looked dreary; the furniture was worn and the pantries were empty. The staff turnover was high. I learned there wasn't enough money to purchase basic items like paper napkins, so staff had cut large towels to make napkins for individuals. At one residence, I was told residents ate in shifts because they didn't have enough plates and other utensils. Staffing was at a bare minimum and with the constant stress, CDS experienced high staff turnover. I knew we needed to generate new revenues if we were ever going to get out of the fiscal crisis.

For our 2000 gala, we wanted to reassure the Rochester community that CDS was moving in the right direction. It was important for local officials to hear about the improvements being made and plans for growth. There were enough reasons to celebrate. We invited all the stakeholders, individuals with IDD, their families, our staff, the local OMRDD staff, and other advocates, filling a ballroom with 250 people. I thought this show of support was important to restore confidence in the community.

When it was my turn to speak, I proudly walked onto the stage and behind the podium in a new navy blue suit, white shirt, and red tie, and addressed the crowd to reassure them of CDS's fortitude and commitment to the community. I implored Sy to provide opportunities for CDS to grow, and he did. We had done what we could to manage costs and maintain efficiency. I knew then that to emerge from our financial crisis and ensure financial health, we needed more revenue, which was only possible through growth. For CDS it was a new beginning. Sy responded to my plea and allowed us to grow. We added five residences within a year, but it was done without the right resources in place. CDS was still operating on a shoestring budget. The new residences were experiencing staffing and quality issues. It would take another year to rebound.

In the meantime, to make matters worse, state auditors appeared for an unannounced visit at one of our intermediate care facilities and sanctioned CDS for inadequate services, which presented an immediate safety concern. They issued a 45-day statement of deficiencies (SOD), which meant CDS had that time period to correct the deficiencies. I had to provide an immediate plan of correction to remain open and satisfy the auditors, which included increasing the number of staff. Audits continued across our facilities, and SODs began to pile up.

It was no surprise to me that our residences came under New York State sanction. At OMRDD's local office, Sy Zielinski reassured me that they were committed to supporting CDS. I had come to trust and respect him, but my staff and I were suspicious that they could be preparing to come in and take over control of our residential operation.

My history working in the field of developmental disabilities had been distinguished by making organizational improvements and fixing problems, but now, being pulled in many directions and lacking funds, I felt impotent. I needed help.

I received the support I needed when we hired a new member to the board of directors, Daniel Crozet, a senior Xerox executive from France. He had been sent all over the world to help turn around troubled Xerox operations. The Crozet family, which included their son, Ian, who was intellectually and developmentally disabled, had recently relocated to Rochester. Before joining the board, Daniel impressed our staff with his insight and intelligent questions as he was making rounds to select a day program for Ian. The staff suggested he could be of help to CDS as we dealt with the mounting problems. After we met, I agreed. He was a fixer, and I was a straight shooter. Together, we were a force to be reckoned with. Or at least, in theory, we should have been.

The serious quality issues at CDS that were raised by New York State were leaked to the press and the response was brutal. There was a huge erosion of trust. *The Democrat and Chronicle* newspaper ran captious pieces on CDS every week. To highlight the problems, they ran a three-page story on CDS, calling attention to the quality issues across the residential programs, as well as complaints from ex-employees and ex-board members. The union that represented our frontline employees pointed to a failure of my leadership.

No one understood or cared that my staff and I had inherited an organization on life support that lacked resources to bring it back to life. This was a culmination of years of sacrificing quality at the expense of badly executed expansion plans, like the downfall of the Sean Donahue Health Center. Misdirected resources, poor planning, and ignoring the problems at CDS's mission-based programs had led to public humiliation.

I worked late into the evenings, both to complete work that couldn't wait and to find refuge from noise after things quieted down to sort out a plan for the next day. I felt overwhelmed. But I never displayed emotion during all of this; I knew that if I showed weakness or lack of trust in my own abilities, it would permeate the organization.

I made my top priority the budget and finances. We found ways to reduce costs while slowly improving the quality of our residential and day programs. To start, we dismantled and replaced the 10-person team responsible for facility maintenance. They were ineffective and lacked any sense of obligation for quality and efficient work. That one change brought about effectiveness and efficiency in facilities maintenance. Yet we were drowning under the unrelenting public and media focus.

To make a bad situation even worse, one evening around 6:00 p.m. I was sitting at my desk at work, and there was a knock on my door. It was CDS's quality assurance director and the director of residential services. They were there to tell me they'd heard gossip that the OMRDD office and the State of New York wanted me to resign from CDS. If I did, the state would show some leniency and go easy on CDS. It was likely this was not a rumor; I'd had a similar conversation with a retired state official whom I had hired to help fix the problems at CDS. He confirmed that the state had lost confidence in my ability to lead the organization, further stating that Sy Zielinski and his team were concerned and wanted to see a change.

Then my two directors gave me an ultimatum. They informed me if I didn't leave CDS, they would resign. I was surprised, and felt humiliated and devastated. A mixture of sadness and anger rose up through my body. This was the time when I needed them most, and they were prepared to abandon me. For the good of the organization, I'd taken on a huge responsibility and placed my whole being into trying to make CDS better, and now I was being told by my employees that I had to leave! I thanked them for their candor and directed them out of my office. The state was asking me to leave; my employees were asking me to leave. I had to face reality.

I didn't do well with ultimatums, so the next day I accepted the directors' resignations. I wouldn't be bullied into a decision that would change both the organization and my life. But what they said gnawed at me. Maybe they were right.

That Saturday morning, I opened my mind to the idea of my resignation. I invited Daniel Crozet, Lew and Phyllis Wolf, and my senior staff to meet me in the conference room of our Unistel facility. I explained the situation and told them I thought it best for the organization if I resign. My senior staff was in tears. They had been by my side through difficulties and success, and they didn't want to see me go.

Daniel, Lew, and Phyllis thought differently. They expressed unequivocal support. They did not want me to leave. Lew said, "Sankar, stay strong. We will get through this." I appreciated their confidence, but I couldn't see a way out. I never made any decision without thinking through every alternative. My mind had been made up. My termination would be effective Monday. Daniel appointed our director of finance as interim CEO. Everyone gave me a hug, and I walked out. Oddly, I felt no relief, and I was still deeply unsettled.

I went home and told Yvonne what transpired. I was conflicted about the entire situation. Yet I remained convinced that my leaving the organization might bring relief. She just sat and listened and didn't say anything.

I knew the decision meant we would no longer be able to stay in our dream home—a home we had recently purchased. I asked our real estate agent to come over to discuss putting the house on the market. She told me she already had people in mind who would be interested. Yvonne remained upstairs while I talked with the agent.

After she left, I went upstairs to our bedroom to discuss our move. I was optimistic, confident I was making the right decision, and that I would find a way to take care of our family. However, when I entered our bedroom, I saw Yvonne sitting at the edge of the bed in tears. It broke my heart, and I tried to comfort her, but she pulled away.

"Please think this over," she pleaded. "We have a nice home. I'm happy here in Rochester with our family. Our kids are settled into their school where they have friends." Yvonne enjoyed her job as the customer service manager at a local supermarket. When I made my decision to resign, I never considered how this would impact my wife and our children.

"If you're worried about money," she continued, sobbing, "I'll work extra hours to help out until you find another job." Then the phone rang.

20
SECOND CHANCES

I ANSWERED THE phone, and it was Lew Wolf. He said, "Sankar, I have news you must hear. I reached out to Sy Zielinski and asked him directly if the OMRDD wanted you out of CDS. Sy told me he didn't want to see you go." Lew explained that while Sy confirmed New York State's reservations about CDS as an organization, he personally had no concerns about my leadership. "I think you should reconsider. CDS needs you," Lew added.

Tears welled up in my eyes, and I began to choke up, but I knew I needed to maintain my composure. I forced a response. "Thank you, Lew," I said, as if we were concluding a business meeting. "I'm grateful for your intervention." Once again Lew had been my strongest advocate, as he had been when Adam Goldstein was eager to get me fired.

With that call, my perspective shifted 180 degrees. I stared out the window into the distance where the sun was rising and thought of the two directors who had resigned. It shook my confidence in myself because I allowed it to, and now I knew that was the wrong attitude. I let rumors cloud my judgement. Now I had to go back to my staff and the board and tell them my resignation was premature.

But before I could do so, I was surprised to find that my senior staff had already jumped into action on my behalf. Each had an inside connection to people at OMRDD and learned that either there was no talk of my need to resign or there was talk of leniency to the organization if I did. OMRDD was aware of problems, but no one doubted my abilities to fix them. The rumor was just that—a rumor.

I felt like George Bailey in *It's a Wonderful Life* when all the people of Bedford Falls whom he had helped over the years came to his aid during a period of crisis. I had made up my mind to rescind my resignation and informed my staff. I was relieved to see they were excited when they heard this news.

I called Lew and Daniel to inform them I had reconsidered my resignation and would stay if they still wished. They were delighted.

Yvonne was listening into my conversations on the phone. Her mood was suddenly buoyant, and she thanked me for changing my decision. She understood I had been juggling so many things at once. Most importantly, she told me she and the kids loved me and would support me in any decision I made. All I could do was embrace her and remain silent as a tempest of emotions swept through me.

On Monday I showed up at our headquarters like any other day, but when I arrived I found Sy Zielinski and his deputies from OMRDD in the lobby. They came to show their support upon learning that I was remaining as the CEO of CDS. The director of finance, who had been appointed acting CEO, cheerfully handed the scepter back to me.

Then another rumor drifted onto the shores of my office. The senior leadership of a highly respected "sister" agency, and one of our competitors, had approached Sy Zielinski with a proposal to take over operations of our two day programs, or at least the program at our Webster location. While this competitor operated a large residential program, it lacked a day program comparable in size to ours. So I met with Sy to ask if this was true.

This time the rumor was true. Then Sy added that he had made it clear to the other organization's leadership that OMRDD wasn't in the business of shutting down organizations and breaking them up. Sy once again had our backs. In another meeting, Sy reiterated his continued support of our organization and his desire to work with me. He advised me not to be distracted by the noise.

As I returned to my office, I thought hard about what had happened and what lessons I had learned. I would not let others shake my own confidence in myself. I should turn a deaf ear to gossip. I should do my own research before making bold, life-altering decisions. Lastly, I should always consider the collateral impacts my decisions had on others, particularly what impacts they may have on my family.

21
LIGHT AT THE END OF THE TUNNEL

WITH RENEWED FOCUS as CEO, my first priority was to hire a replacement for the residential director who had resigned in the fog of rumor. My search extended beyond the geographic boundaries of Rochester. Eventually, I hired a fellow who lived outside Buffalo, about 50 minutes West of Rochester. He was a very qualified candidate with great experience in the IDD field and didn't mind the commute. He was upbeat and affable. He was eager to roll up his sleeves and get to work. Under his skilled directorship, our situation gradually got better.

Despite my leadership successes, I still felt like an outsider and an unknown quantity in the not-for-profit IDD world. I was often blunt and standoffish, possibly a patrimony of my culture and upbringing. I wasn't gregarious. I didn't readily make friends. I lacked the skill to walk into a room and take over a conversation. My style instead was to enter a room and scan the audience, then approach people I knew before engaging people I didn't know. If I was going to be a successful CEO, I knew this had to change.

The people I dealt with on a business level often told me that they appreciated me for being straight and to the point. But I could skirt social propriety when I used the same approach in social situations. I also developed a reputation for keeping my word and never going back on an agreement. Together, I believe these qualities assisted me in my role as CEO. I always gave priority to the business of running the organization. We could be friends, but business was business, and I knew how to separate the two.

We had regular meetings at the OMRDD local office. One day I arrived early and was approached by Sy's deputy, Marie O'Horo. Marie worked closely with my staff on rates and finances. She was strikingly elegant and professional, and as she extended her hand and smiled, she told me she had something important to tell me. Marie was not the type to engage in casual conversation, but now she seemed to want to talk to me in earnest, and I sensed it wasn't about business matters.

One of her best friends, a teacher at the Penfield Middle School, had shared with her a story about one of her students, a young man who was shy and yet eager to learn, who had captured her attention and affection. With some guidance, in a short time the young man came out of his shell and was blossoming. He was always kind and considerate, and he always listened to her. Marie paused and searched my face for a reaction. I had no idea where the conversation was headed, or who she was talking about, so I had none.

"Come on, Sankar, you know who I am talking about," she said. "It's your son, Andrew."

With all that had been on my mind, I didn't at first make the connection. What did I have in common with a young student at Penfield Middle School? Of course, it was Andrew, and I beamed with pride.

My memory drifted to a moment when Andrew was only five years old. We were at a family get-together, and all the kids were running around the house, waiting for supper to be ready. My father-in-law was coming down the stairs and stubbed his toe against one of the railings. He was in a lot of pain, and he had to sit on one of the steps, waiting for the pain to subside. All the children were oblivious except Andrew. He rushed to help his Grandpa, saying

"Papa, I saw that you hurt your foot. Are you OK? Can I bring you something?" Somehow this impressed Yvonne's father, and he would frequently recount how Andrew's empathy and kindness was unique, and evident at a young age.

I thanked Marie for her kind words and told her that I would pass on what she said to Andrew. That evening, I shared Marie's account of Andrew with the family. He was expectedly humble. This event opened a door to a greater friendship with Marie and, indirectly, Andrew had helped his father's professional relationship without knowing.

As we put the CDS residences on the path to financial restoration, I focused on Unistel, our employment services division, which had operating losses of about $500K a year. We wondered how this was possible. The capital expenditure to purchase the Blossom Road facility to accommodate a planned expansion of the contract to assemble Kodak disposable cameras was certainly a factor. This facility acquisition occurred right before Kodak canceled the contract and sent the business to Mexico. How could CDS not know that was coming? CDS was left holding a large mortgage without the revenue to cover the mortgage payments. With the loss of the Kodak contract, Unistel was limited to light manufacturing, such as stuffing envelopes and other collateral materials for companies. That was not going to dig Unistel out of its financial hole.

To further exacerbate the financial issues, the cost associated with serving people with IDD was more than envisioned. The Unistel plant was intended for higher-functioning people with IDD. This meant it should be a more efficient operation where fewer employees were needed to complete work, keeping labor costs down. However, that was not the case. Unistel employed people with IDD who had high social and behavioral needs that required close staff supervision throughout their day. The New York State revenues were insufficient to cover all the support staff salaries and those of the IDD workforce. This all contributed to a negative P&L.

After a preliminary analysis of the data, I realized this model—employing individuals with high needs—was not sustainable. Under the current funding structure, Unistel would never become profitable. But I needed more data. I met with my staff and asked them to build a profile of every individual attending Unistel, including the level of support needed and the cost of providing this support. The data confirmed what I suspected: serving people with severe difficulties without adequate funding was bankrupting Unistel. Without Sy's help, I feared there was no future for Unistel.

I went to his office to discuss the findings. With characteristic bluntness I told him, "Without a significant rate adjustment from New York State, Unistel will be forced to lay off 45 individuals with IDD in 30 days."

He seemed surprised and asked me to elaborate on my findings. I provided some examples but I also sensed that he wanted to move slowly. OMRDD's standard practice was to expect CDS to spend money up front and hope to be repaid later. However, I explained to Sy that CDS was in no position to incur further deficits since our line of credit was already fully extended. I added, "Hoping that someday CDS will be reimbursed for deficits is not a solvency strategy."

Sy knitted his brow in thought. Then he asked for documentation on each individual who would be affected by the layoffs. We compiled the information and sent it to his office. Within a few weeks, Sy's office notified CDS of new rates. OMRDD *quadrupled* the funding that Unistel received for the 45 people who would have been impacted. The effect was dramatic. The financial forecast tilted from a steady descent into bankruptcy to a trajectory toward profitability. I was grateful to Sy for helping me to turn a problem into a success. I also realized the key to our financial future was working with our state partners.

After 21 months as CEO, I felt the ground beneath CDS solidifying.

22
THE TURNAROUND

AMIDST OUR GROWING pains, we received heartbreaking news. By early 2003, Lew Wolf, the founder of our organization and the person who had advocated for me on multiple occasions, was diagnosed with Alzheimer's Disease and stepped down as president of the board of directors. The news hit me particularly hard. I loved that man and admired his resolve throughout this difficult time. His sense of purpose, decency and hope shone through. Lew agreed that we needed to transition board leadership, which I was already anticipating.

Daniel Crozet seemed like the natural replacement as president of the board of directors. He was an active board member and already felt like he had become part of the CDS family. His son, Ian, had been placed in Unistel and, per my request, Sy had found a way to fund the cost of his services. Daniel agreed with me and accepted the President position. He became my mentor and coach, teaching me the strategies he had learned at Xerox to boost performance and quality. Daniel led strategic planning sessions at CDS, focusing on five essential areas: (1) provide world class service; (2) recruit and retain highly skilled and dedicated people; (3) market CDS's services and develop opportunities to promote its mission; (4) maintain an effective IT system, using it to empower managers; and (5) maintain and promote financial strength. These five strategies served as our framework for developing and executing management plans during my tenure as CEO.

To further develop our team, I took our senior staff to a leadership seminar in Las Vegas with Shane Yount, a renowned corporate trainer, who introduced us to process-based leadership. Strategy is good, but without good process, there is no progress. We blended the Xerox business approach with Yount's process-based leadership and developed a custom approach that proved effective and remained our approach to management during my tenure. Operational discipline became a key element of our culture. We were building the business foundation CDS had lacked, and in a relatively short period of time, we completed our financial turnaround from losses to profits.

Pulling out of the financial crisis, I was committed to improving our strategic planning process. Before I became CEO, the CDS executive team and the board of directors engaged in strategic planning sessions every five years. But these sessions became little more than an exercise, since none of the strategic goals ever left the conference room.

It was a disciplined process. We moved the sessions to an annual, rather than a five-year, schedule, followed by meetings between the staff and the board of directors to update our strategic goals and keep them in focus. The goals were formulated around a three-year business projection and plan.

These sessions were facilitated by Cenette Burdine, a consultant who became a good friend. Her role was to be an "honest broker" and challenge assumptions and decisions. After the annual sessions, Cenette updated the strategic plan and prepared it for my review, ensuring that the plan aligned short- and long-term goals. This plan was shared with key people within the organization. Once the plan was agreed upon, it was used quarterly as a tool to measure progress. This process became the foundation for our growth and diversification.

Over the next 23 years of my administration, our financial statements showed strength and fiscal health. Early on, untangling our finances was so traumatic that I never had time to enjoy the financial improvements we experienced. I believed that without maintaining sharp focus, pressure, and a sense of urgency, we could become complacent—and I believed complacency was the slippery slope to disaster. I expected every employee to work hard, and smart, with the senior staff setting the example. Our key stakeholders—from our individuals to the state regulatory bodies—expected more from us, and I expected the same from my team and myself. This translated to excellence, but left little time for celebrating our successes.

I always did my best to recognize everyone in the organization, especially our frontline staff. I prided myself on remembering everyone's name. I benefited from a good memory, but that was not enough. *It was important to me to remember people's names.* People visiting CDS were impressed that I could call our staff members, people with IDD, and our volunteers by their first names.

Over the years, I recognized several mid-level management staff with potential for growth, and encouraged them to go to school and further their education, just like the encouragement I had received from the chief chemist at Coca-Cola years ago. They all did, and I saw that they were promoted to senior-level positions. I'm proud that the majority stayed with me during my duration as CEO at CDS.

While I showed my staff how much I valued them by making sure that they were paid at the top of the industry pay scales and that they had strong performance incentives, I realize now that spoken words also mattered. I would often tell the staff not to take my frequent, critical feedback as lack of confidence in them. I was just encouraging them to be better. They knew very well that if I didn't want them in the organization they wouldn't be there. In hindsight, it would have helped to sit down with my staff and sing their praises when they did well. But instead, I led us from one fire hose to the next without catching our breath.

I lived by a sense of urgency that made me think of the job only. That led to a stressful life that sent me into a medical crisis in 2002, resulting in open-heart surgery. In the scheme of things, I have no regrets. You're never too old to learn. I did the best I could with a sense of peace in who I was and what I brought with me to the job every day. I suspect the staff who left the organization had a different perspective but I hope that they would say that whenever there was a departure I ensured everyone had a soft landing. It was the least I could do.

PART III

MOMENTOUS DECISIONS

PART III begins in 2002, after the heart bypass surgery I wrote about in Chapter 3. Looking back, with CDS suffering through, and surviving, so many turbulent events, I feel even more grateful for my own chance at a new life. In Chapter 25, I lay out my strategy and organizing initiatives that laid a strong foundation that contributed to CDS's growth. The subsequent chapters give an overview of how I connected political operatives and business leaders with CDS, as I pursued some of my most ambitious projects: building a new headquarters, founding iCircle-managed long-term care services, building Warrior Salute Veteran Services, and growing Unistel's global reach. This growth occurs under the shadows of a lawsuit, changing federal and state regulations, local objections, and international shipping fines. By 2018, CDS leads the establishment of a care coordination organization, which shows early signs of trouble. I begin to wonder if I have committed hubris by taking the organization too far.

23
A NEW BEGINNING

AFTER HEART BYPASS surgery in 2002, I stayed at home for six weeks, carefully following the doctor's orders. Finally, I felt well enough to return to work, and gradually eased into a full-time schedule. The first day, a bright and crisp winter morning, I drove my regular route, but very slowly because my chest was still healing. I didn't want to risk making unexpected stops or sudden turns. I tried to avoid every bump and pothole. I lived close by, so the trip lasted only 15 minutes, but it felt more like an hour.

At the office, I settled in for the day with my assistant, Cindy. I decided to follow everyone's advice and return to work part time at first. My limited schedule forced me to delegate some work to others, which relieved some stress, something strongly recommended by my doctors. I stopped trying to "own" everything. I needed to trust my staff members to do their work, and to give them the space to do it, which in turn required their loyalty. Some staff who undermined my leadership were replaced. The new staff looked to me as a leader to support and empower them to make good decisions, not as someone who would solve everything for them.

While these changes to my leadership style helped to reduce stress, I found I had more time available to imagine the way things ought to be at the organization, focusing on the mission. Removing myself from day-to-day operations was pivotal in allowing me to approach the CEO position like a CEO.

If I expected to stay healthy, the doctors insisted that I make changes to my activities and lifestyle outside of work too. I was disciplined, and took action to reduce stress, maintain health, and improve strength. My priority was to attend to my spiritual life. I started to go to church and read my Bible regularly. I believed that God had spared my life, and for that I was grateful. I paid more attention to my family. I promised them I would start taking time off every three months so we could go on vacation together, which we continued for years. I paid attention to my diet and began an exercise program designed to strengthen my heart. I spent at least 45 minutes on the treadmill at least five days per week. While walking on the treadmill, I prevented monotony and I made use of the time by reading a wide variety of books, which took my mind to faraway places. All these things together helped me tremendously to manage my stress. Last but not least, I picked up golf again to augment my time on the treadmill. As the weeks and months passed, these activities became routine.

On the golf course with my friends, I developed a reputation for getting more lucky breaks than they thought I deserved through chance alone. After our games, they would grumble on their bar stools about impossible golf shots that started out bad but miraculously turned out good. For example, I would tee off with a ball that was pulling left, watching it curve in a direction away from the hole. Physics dictated that, after it landed, the ball should continue to roll to the left, but my ball would defy Newton and take an unexpected jump to the right. Or I would hit a "duff shot," where my club would graze the top of the ball, and instead of stalling after a few yards, the ball would continue to roll and roll in the direction of the hole, as if moved by some invisible force. But it was the top spin that helped the ball roll well beyond where it should have stopped. Or a ball would head for the water, and rather than disappear below the surface, would skip along the surface effortlessly like a water strider, and settle on the fairway. These shots became affectionately known as hitting a "Sankar Ball," a term which took its place in our golfing lexicon, along with duffs and flubs and yanks and hooks.

With practice and improved strength, my golf game improved and I relied more on skill and less on Sankar Balls, to the satisfaction of my golf partners. And although they passed off the Sankar Balls as incredibly good luck, my interpretation was different. They were providence. In the same way that God had provided me the assistance I needed to survive cardiac surgery until I could take control of my own health, He provided me assistance on the golf course until I could regain competence.

He was not done with me yet.

24
STRATEGY AND INNOVATION—UNISTEL'S REBIRTH

ALTHOUGH MY DOCTORS had cautioned me about the dangers of stress on my heart and health, returning to work meant returning to a demanding job. I was committed to CDS's growth plan, which included Unistel. Just before CDS lost the contract assembling Kodak disposable cameras, Unistel had moved from headquarters to a different facility with a large mortgage. With new resolve, I decided to visit the new Unistel plant to determine if we could restore it to profitability and growth.

A staff member gave me a tour of the facility. Midway through, standing in the hallway, he opened an adjacent door, and a strong scent wafted over us. It was the unmistakable smell of garlic, and it immediately carried me to warm memories of my home in Guyana. It acted like a spell.

I learned that Unistel was in the spice business. Inside this room, three individuals with intellectual disabilities were manually packing spices into bottles. Unistel branded the spices "Sensational Seasonings." Its primary customer was the US military, to which we provided a limited quantity of 10 spices, one being garlic. The revenue grossed about $100,000 annually.

I was intrigued, and asked to speak to the person in charge of the contract. I was introduced to Jack Pipes, a former procurement officer for the US military, who had come out of retirement to work at Unistel. As the liaison to the military, Jack collaborated with the National Institute for the Severely Handicapped (NISH), which facilitated federal contracts to private nonprofit IDD organizations and secured the spice contract. But it seemed so small.

Jack explained that CDS management had decided to contain the size of the contract. CDS lacked the finances to invest in equipment and procure a larger volume of products needed to expand the business and wanted to avoid another costly mistake. The challenges at the residence for individuals with severe autism, and the debacle with the Sean Donahue Health Center, had left them cautious and shaken.

I immediately saw the opportunity to transform and grow Unistel. I asked Jack if we could renew conversations with NISH, and he expressed confidence that we could.

"We must grow Unistel, Jack" I said. "I think the spice business is the way to do it."

Jack was giddy. No one before had proposed expanding the spice business with such conviction. He was thrilled.

To purchase new equipment for the spice business, but with no cash to do so, I contacted Ann Costello, the executive director of the Tom Golisano Foundation. A Rochester native, Tom had established his foundation with a mission to support organizations that worked with people with IDD. He had a personal interest in organizations like CDS because his son had intellectual and developmental disabilities. Tom agreed that investing in our spice packaging equipment could be profitable, while providing meaningful work opportunities for individuals with IDD. He agreed to fully fund the purchase of equipment, setting up four semiautomatic production lines. This decision helped create 40 well-paying jobs. Tom and his foundation came to the rescue, and for that I am eternally grateful.

With the spice business growing, I encouraged the team to generate more ideas to grow Unistel. The general manager suggested that we get into the pizza making and packaging business. The goal was to provide frozen pizzas to the US Military, like we did the spices. The problem was, we had absolutely no knowledge of commercial food cooking and packaging. But I didn't want to extinguish creativity. So I indulged in the general manager's idea and visited a local bakery that made and packaged baked goods on a large scale. We contracted with the bakery to provide frozen pizzas to the New York State prison system. To provide frozen pizza to the prison system was one thing, but to sell to the military was another. We had to be cautious. We lacked expertise and capacity to sustain this venture. Sometimes I laugh when I think about Unistel selling frozen pizzas to the military, but sometimes risks must be taken. Taking a different direction, over a 10-year period, Unistel expanded its spice business from just 10 spices to more than 50 spices, with total revenues of $10 million and a healthy margin.

Across the board, CDS grew organically. I attended the groundbreaking of the new residential sites. We also increased the day programs from two to five. Our efforts were paying off. To drive growth and quality, CDS developed a strategic planning process that aligned its operations, overall strategic objectives, and mission. There was no room to stray from the plan.

Employees operating Unistel's spice packaging machine and labeling bottles

25
THE RIGHT HIRE AT THE RIGHT TIME

I CONTINUED TO collaborate with Sy Zielinski in his role as OMRDD's local director. By 2005, as he approached his 55th birthday, he casually mentioned that he was thinking about retiring as soon as he became eligible for retirement with full benefits. At the time I was thinking of adding another executive to the executive team, but I was hesitant. I believed in a "flat" organization, where I, the CEO, wasn't far removed from the operations. Now, with CDS growing, I saw the benefits of hiring a chief operating officer to supervise the day-to-day operations. None of us on the executive team had the experience or longevity in the IDD field that Sy did.

Sy would more than fit the bill as COO. As OMRDD's director of the local DDSO, he had accumulated great institutional knowledge, experience, and operational expertise. In addition to overseeing nonprofit organizations in upstate New York, he was responsible for overseeing more than 100 state-operated group homes and many state-operated day programs. He worked with several major unions representing the direct care workforce. He had exposure to the state legislature and the governor's office. If Sy joined me at CDS as our COO, he would bring a wealth of knowledge, experience, and maturity. Adding him to the executive team would also likely mitigate concerns about CDS at the state level.

THE RIGHT HIRE AT THE RIGHT TIME

Sy joined me for lunch one day at a local Italian restaurant in Penfield. As soon as we were seated, I got straight to the point. "After you retire, you should join CDS as COO," I said. He sat up straight and his eyes lit up. Clearly, Sy was interested.

"What might that look like?" he asked, his interest piqued.

I listed the scope of the job as I envisioned it. He would have authority for all day-to-day operations. He would participate in the executive team's strategic planning and advise on any matters that involved OMRDD. This role would also require him to attend board meetings and advise the directors on governance issues.

The more I spoke, the more animated Sy became. He quickly made a list of the conditions under which he would retire from his job with New York State and accept the CDS position. We easily agreed on each item on both our lists. Before the server could offer us dessert, we had decided on a compensation package and shaken hands.

Then Sy decided to make a statement. He looked me in the eyes and paused before saying "Sankar, there is only one boss in an organization. I have had my turn running a large organization. I have no need for the CEO job. You can rest assured that you will have my loyalty and support." It was uninitiated, but somehow Sy felt he needed to say it. I am proud to say that Sy kept his word.

Within a few months, Sy retired from OMRDD and assumed his position at CDS. He immediately fit into our executive team like a missing piece of a puzzle. I predicted his addition to our team would allow me more space to plan for the organization, take better care of my physical and emotional well-being, and reduce my stress. Paradoxically, Sy's presence did just the opposite. Sy was intellectually curious, so we frequently engaged each other in high-level, in-depth conversations. I became even more involved in the business, but now with a wise partner to provide valuable advice, it freed me up to explore growth, diversification, and innovation. It reinforced my confidence that we could accomplish greater things.

26
REBUILDING AT THE TOP

IN 2024, I attended a meeting of CDS's leaders and donors in Florida, and when we went around the room introducing ourselves, Mark Peterson spoke: "You all should know that I've been on the CDS Board for more than 20 years, after first telling Sankar 'No.'" There were others in the room who felt precisely the same way, and it invoked laughter among all of us.

We had been brought together by a common mission—to support our most vulnerable and needy citizens—and we stayed connected to each other because there was more good work to do. I can't shake the conviction that providence had a role in bringing these talented and compassionate people into my life, usually through some fortuitous chain of events.

When I met Mark, CDS was looking for a new board chair (previously, president), but we crossed paths in an unlikely way. Five years after the CDS Foundation's demise, I hired a director of development, Bill Kennan, to oversee fundraising. He and I carefully pondered how to reintroduce CDS to the community to help with fundraising. I wanted to get it right this time. I was confident in Bill because he was well known in Rochester and knew the local "who's who."

One of the first people Bill suggested I meet was a good friend of his, Mark Peterson. He managed investor relations at the Greater Rochester Enterprise (GRE), a private organization that served as the regional local economic development group and worked closely with the state government in Albany. The organization's members were business leaders who paid a yearly fee to sit on GRE's Board of Directors. Mark's job was to keep all the business leaders engaged. He also served on several nonprofit boards in the Rochester area. He seemed like an ideal addition to our board of directors.

We met for breakfast at the Browncroft Family Diner in Penfield. After ordering breakfast, Mark said to me, "I'm only meeting with you out of respect for Bill." He explained that, in addition to his job at GRE, he served on several boards in the area and didn't see how he could accept another volunteer role.

His frankness placed me a little on my back foot. I hadn't shared anything about CDS with him, yet he preemptively shut me down. But I wasn't discouraged. I never took no for an answer. I told him about myself, which included my immigration story, the problems I had overcome, and how my family arrived in Rochester. His attitude softened.

Then I transitioned the conversation to CDS and the shape we were in when I became the executive director. I told him about all the changes we made to the organization and the growth that came from those changes. He leaned in and asked questions as I went along. He became engaged, and occasionally offered a suggestion and referenced his experience.

Eventually, our plates were cleared, and the meeting was ending. Mark turned to me and said, "I can't believe I'm saying this, but how can I help?"

I whimsically told him he could really help the board of directors.

"OK," he responded without pause. We shook hands on it.

Besides, I was filled with hope that Mark could be of enormous help to me as we looked at CDS's future. That hope turned to reality: for the next 10 years, as board chair, Mark gave me unwavering support and helped accelerate the growth of CDS. To this day, he continues to serve on the board of directors.

The next person providence placed in my path appeared during an event sponsored by KeyBank. They had a suite at Bills Stadium in Buffalo, and our relationship manager invited my CFO and I to a Sunday game. We were told we would make one stop as we headed to the stadium. On the way, the driver stopped at the corner of Douglas and East Avenues in the City of Rochester, in front of an elegant, historic mansion. Waiting for us was Dennis Buchan, a retired regional KeyBank president. He and his wife, Mary, had moved from Albany to Rochester and traveled with the upper echelon of the community. Dennis had served as the chair of the Republican Party in Albany and continued his involvement with the Republican Party in Rochester. He also served on several philanthropic boards. Clearly, he would be an ideal board recruit.

After the football game I asked Dennis if he would join me for lunch sometime, and he agreed. Then he invited me to lunch at the Country Club of Rochester, where he was a member. A CDS Board member, Rich Ferrari, who had a career in banking, knew Dennis very well. Rich provided sage advice: I should spend more time listening than talking, asking questions more than sharing information. I took this advice to heart.

Dennis had a refined but comfortable manner and put me to ease as soon as we were seated. He educated me on the politics of New York State, Albany, and Rochester. I followed politics at the national and local levels, and his knowledge of the political landscape was quite astute. He explained how charitable foundations operated, and what types of fundraising activities were—and weren't—successful. Dennis was not a proponent of fundraising events. He targeted galas, emphasizing the inordinate amount of time in planning and energy that were required to produce galas that usually resulted in raising funds, most of which went to cover expenses. "Galas are a dime a dozen in Rochester," he said. "And they don't raise money."

I nodded, recognizing that I was being given a master class in politics and fundraising, among other things. The more he spoke, the more certain I was that, with his knowledge of the local community and his expertise in fundraising, we could create a brand-new foundation. By the end of the meeting, I saw exactly why CDS needed Dennis. "Your insights on foundations illuminated several problems with our former CDS Foundation," I said. "I would love for you to chair a new foundation board for CDS. We need someone with your character and extensive experience."

Dennis agreed to come on board. We worked with our legal team to establish the new CDS Wolf Foundation as a nonprofit organization, applying Dennis's wisdom and my lessons learned from the CDS Foundation. This time, CDS would be the foundation's controlling member and retain the right to approve and remove its directors. We would never again make the mistake of creating a totally independent and self-governing entity. Further, CDS would approve its budget and be informed of key decisions. To complete the loop, the bylaws stated that the foundation's chair would also serve on the CDS Board of Directors, with a standard agenda item to update the CDS directors of the foundation's activities.

Next, Dennis advised me on how to structure the foundation around corporate giving, individual giving, and community giving. We developed charters for each area and sought candidates to serve on the foundation's board of directors. Soon we assembled a board of nine people, with Dennis as the board chair. I followed his advice for the next several years, and with his leadership we developed the CDS Wolf Foundation into a world-class fundraising organization.

Over time, as I got to know the Rochester business community and especially the law firms, I was introduced to Richard Yarmel, a partner at Harter Secrest & Emery. Rich was very interested in the CDS services because he had an uncle with IDD who lived in another part of New York State. He gladly joined the board of directors and has been tremendously helpful these many years. When the opportunity presented itself, Rich used his influence to convince a private philanthropic organization based in New York City, on which he served as a board member, to donate major funds to the Warrior Salute program every year. I am forever thankful for his unwavering support, his wisdom, and his continued interest in the CDS mission.

At some point, I learned of Bill and Kathy Woodard. Their daughter, Angelica, was accepted at CDS's Turk Hill Road apartments. Bill was retired from the private, for-profit industry, and besides looking for a place for Angelica to live, they wanted to get involved and provide their support. This led to Bill serving as the chair of the finance committee for years. Kathy served on fundraising committees. They also made generous gifts to the organization. The CDS mission remains strong because of parents like Kathy and Bill.

I've written about Rich Ferrari and Greg Gribben in this book. Their service, as chairs of the board of directors through the many crises and challenges, and the tremendous growth and diversification of CDS, has been exemplary.

Mark Peterson, Dennis Buchan, Rich Yarmel, Kathy and Bill Woodard, Rich Ferrari, Greg Gribben, and so many others have contributed immensely to CDS. I am forever grateful for their service and support. They exemplify the chance encounters and chains of events that kept unfolding in a way that showed me that my life mattered. I had a purpose, and as I moved toward it, the right people continued showing up at exactly the right time.

27
GIVING MY CHILDREN OPPORTUNITY

LIFE CAME FULL circle unexpectedly when my children showed interest in working at CDS. In 1987, I entered my first job in the intellectual and developmental disabilities space in large part because I was seeking help for my daughter, Abigayle. By 2005, she had obtained an associate's degree in administration. Immediately following her graduation, the subject of finding a job arose. She asked if she could work at CDS. I was very proud to hear that Abigayle wanted to work there, and I encouraged her to apply.

She was offered a position in the human resources department and has worked in that department ever since. Abigayle loves her career at the CDS, performing duties at the headquarters that require her to interface with the employees and guests as she coordinates the front desk activities. Since day one, Abigayle thrived on going to work every day and she has done an outstanding job.

Abigayle has plotted her life's path in an exemplary manner. While both of our children were encouraged to explore their musical interests, Abigayle showed a talent for playing the violin. Andrew kept up with the saxophone through high school, but dropped it after he went to college. Abigayle loved playing the violin, became very proficient, and has been a volunteer member of the Penfield

Symphony for more than 20 years. She volunteers at her church and participates in groups and missions trips. Yvonne and I are grateful and proud that Abigayle has found meaning in her life and never let her mild learning disabilities stop her from living her American dream.

Andrew joined CDS a short time after Abigayle. He returned home the summer after graduating college with a BA degree, expecting to begin graduate school in divinity studies that fall. To keep him busy, I advised him to get a summer job like every other college student. He found a part-time job working in the classrooms at one of CDS's day programs. He liked his work, and the people liked him. Andrew had a great personality. He was honest, caring, and compassionate. Yvonne and I felt that he could do whatever he put his mind to doing. He returned to CDS every summer until he graduated from Northeastern Seminary with an MA degree in divinity.

Upon finishing graduate school, Andrew continued to work at CDS, changing to a full-time position. I expected that he would naturally pursue a career in theology and either become a pastor or complete a PhD in theology and maybe become a professor. That was our hope, but he had different ambitions.

After several months, I mentioned as nonchalantly as I could that if he wanted to start a PhD program in the fall, he should apply soon. He told me he wished to stay at CDS. He didn't consider CDS a temporary position and wanted to make CDS his career. I had misjudged the situation.

As Andrew advanced through our organization, I became concerned about the potential conflict of interest his employment posed with me as CEO. From time to time, he sought my advice on how to handle his career. Of course, any father would want to counsel his son given the opportunity, but as the CEO, might I be giving him an unfair advantage? At home, we stopped speaking about what was going on with his job at CDS. It created distance between father and son, which I had to accept. If he worked somewhere else, we would probably have normal conversations about his work. That wasn't happening because, as CEO, I had to be mindful of the appearance of conflict of interest.

Life wasn't easy for Andrew at CDS as he assumed more responsibility. People were hesitant to socialize with him because of his relationship with me. He had to work harder than anyone else. Later in his career, Andrew became the director of the day programs. The HR department worked with his supervisor to document every step in the promotion. There, Andrew developed his own management style and shined as a valuable member of the team at CDS. Board members who had known Andrew as a young boy saw him as a capable leader in his own right. I'm grateful that CDS looked beyond the potential conflict of interest and gave him opportunities to grow.

From time to time, people have asked me what I expected of my children. I repeatedly said that all Yvonne and I ever wanted for both Abigayle and Andrew was for them to be good citizens. We are proud parents.

Our daughter, Abigayle

Our son, Andrew

28
AN ERROR PROVIDES AN OPENING

WHEN I JOINED CDS in 1989, its headquarters was in the Town of Perinton on the east side of Monroe County, and remained so until I became CEO. It was a 50,000-square-foot commercial property, built and leased to accommodate CDS's administration and its day training programs. By the close of 2005, we had grown out of the building and needed more space. Many people CDS served lived on the west side, so I began to consider a more central location. Staying in Perinton no longer made sense.

Furthermore, that location became a dinosaur. Services for people with intellectual disabilities were transitioning toward community integration and less segregated settings. The classroom setting was no longer functional, and the facility's age showed. The landlord did as little maintenance to the facility as he could, while the lease payments increased every year. To maintain a good physical environment for its staff and individuals receiving services, CDS took on the responsibility of making the regular improvements and repairs the landlord had failed to do. I made the decision to relocate our headquarters.

I voiced my reasons for relocating in early 2006 at the CDS Board of Directors meeting. They unanimously supported my vision to move from the Perinton facility into a new, modern, and progressive environment, even though I didn't have a clue how we would finance the project. CDS wasn't in a strong financial position, and we moved ahead with the knowledge that funding wouldn't be easy. I set out to assemble a team for the project, including a real estate company to secure the land, an architectural firm to design the property, a CDS team to develop a proposal that we would present to OMRDD and a finance company to obtain financing. With the right people in place, what could possibly go wrong?

We identified a parcel of land of which we would need 10 acres in the Town of Webster off of route 104, a state road connected to the major highways stretching across the Greater Rochester area. This was an ideal location because, since 1987, CDS staff had to drive at least 10 or 15 minutes, depending on traffic, from the location in Perinton just to reach the highways. With this new location, we could get to any other location in the area within 20 minutes. Dave Christa of Christa Development owned the land and we negotiated a purchase of the 10 acre parcel. He also committed to helping us obtain the state funding to build our headquarters on it.

Next, we needed a building designed to accommodate all our services; for that we needed an architect to put our vision on paper. We selected Harrison Bridges, a local architectural firm. Over several meetings, we discussed how to best relocate the day program and the Unistel vocational program, presently at the Perinton location. More importantly, for the day program, we envisioned a more functional, natural, and progressive environment without classrooms. I wondered what this might look like. The CDS team imagined a "Town Square," around which we could structure individual activities. It helped me envision how this Town Square concept would help bring people together.

We sketched out what the setting would look like. One end of the building would house administration; Unistel would be at the other end, and the day program, with all its exciting features, would be in the middle. Also centrally located would be the cafeteria, which would be operated by the individuals who worked at Unistel. At the very end of the building would be an industrial facility, with its own loading dock, to service Unistel. Behind the facility would be an area designated for our fleet of transportation vehicles. We gave Harrison Bridges full creative authority for laying out our concepts.

A couple of months later, I excitedly sat down with the firm to review their preliminary drawings. As I flipped through their packet of materials while they made their presentation, my heart sank. It was conventional and sterile. Clearly missing was any attempt at innovation or creativity. Ten minutes into the hour-long meeting, I stood and said, "You must go back to work. I want to see the Town Square where the activities would take place. Right now, I don't." The architects were stunned, and mumbled apologies before they quickly left. I expected that, like my staff, they would learn that my criticism meant I knew they could do better.

The Harrison Bridges team returned a month later. The message had gotten through: this time they had captured every aspect of our vision. The design included windows with bright and natural light all throughout open spaces. The Town Square, positioned in the middle of the day program, had a vaulted ceiling with skylights, inviting in the sunshine. An elevated area in the Town Square could be used as a stage for entertainment, and the space facing it would easily hold about 100 people.

On the side of the stage was a room for art therapy, which would have a kiln where individuals and staff could create pottery. Next to the art therapy room was a small room with a lot of lighting, ideal for gardening. It had a door to the outside, opening to a large porch and a beautiful garden.

Adjacent to the Town Square was an apartment with a kitchen, bedroom, bathroom, and living area. A key feature was the cabinets installed with a hydraulic system, allowing someone in a wheelchair to press a button and have the shelves go up and down, making cooking items accessible. The purpose of this area was to provide a meaningful environment to train individuals on how to live in an apartment and acquire skills that they could bring to a residence or their own independent living setting. Across from the apartment would be a dance and music room with a technology room adjacent to it.

To access the Unistel from the Town Square, one would pass a fitness facility to help individuals stay active and fit. Further down that hallway would be the cafeteria with a kitchen and beautiful chairs, cubicles, and tables. Behind the cafeteria was a courtyard.

Harrison Bridges had hit the design out of the park. Staff loved the new design. But we still had no money to fund the project. We had to secure an avenue for funding because the Perinton facility's lease agreement was ending soon. By 2005, CDS was paying the landlord $50,000 per month. I told staff that we would never do a lease arrangement again; it was outrageous that, at the end of 20 years, CDS would have paid millions of dollars to the landlord and we wouldn't own the building. I was resolved that CDS would own our new building.

Our only hope for funding was OMRDD. We developed an attractive request and laid out the financial *pro forma*. I instructed my staff to build the *pro forma* based on our monthly lease payment. Shelley Miller, our local contact, helped compile and submit the necessary paperwork to the OMRDD office in Albany, which was packed into three two-inch-thick binders. The documents were painstakingly assembled, from program design to architectural drawings to the financial *pro forma*. Everything was accounted for. I held my breath as my staff took the binders to the post office.

With our submission en route to OMRDD, I contacted Justin McCarthy, Senator Nozzolio's Chief of Staff in Albany, to discuss next steps. Dave Christa had introduced me to the good senator, who committed to helping us to obtain the funding. Justin told me to be patient; the bureaucracy in Albany moved slowly. This did not help. It only increased my sense of urgency.

Midsummer was already upon us, and elections for the next governor would be held in November. I didn't want to take any chances with the new administration, and I was determined to push hard to secure the funding.

We waited a month and then called the OMRDD central office and left a message. No one returned our call, so I called Shelley and asked her to confirm with OMRDD that our package reached them. A few minutes later she called back to reassure me they had received the package. I felt encouraged.

By the end of August, we still hadn't heard from OMRDD, and worry was setting in. I reached out to Justin McCarthy and asked him to speak with his contact at OMRDD. He did, and called me back later that day with a surprise. "Apparently, the CDS package is incomplete," he said.

"What?" I yelled out, dumbfounded. We had double- and triple-checked all the information and carefully followed OMRDD's template.

"OMRDD staff are saying they can't decide on the financial plan because they don't have enough information," he said.

I thanked him and hung up the phone to collect my thoughts. CDS had no backup plan. I had met with my staff multiple times to review the documents, and I was confident our package was complete. Justin and I spoke again a short time later, and we decided to request a meeting with OMRDD's staff. He secured an appointment for us, and my team and I traveled to Albany.

At the OMRDD office we were ushered into a meeting room. I felt like we were on a movie set for *The Godfather*. The lighting was dim and there was a single, rectangular table in the center with six chairs. The only thing missing was cigar smoke. Since becoming CEO, I had always looked on negotiations as psychological exercises, and this room's mood only heightened my readiness to go toe-to-toe. There were three of us from CDS, and Justin had brought a good friend from New York State's Division of the Budget as reinforcement. We waited in the room where, eventually, two gentlemen emerged from the shadows. Both were senior staff in OMRDD's finance office.

AN ERROR PROVIDES AN OPENING

Shortly after introductions, one of the men addressed us.

"Before we get into this meeting," he said, "I need to share something with you. Justin, I know we told you that the CDS package was incomplete." Then he sat and looked at us in silence, as if he was waiting for a response.

I was on high alert, poised to observe their body language, prepared to act at the first sign of weakness. This was my usual stance in meetings where much was at stake.

But it turned out to be unnecessary. "We told you the package was incomplete," he continued. "That was an error. In fact, the package is complete."

His words have echoed in my memory to this day. The entire meeting pivoted 180 degrees, just like that. Their error clearly had given us an advantage.

Justin and I looked at each other and nodded. He was astute and knew how to play the situation. We had agonized over the reams of documents, and driven all the way to Albany only to hear they had the documents. Something good needed to happen. Justin simply replied, "No problem. Things like this happen," as if they were apologizing for a missed phone call. Then he squared his shoulders. "We just need to figure out how we should move forward."

The conversation shifted to CDS's needs. After some back and forth, one of OMRDD's men looked at me and said, "We looked at your financial *pro forma* and saw no issues with it. What are you looking for?" I was surprised. My confidence was lifted.

That was just the question I wanted to answer. I said, "CDS needs a prior property approval (an OMRDD term), containing the numbers we submitted to you, as soon as possible."

"How soon?" he asked.

"Two weeks," I said. Two weeks would bring us to the middle of September. The election cycle was well underway, and spending usually came to a halt right before the election. I hoped I was giving them enough time to process the approval.

Two weeks later we received a fax from OMRDD central office containing a copy of the prior property approval with all the numbers we had submitted. They approved our plan in its entirety. We were elated. I contacted the board chair and shared the news. He congratulated me, saying, "Sankar, I have to admit this was your vision, and you pushed to get it done. You have every reason to be proud."

I remained humble. "It was a team effort," I said, internally feeling quite pleased with myself. Once again I believed providence had intervened on behalf of CDS. Who knows what might have resulted if OMRDD had acknowledged they received a complete application from the start? Would they have approved it? I was grateful their mistake ironically paved the way for our successful outcome. Things started out one way and ended up in another. I had hit another Sankar Ball. It also reinforced my belief that there is some divine order to the world, and that when you're successful, and contribute to society, good things tend to happen to you.

With funding for our new headquarters secure, Harrison Bridges solicited proposals (RFPs) from local construction companies to build the project. When the bids were returned, we met in our CFO's office to review them. Our main concern was the cost of the project. We settled on the lowest bidder, Javen Construction, and moved full speed ahead with no time to waste.

29
GRAND OPENING

CONSTRUCTION OF THE new headquarters started on schedule in early 2007. I drove out to the location every week, excited to watch the two-dimensional drawings become rendered in a concrete and steel structure on a 64,000-square-foot foundation.

During the early phase of the construction, staff who came to observe the construction hinted that something seemed to be missing: a full-length, heated therapeutic pool. Not only would this be a benefit to our individuals with disabilities, but it would also be used by the staff. I considered it an unnecessary luxury that would strain our budget. But then I thought of how the staff had made a good argument: it would enrich the individuals' lives at the facility. If we were going to erect a state-of-the art facility, then that is what we would do.

I estimated it would cost about $300,000, plus or minus a small margin, to install a pool, and felt comfortable that we could raise that amount of money through fundraising. It was a gross error. The architect designed the pool and sent out the request for proposals. When the bids came back, *the lowest was $1.2 million.* I was shocked. Now I was faced with a dilemma, and everyone looked to me for a decision of whether or not to move forward with the project.

My first thought was to humbly crawl back to OMRDD and ask for additional funding, but that didn't feel right. The State of New

York already gave us $10 million. Going back for more seemed downright greedy. After all, we needed to have some skin in the game. I reasoned that if I could raise $300,000 in one year, then I could certainly raise $1.2 million in three years. We moved ahead with the pool, and the backhoes went to work digging a hole. We were particularly grateful to the Golisano Foundation, which gave the largest gift—$125,000.

Adding the therapy pool prolonged the construction project by three months, and as a result, we had to extend the Perinton headquarters lease. The problem was that our landlord wasn't cooperating. He was already angry that he had to find another tenant that would pay the ridiculously high $50,000 per month rent we had been paying. Now, to "graciously" allow us to remain in the building, this brigand wanted to shake us down for an *additional* $35,000 a month—totaling an exorbitant amount of $85,000 for each additional month. It was extortion. He was unyielding. Thankfully, Shelley Miller at the DDSO came to our rescue and she obtained approval to pay him the obscene monthly payment until we moved out.

Finally, after 18 months, the construction of the facility was complete. The facility included a beautiful therapy pool. It was constructed with concrete blocks rather than steel, and its roof was held up by heavy wooden beams. Overhead, decorative wooden planks lined the ceiling. Harrison Bridges assured us that in the years to come we would thank them for their design. We faced more upfront costs because of the concrete, but they assured us we would save more money on maintenance. That proved to be true. And, yes, within three years we raised the money to pay for the pool.

The first time I walked into the new Town Square, the heart of the new facility, I was overcome with pride and emotion. I imagined our staff and program participants filling the space with activity. The skylights and floor-to-ceiling windows that made up one wall filled the square with natural light. We named the apartment adjacent to the stage "One Town Square"—a nice touch. Then we decided to personalize the other rooms around the square. I proposed that, in honor of the founders of CDS, Lew and Phyllis Wolf, we name the new facility "The Wolf Life Transitions Center." The board of directors unanimously agreed.

A month after we began operations in the new facility, we engaged an events company to organize a grand opening. We sent invitations to our partners and the community at-large. This included every former board member, our former executive director, Bob Rosenborg, and the local and state legislators who supported us.

The mood of the grand opening was spirited and festive. Each guest commented on the design, the style, and the brightness and openness of our facility. It was more than a building—it was a symbol of innovation and optimism in caring for our constituents. It was a place in which our staff would find pleasure to work. I greeted everyone with earnestness and pride, especially Lew and Phyllis Wolf. Lew's Alzheimer's disease was progressing, but I privately hoped that he still had the ability to recognize in some way how this building honored his and Phyllis's legacy, and the Wolf family.

The grand opening ceremony was conducted in the Town Square where about 200 people had gathered. I gave the final address, and as I stood at the microphone, scanning the cheerful faces in the crowd, my eyes stopped at one face. It was our former president of the board of directors, Adam Goldstein. I had made sure to invite him, although our relationship had ended badly almost a decade ago. I couldn't ignore the contribution he had made to CDS over many years. In my opening remarks, I expressed great appreciation for everyone in attendance and their support. Aware of some of the people present at the ceremony, I abided by the sentiment "Let bygones be bygones." I would not let the past, or anyone, stifle my spirit.

At one point during my address, I paused, as I became overwhelmed with gratitude for the people who had made this possible. My throat tightened, and tears of gratitude welled up in my eyes. All the hardships we had endured in the years leading up to the building flashed through my mind. I took a deep breath to keep my emotions under control. I was astonished at all the wonderful people who had shown up for the grand opening. In the first row I saw Ann Costello, the executive director of the Golisano Foundation, who was instrumental in the approval of the $120,000 for Unistel equipment and the gift of $125,000 toward the pool. I was tremendously grateful for their support. Somehow, I got through the speech.

At the end of the ceremony, our events company led everyone outside to the front of the building. Cages containing hundreds of Monarch butterflies were brought forward. Then, after a brief countdown intended to build excitement, the butterflies were released and the sky became a kaleidoscope of orange and black wings against a blue sky. The guests gasped at the spectacle. The flickering colors spread out as they flew away, and my mind drifted with them, to the early days when I had started at CDS. The Monarch butterfly is said to symbolize transformation, rebirth, a new life, and new opportunities. It is said that when a Monarch butterfly crosses your path you should embrace all the changes that are about to happen in your life. I thought how this had been emblematic of my life over the previous decade. But even more so, it symbolized the changes that had happened and were about to happen in CDS—a new beginning. It symbolized the lives of those who were attending our programs. It was a fitting way to end the ceremony; our new name was befittingly changed to CDS Monarch.

A new beginning was dawning. We were more strategic in offering opportunities for people to participate in life at its fullest, challenging existing norms—especially that people with special needs had to live in group homes and attend segregated programs. We committed to transforming CDS Monarch into a diversified, multipurpose special needs organization, striving for growth, innovation, and long-term sustainability.

CDS headquarters (Wolf Life Transitions Center) and the Town Square, which opened in 2008

Therapeutic pool at the Wolf Life Transitions Center

30
CDS MONARCH VS. NEWSLETTER

FROM ITS INCEPTION, our organization was named "Continuing Developmental Services," and it was identified by a plain and uninspiring logo. Our tagline, too, "Empowering people for life," was vague. Neither the name, logo, nor tagline evoked an organization that was growing and on the cutting edge of its field. We were still stuck in our cocoon; figuratively, we needed a butterfly. With the opening of the new Wolf Center, I petitioned for a new name, as well as a new logo.

When we proceeded to change the organization's name from Continuing Developmental Services to CDS, and finally to CDS Monarch, I couldn't have imagined the drama that would follow.

During construction of the Wolf Center, I had engaged a marketing firm to review and make suggestions for changes to our brand. We prioritized improving the company's name and logo, hoping to use them on signage for our new facility. The marketing firm conducted its research and proposed a new name for the company: CDS Monarch.

The firm's representatives walked us through the rationale. They imagined the life cycle of a butterfly when reflecting on how people with IDD in our environments were escaping the stereotypes and restrictions that had been placed on them and were making progress toward living more independently. Similarly, a butterfly begins in a cocoon, and at maturity it breaks out and flies away to enjoy a new, independent life. I loved the imagery and symbolism. "Monarch" best captured the vision. So Continuing Developmental Services would be shortened permanently to CDS, and CDS Monarch would become the new name.

Next, the marketing firm produced renderings of the butterfly for our new logo, and we landed on one that has served us for 20 years. As we added businesses, we simply designated a new color for that entity's butterfly to distinguish one business from another. Finally, before construction of the headquarters was finished, we drafted a new tagline: "Celebrating the everyday of life." This completed the rebranding of our company.

Then, in 2009, during the first year of operations at the new facility, trouble found us. The Arc of Monroe, a competing nonprofit organization where I had worked before coming to CDS, decided to bring a lawsuit against CDS Monarch for use of "Monarch" in our new company name. Evidently, the Arc of Monroe published a newsletter called *Monarch News*. They were concerned that their donors and others in the community would be confused by CDS's new name, and their fundraising efforts would be diluted.

I was incensed. As part of the branding and trademarking of the new name, our legal firm had conducted thorough research and given us clearance to use the name "CDS Monarch." We had invested heavily in updating our website, printing brochures and other materials, and manufacturing signage for the road, the front of the building, and the public areas inside the building. If we were intentionally stealing a name, we certainly weren't being secretive about it. Our logo was on full display. Case managers from the Arc of Monroe and other organizations had visited our headquarters and seen the new branding, but no one ever said anything. The staff agreed that we must defend our new name.

I immediately reached out to the Arc of Monroe's executive director to discuss the matter. She was unavailable and the waiting began. One morning, while at my desk, the phone rang. It was the Arc's executive director, whom I knew, and she wanted a word with me. I was prepared for the call; I knew it wasn't going to be a friendly one.

"I am sorry for pursuing legal action," she said coldly. "But we're concerned about your new name." She proceeded to describe the potential confusion that would be generated between "CDS Monarch" and their newsletter, *Monarch News*, as well as the financial impact on their organization.

After regaining my composure, I laid out our defense. We had done our due diligence to ensure that we didn't infringe on anyone's name. Only with clearance from our legal team did we commit to using the name "CDS Monarch."

She remained unmoved. "If you don't change your name, we'll see you in court," she said as she hung up the phone.

That was highly unfortunate. In Rochester, four organizations—CDS, the Arc of Monroe, Lifetime Assistance, and Heritage Christian Services—were regarded as "sister" organizations. We were non-profit organizations with a shared mission to support people with IDD. The lawsuit was like suing a close family member over the name on a mailbox. I expressed concern to the executive director that the community would denounce the lawsuit and reproach our organizations for spending money in court when we should be spending it on our missions. That argument became moot when, a month later, Arc served CDS Monarch the papers for the lawsuit. We had no choice but to defend our position.

A board member recommended the Woods Oviatt Gilman law firm to represent CDS Monarch. I reached out to a partner, Dan O'Brien, and hired them. The case was scheduled to be heard in a couple of months, so Dan and I put our heads together crafting our defense. He poured over all documentation and all the processes we had followed. I was skeptical that our name was somehow a "surprise" to the Arc of Monroe since their staff had visited the facility and had seen our signs, yet never mentioned anything about them. They didn't appear to make any connection whatsoever about our name and the Arc's newsletter. Dan shared my skepticism. If that were the case, why would the community make any connection?

Then the Arc of Monroe struck again. They filed an injunction to force us to cease using the name "CDS Monarch" while the case was waiting to be tried in court. We moved fast to respond to the injunction. Our defense team remained resolute that we had done everything appropriate to avoid trademark or brand infringement before choosing our name. We were unconvinced that CDS Monarch, the name of a large organization, was being equated with the title on a newsletter seen only by subscribers. Dan submitted our written response to the court, and soon after we had a hearing date.

The morning of the hearing, I entered the courtroom and wasn't surprised to see the executive director from the Arc of Monroe with their attorney. When his turn came to present their case, he put on a great performance, orating and making dramatic gesticulations of his hands, as if he were portraying William Jennings Bryan in a stage play. There is no doubt that he was thorough, and he did a good job of making Arc look like the victim. I was becoming concerned. At one point he said, "CDS gambled with the public's money and lost. Now they should pay. Your Honor, you must find in favor of the plaintiff."

The judge responded to the attorney, asking precisely the question that we had: *Why had none of the staff from the Arc of Monroe who visited the CDS Monarch facility complained about the new name?*

"Your honor, it wasn't their job to do CDS's work for them," he rebutted. This exchange made me hopeful that their argument didn't quite resonate with the judge.

Dan lacked the dramatic delivery of the Arc's attorney, but he was thoroughly prepared and did an excellent job of laying out our defense. Both attorneys then made their closing remarks, after which the judge announced that he had made his ruling. He handed copies of his ruling to both attorneys and chased us all out of the courtroom as he prepared for his next case. Meeting with our attorney outside the courtroom, I learned the judge had ruled in our favor. *And just like that, the lawsuit was over.*

After the trial, both organizations moved on. The attorneys confirmed we could continue to use the CDS Monarch name.

Our legal victory reaffirmed my belief that you should never give in when obstacles are thrown in your way, especially when those obstacles can come from places you don't expect. You should continue to forge ahead, motivated by the knowledge that you are doing good and important work. Even when you suspect defeat, don't give up.

Despite our win, I encouraged everyone to remain humble, for there was no virtue in rubbing Arc's nose in their loss. Instead, we focused on our business.

31
INNOVATION IN HOUSING

THROUGH OUR RELATIVES in Florida, I became acquainted with Kapil Bhatia, the CFO of the Raymond James investment firm. I'd long known that Raymond James had a division that financed housing options for seniors. Then one day in 2010, while thinking about housing, the wheels in my head started spinning. *Maybe CDS could provide housing options for people with IDD.* I floated the idea to Kapil, and he endorsed it. Soon a few key staff members and I traveled to Tampa to meet with Kapil's associates who oversaw the Raymond James Housing Finance Department.

This was timely because New York's Office for People with Developmental Disabilities (OPWDD) had announced a moratorium on the development of new residences for people with IDD. The announcement put the future of independent community living for people with IDD in jeopardy; this, in turn, placed pressure on families. The situation was unacceptable. We needed to find a solution. Maybe we would learn something helpful from the Raymond James team.

While the Raymond James team educated us on the housing development process in Florida, we learned that they were interested in having CDS establish a housing project in Tampa. They even presented us with a tentative budget for construction of a new 50-unit apartment building on a $1 million piece of land.

But the seller wanted cash to move forward, which for us was a dealbreaker. CDS wasn't ready to shell out cash for a brand-new initiative in Florida, a state in which we had not yet done business. But the education was useful.

Just because we didn't want to enter the Florida market didn't mean we should give up on housing. Why not apply what we learned and start in New York? My team and I explored different options for subsidized housing in New York State, looking for the right opening. CDS Monarch already operated traditional residences funded directly by OPWDD. We also had three residences funded by the US Department of Housing and Urban Development (HUD). We relied on our expertise as we considered options. We sought information on opportunities at the state level and identified the New York State's Homes and Community Renewal (HCR) department as the place to go for funding. It awarded tax credits to developers, who then sold them to investors to finance their projects. HCR was the most viable option. We learned that HCR housing opportunities were very competitive, but I wasn't deterred. CDS would compete.

Being an affordable housing developer could be another revenue source for CDS Monarch. One of the most lucrative aspects of being a developer in the affordable housing business is collecting a "developer's fee," a 10 percent fee awarded for completing a project. For example, if a developer built a housing project for $10 million, they received a $1 million fee upon completion. It was a pragmatic approach to IDD housing.

To submit a proposal as a new developer, securing a partner with experience was necessary. Our goal was to build our first 50-unit apartment building, integrating people with IDD into the facility. After much research and consultation, we found the Cornerstone Group, headed by a gentleman who was well-known in the community. We met with him and reached a 50/50 agreement to move forward. There were no warning signs of potential trouble working with this individual.

To apply for an affordable housing project in New York, we needed land on which to build the facility. We learned of a local entrepreneur, Peter Landers, who had a parcel of land for sale. We offered him a good price, and he agreed. However, I quickly learned that Mr. Landers was what people called a "nibbler." He found additional reasons to increase the price he agreed to. The money didn't matter to me as much as the principle. But I sucked up my pride and agreed to the additional costs. Besides, I liked Mr. Landers.

Finally, we selected Lecesse Development to construct the facility. The application was submitted to HCR. Then the waiting began.

One Sunday evening, our co-developer called to inform me that we were two weeks away from hearing HCR's decision. He reminded me that after HCR reviewed each submission, their recommendations were sent to the governor's office for approval. He added, "If you know anyone in the state legislature, ask them to contact the governor's office and advocate for our project."

By then, CDS Monarch had retained Justin McCarthy as our government lobbyist. Justin had been Senator Michael Nozzolio's chief of staff, and left to set up his own company. He informed me that he would make the calls. Two weeks later, we received the great news that we were awarded our first housing project. As we envisioned, it was a 50-unit apartment building where 10 people with IDD would live on their own in an integrated setting with minimal support. This was the first project of its kind in New York State, paving the way for others to get into the business of helping people with IDD access housing. It was a moment to celebrate.

Before architectural drawings were developed, I asked our co-developer to visit one of his facilities. He built affordable and low-income housing communities, and we wanted to get a sense of the environment. Hopefully, it would give us ideas for our facility. On the tour, I noticed that the apartments were ordinary, and not aesthetically pleasing. To me, the facilities were designed for people at the bottom of the socioeconomic scale. Bare minimum.

I was glad we went, because I was resolved we wouldn't build our facility that way.

We invited our architect to our headquarters to sketch out and discuss ideas. He received a tour of the facility before we sat down together. I opened the conversation, saying, "Take notice of how CDS builds new properties. You're sitting in one right now. Any apartment buildings we build must appeal to the eyes, and they must have first-rate construction. I want people living there to be inspired and be uplifted."

He agreed, and we began discussing the lobby and foyer areas. We wanted to give people a strong first impression of our organization as they entered the facility. The foyer would have high ceilings, with a sitting area and fireplace in the lobby. A wooden staircase would go from the first to the second floor. We also included a fitness area, a community room where people could congregate to celebrate special occasions, and an area equipped with computers for people to search the internet and stay connected with loved ones online. We would have plenty of natural light and bright colors throughout the facility.

We all seemed to be going well with the design when we came to a matter of disagreement with the architect. He insisted that, for the second-floor apartments, the most efficient place to install the air conditioning units would be on the balconies. He must have misunderstood, thinking that we were like other builders of affordable housing who valued efficiency above quality. I stared at him and said, "If you were a resident living in one of these apartments, would you want to sit on your patio listening to your air conditioning unit?" His lack of response answered my question. I told him to reengineer the placement of the air-conditioning units. Like magic, the air conditioning units suddenly appeared in an unobtrusive location.

Then our co-developer made a fatal mistake. During the construction, he wanted to renegotiate our arrangement, which involved the agreed-upon fee structure. He maintained that the contract he signed with us made him responsible for certain guarantees, such as keeping within the construction budget, hitting the target to complete construction, and having all apartments occupied with renters on schedule. We equally comanaged every aspect of this project. He had no risk. Yet now he was demanding we divide the developers' fee differently: rather than each sharing 50 percent, he demanded *70 percent*. I was fuming mad. He had forgotten our political advocacy that was brought to bear. He became greedy.

My staff and I met him at a restaurant where he dug in his heels. I finally said, "This isn't good. We came to you in good faith. You can't change the rules midstream after we signed an agreement. This isn't how we do business." I made it clear that his way of doing business would jeopardize any long-term relationship with CDS Monarch. He didn't care. We eventually agreed on 55 percent for him and 45 percent for us. I left that meeting determined that we would never do business with that co-developer again. We never did.

But I didn't let this co-developer spoil the big picture: CDS Monarch provided people with IDD housing opportunities when there seemed to be none. We did so by creating a new housing model in upstate New York, leaving a butterfly-shaped housing footprint. Housing 10 people with IDD in a 50-unit apartment building was like opening a group home. And because we provided this housing for seniors, families, and veterans as well as people with IDD, we were offering people more natural settings where they could experience life in an integrated community.

Each person with IDD who moved into the apartments saved the state of New York $80,000 annually. For residential care, the state was paying private, nonprofit providers like CDS an average of $100,000 annually *per resident*. This new housing model cost the state only $20,000 per person each year. At this project's scale, CDS saved the State of New York $800,000 for 10 people on an annual basis, and that was just the beginning.

For years to come, CDS Monarch employed this model to build more housing communities with HCR. We established new partners and enjoyed much success. Our winning approach benefitted all parties involved—especially our residents, whose lives were enriched with community living.

Edna Craven Estates, Rochester Affordable Housing Community

32
I WILL FIND A WAY

SIX YEARS AFTER the Golisano Foundation awarded Unistel a grant to install four new production lines, we submitted another proposal to the foundation. In the interim, from 2004 to 2010, Unistel's spice business had grown exponentially. We expanded its spice offerings to the US military and embraced a new opportunity to provide spices in small bottles. To do so, Unistel needed an automated production line. These small bottles of spices were included in the unitized group rations and food packages that soldiers received in the field across the world. For efficiency and consistency, packaging these small containers was best done on an automated production line. An entire production line with a bottle feeder, conveyor belts, sensors, filler, labeler, sealer, and a metal detection machine cost $375,000.

While our cash position was still improving at Unistel, I believed we needed to access philanthropic dollars to assist us with the purchase. So we submitted a request to the Golisano Foundation for a grant. A meeting was scheduled with the foundation's trustees to discuss the details of our plan.

During the interview, Tom Golisano, instead of discussing our request, asked germane questions to gain a broad understanding of CDS Monarch's funding of its 27 residences. He shared with me his recent meeting with the CEO of another IDD nonprofit on the west side of Rochester that operated an even larger number of residences. That organization had submitted a grant request to make repairs to their residences, including roofs and parking lots. Tom wanted my perspective. He said, "After hearing that CEO's pitch for the grant, I asked him how much the State of New York gave his organization to operate a residence, on average, per person per year. The CEO told me $100,000. Do you know what you get at CDS?"

The question caught me off guard. I came prepared to discuss Unistel, not the residences, and I paused, trying to recollect our residential rates. Then I confidently replied, "Tom, as far as I know, we get about $80,000 per person per year." I recognized my figure might be off a bit, but I wanted to prove that I was knowledgeable about our finances.

Tom shook his head in disbelief. "How can that be?," he asked. "That's 20 percent less than what the other organization gets from the state. Please go back and double check. Let us know if the number you just gave me is correct." Then he glanced at our application on his desk and seemed poised to ask me the next question regarding our request, but he didn't. Tom put down his papers. He seemed upset and wanted to get something off his chest. He said, "I must tell you something. If I paid $100,000 to an organization to take care of my loved one in their residence, that residence better have good roofs and parking lots." I thought to myself, *I couldn't agree more.*

Finally, the conversation returned to Unistel. I wasn't prepared for his next question. "But won't an automated line take jobs *away* from people?" he asked. His foundation's previous gift had created 40 new jobs, and this operation threatened to do the opposite. Tom was smart, and I hadn't fully anticipated his questions. Furthermore, he wasn't convinced the automated production line provided an acceptable return on his investment.

Back at the office, I immediately went to our business office to double-check the figure I had told Tom about the per-person cost for residential services. Our vice president of finance, Judy Consadine, did a quick calculation, which came to exactly what I had stated. So I contacted Ann Costello, the Golisano Foundation's executive director, and relayed the information.

Soon after we left our interview, I learned our request had been denied. I was told that I gave the wrong response to one of Tom's standard interview questions. He had asked, "Sankar, if we don't provide you with the funds, what will you do?"

Out of frustration, I said, "Tom, if you don't support the request, I will find a way." My answer was not out of vanity; that was how I had always approached a problem. The irony of the situation was, that was why I was there—trying to find a way. And in fact, we did just that. We used cash from our operations to purchase the equipment, and I didn't look back. In hindsight, I should have shown deference and said, "Tom, we really need you. If you don't help, we can't do this." *This was a lesson learned dealing with Tom Golisano.*

History repeated itself when Tom paid an auspicious visit to the spice plant to celebrate his foundation's 25th anniversary. As he finished the tour, he advised me to install air conditioning in the building—a building poorly designed to accommodate air conditioning. Since he made the recommendation, everyone thought we should approach the Golisano Foundation for funding. I thought not. Unistel was operating profitably, and it didn't escape me that Tom and his foundation had given us the seed money to achieve Unistel's growth and profitability. I couldn't bring myself to make the request. CDS fully funded installing the air conditioning system.

33
CDS MANAGED CARE COMES TO UPSTATE NEW YORK

MY MEETING WITH Tom Golisano to discuss Unistel's funding request, although unsuccessful, was fortuitous. This was a pivotal moment in the IDD field. Tom and his foundation had reservations about the long-term financial sustainability of the IDD residential system. Chief contributors were the rising costs of labor and other operational costs, alongside federal and state limits on Medicaid spending.

Tom and his trustees were leading the conversation on how to reengineer the IDD service system to be more sustainable. His interrogation about the amount and use of state funds gave me insight into how he viewed the nonprofit agencies, CDS included: that we mismanaged the funds New York State gave us.

The meeting was prescient: in the coming months, concerns about the system's sustainability became the focus of conversations between the governor's office and the commissioner of OPWDD. (By this time the Office of Mental Retardation and Developmental Disabilities [OMRDD] had been renamed the Office for People with Developmental Disabilities [OPWDD]). There was growing talk about a new model of care delivery, and I wondered what that would mean for our organization and the individuals we served.

We soon learned that the state's goal was to transform the service delivery system for people with IDD from a fee-for-service model to a managed care model. New York intended to place management of the system into the hands of insurance companies, preferably operated by consortiums of IDD providers.

A group of providers of services in Western New York, based in Buffalo, created an entity called Person Centered Services (PCS) that would potentially be that managed care insurance company. The group conducted quiet outreach into the Finger Lakes region and convinced two of CDS's competitors to join their effort. Those organizations were considered founders of PCS and arranged an equity interest in the new company. CDS was never approached.

I consulted with Sy, former director of OPWDD's local DDSO and now our chief operating officer. He was shocked and disillusioned that two large Rochester-based organizations would join forces with a group in Buffalo on an enterprise that would impact providers and individuals in the Finger Lakes. To him, this betrayed his efforts to align the Finger Lakes IDD providers as a group with common interests and undermined the collegiality he had fostered among competing organizations.

To drive the move to managed care for people with IDD, OPWDD published the Developmental Disabilities Individual Service and Care Organization Statewide Comprehensive Plan referred to as the DDISCO Plan. It outlined the requirements to establish managed care entities and represented New York State's first full-throated attempt to control Medicaid costs in the IDD population. The document triggered an avalanche of questions from providers, families, and advocates. The term "managed care" had negative implications, and conjured up a system of cost controls, juggling of limited resources, and denial of services. Further, people feared the quality of services would suffer. Individuals with IDD, lacking the ability to navigate the system, would suffer the most. CDS Monarch and our fellow service providers in the Finger Lakes felt compelled to do something; we just weren't sure what that was.

The CEO of one of the two organizations that joined Buffalo's managed care effort, with whom I had an amicable relationship, contacted me and asked for a meeting. The intent was to petition CDS to join their cause, thereby eliminating any competition. We met at a restaurant in the city; I brought Sy, and the CEO brought his deputy.

Our conversation remained cordial while we attended to our pizza and salad. Then, as we were finishing up our meals, the two gentlemen attempted to convince us why it would be beneficial for us to join forces with PCS in Buffalo, and the mood took a turn. We were prepared with a response. Sy began, expressing strong disappointment with the two organizations' actions. He drove the point home, ending with, "You betrayed me and the providers in the Finger Lakes region."

Sy's indictment of their actions caught the CEO and his deputy by surprise. They immediately became defensive, arguing that Sy had mischaracterized their intentions.

Their argument fell flat. Sy and I didn't see how we could possibly join forces with them. The federal government had stipulated that any insurance arrangement at the state level must provide consumers with at least two options in every county. What PCS was proposing, in essence, was the creation of a monopoly. Its goal was clearly to smother and eliminate any competition.

By the end of the meeting, any cordiality was gone. The CEO and his deputy did not anticipate our counteroffensive and concluded the meeting. His parting words were, "The train has left the station. You can either get on or stay off." If the train had indeed left the station, we were not getting on it, and we were not getting off at Buffalo. Sy and I, and CDS, were determined to lay our own tracks.

34
GETTING INTO THE INSURANCE BUSINESS

FOR SEVERAL YEARS after 2010, when OPWDD announced that the IDD system would move to managed care, deliberations about how to accomplish the goal continued at a snail's pace. I applied myself to studying managed care and its impact on the future of IDD services, and came to one conclusion: CDS needed to get into the insurance business. I determined that New York State would need an alternative to the Buffalo based IDD managed care entity called Person Centered Services, and CDS would be it. If not, CDS Life Transitions and other providers could suffer the same fate as the woolly mammoth in New York State. A new age was coming, and it would determine who would survive and who were going to become the leaders and the followers in the industry—whether we were prepared or not.

In 2013, we quietly reached out to key people in the governor's office for advice and counsel. The state's deputy director of health and human services, Jim Introne, knew Sy very well. With Sy's introduction, Jim agreed to speak with us and we headed to Albany.

We explained to Jim that CDS was responsible for the care of 1,000 individuals with IDD, and with our group of providers, we touched the lives of more than 7,000 individuals. We expressed our hope that we would be considered one of the leaders of the managed care transformation and shared our plan to create a managed care entity for people with IDD. Jim listened and was not prone to say much. I wanted to know what he thought. So I broached the subject, asking him, "Are we on the right course? Is this the right timing?" I held my breath. His answer would help me decide what path to take.

"You have more time than you may think," Jim responded. "The governor is in no hurry to make this change." He explained further that the governor wanted key stakeholders to be "brought along" so that they supported this transformational plan. CDS was in a good position. It had already entered the New York State insurance market with the creation of iCircle, a grassroots-managed care entity representing a broad cross section of IDD providers in the Finger Lakes. Working with the state to add managed care for IDD sounded wise.

"CDS would like to be one of the IDD managed care entities," I insisted. Again, Jim didn't respond. However, as we got up to leave, he suggested that we obtain a New York State Medicaid Managed Long Term Care (MLTC) Plan license in preparation for IDD managed care. He felt it would better prepare us because the requirements contained in OPWDD's DDISCO plan were nearly identical to those in the MLTC plan. Sy and I left that meeting feeling a bit more encouraged and confident. However, my mind already shifted to what it might take to establish the MLTC plan.

CDS had built its nest egg for such an opportunity. Spending $1 million to obtain a managed care license was a no-brainer but I had to educate the CDS Monarch Board of Directors and the iCircle Board of Directors about the MLTC business and convince them that it would provide us the means to operate the IDD managed care company whenever the opportunity came. After much consultations and deliberation I was relieved when the iCircle Board of Directors in collaboration with CDS Monarch Board of Directors, approved the application to the NYS Department of Health for an

MLTC Plan license. The insurance licensing process was long, costly, and time-consuming, but we were determined to make this happen.

The MLTC Plan required that iCircle provide care management services to its members. With no experience in the insurance managed care space and to expedite this requirement, we met with a health care consulting company called Independent Living Systems (ILS) that offered to provide these services as a subcontractor. ILS was based in Florida, but they were making inroads in New York, delivering support services to seniors. My team and I visited their headquarters in Miami to discuss the arrangements.

We met Jose Planta, the CEO of ILS, Mary Ferman, their representative assigned to the iCircle relationship and several staff members and consultants. I was impressed by their knowledge of the insurance industry. They explained the relationship between the federal government and the States relative to medicaid spending. ILS appeared to have a long reach in the federal government, and they had key relationships in New York State. We were impressed. I left feeling like this was going to be a good partnership. Naively I signed a contract giving ILS pretty much what they wanted, including a profit-sharing arrangement, should the care management function drive profits.

ILS, because they had expertise with Medicaid, also committed to helping us with our MLTC application to New York State. The application was extensive. Among other things, it required that iCircle establish a network of providers that could deliver prescribed services; personal care services, durable medical equipment such as wheelchairs and hospital beds, access ramps, home delivered meals, incontinence supplies, etc. We were also required to establish a network of transportation companies to take members to and from appointments. It was a lot of work, but operating the MLTC Plan laid the essential groundwork and infrastructure to establish an IDD managed care company. Through collaboration with ILS, and spending more than $1 million, iCircle obtained the MLTC license to operate in 22 counties in upstate New York.

As prepared as we now were, OPWDD hadn't yet agreed to pull the trigger on managed care for people with IDD. Even more unpropitious, providers that joined me in the creation of iCircle were pessimistic that OPWDD was moving ahead with managed care at all. And even more alarming, the iCircle independent financial auditor informed me that if CDS Monarch remained the only financial contributor at iCircle, it had to bear the burden and take responsibility for the company including any losses incurred by iCircle. This now placed CDS in a very risky position. In order to attract providers, I assured them that they didn't have to make a financial commitment, naively thinking that CDS would do so, and iCircle could maintain its independence. Now I had to awkwardly approach the providers for funds, reneging on our original arrangement and hoping they would make a financial contribution. A meeting was held with the iCircle Board of Directors to share this sobering news and when the time came for the IDD providers represented in the room to commit to any level of financial contribution, no one would. I could not blame them. The organizations were much smaller in size and did not have the finances to contribute to a venture that had risks and no clear path to success.

At a CDS Monarch Board of Directors meeting, I broached the subject of iCircle's financial exposure, reassuring the directors that there was no need to be concerned. CDS had conscientiously and steadily built its assets in the CDS Wolf Foundation over the years, and we were prepared for this opportunity, one we shouldn't let pass. My perspective was the nest egg was built on funds gained from operating medicaid programs. CDS was the steward of the funds and it was our responsibility to invest that money in services that would improve the well-being of the most vulnerable members in our community. I was confident that in the long run, CDS Monarch's investments would pay dividends in the lives of people with IDD.

Thankfully I convinced the board to support the MLTC initiative. What's more, they voted to take full financial responsibility for iCircle. I was grateful and relieved. I also expressed gratitude to the executives from the many IDD organizations who continued to sit on the iCircle Board.

iCircle now had a license to operate a MLTC plan and we knew we could not sit on it. Soon enough, the NYS Department of Health pushed iCircle to execute the MLTC Plan. This placed CDS in a new predicament. Other than the license, we didn't have any experience running a managed care plan. We were apprehensive but committed to the path. Ramping up for the launch, we hired several business developers to do outreach with physicians' offices and other service providers in our network, the goal being to educate them about iCircle and hoping they would refer members to the Plan. Then we hired the staff for all the back-office functions. The ground floor of the administration section of CDS Life Transitions' headquarters was renovated to house the iCircle management and we allocated space to accommodate an in-house care management team at some point in the future. An IT team then installed all the necessary IT infrastructure to support the plan's functions.

The iCircle MLTC Plan would be our incubator where we developed the necessary knowledge and skills to operate a managed care plan for people with IDD. Whenever NYS was ready to move forward we were prepared. Looking back at these early years, as we entered the health insurance market, the adage "You don't know what you don't know" fully applied. We had no prior knowledge, experience, or expertise. We were relying solely on our reputation in the IDD field and our word.

We set a launch date, and with a multimedia marketing plan, advertised our iCircle "grand opening" in all 22 counties and made special visits to our network of community providers. When iCircle's lights came on, we prepared for a tidal wave of new enrollees.

The tidal wave came more as a ripple. In its first month, iCircle received only four referrals. I asked for a meeting with the iCircle management and asked tough questions: Did we execute the plan as outlined? Was the information upon which we relied accurate?

Were the business developers doing their jobs? iCircle management reassured me that we had done everything. I was reassured.

I knew the risk: Without significant improvement in enrollment, and subsequently no per-member revenue from NYS to support operating costs, iCircle would likely shut down within a few months. We would lose millions of dollars. Yet, faced with this crisis, I didn't panic. I trusted my staff and the staff trusted me. We were "all in." The following month iCircle received six referrals and new leads continued to trickle in as we entered the third month. iCircle's future began to look bleak, and doubt began to creep in. Then, in the fourth month, something unexpected and special happened: iCircle received 60 referrals, and from there the enrollment continued to steadily roll in month after month. The clouds that had been gathering over iCircle had lifted, and the future of iCircle suddenly looked brighter.

35
PROTECTING THE SPICE BUSINESS LONG TERM

IN THE SAME year that CDS purchased the automated production line for Unistel, it was slapped with an almost $300,000 penalty by the Department of Labor after it conducted an audit, as it did periodically, of Unistel's minimum wage certificate. The certificate allowed Unistel to pay below minimum wage to individuals with IDD who could not work at a standard productivity level. Each worker's wages were determined by their production rate, or "piece rate," compared to that of an average worker without IDD. Staff conducted quarterly time studies, documented them, and provided payroll information to our business office, which calculated each person's hourly rate and wages.

The Department of Labor's review included all the documentation associated with our processes for the minimum wage program, for which the Unistel general manager (GM) was responsible. When he informed me of the audit I asked him if everything was in order. He gave me a thumbs-up stating there was nothing to worry about, which did not ease my mind.

I was not reassured, especially since the GM was known to operate in isolation. He was my direct report, and although he was well-respected by the staff, they had repeatedly reported a troubling pattern to me. The GM often took unilateral actions without my approval, and when he was caught, he would "fall on his sword." His outlook was that it was better to ask for forgiveness than permission—to the extreme. I was losing patience.

I contacted the Quality Assurance Department and asked Carrie Carra, a long-time employee who I trusted and who now worked as an internal auditor, to review all of Unistel's minimum wage documentation and report back to me. Within a day, she was in my office with a report. "The documentation is a mess," she said. "It's totally unorganized, and some of the documents are missing." This was unacceptable. The general manager had failed in his basic duty in this area.

The Department of Labor's auditors agreed with Carrie. Unistel failed to produce the proper documentation for its determination of sub-minimum wages for the workers with IDD. The resulting penalty of almost $300,000 was to be paid as back wages to the employees. While I was happy that the penalty was going to the individuals we served, I was livid about the GM's failure. He not only lied to me, but he failed to protect CDS. Even with all the success during his tenure, I felt it was time for him to leave the organization, and he and I reached an agreement for his exit.

Next, the search for a new GM began. Advertisements in the paper and engagement with a search firm yielded very few applicants. One day Mark Peterson, who was serving as CDS Board chair, emailed me a resume for retired Major General Robert Mixon. As I reviewed his experience, I began to warm up to the idea that having a new GM from the military oversee Unistel seemed might be the solution. I cautiously made a call to General Mixon.

He answered the phone gruffly, saying, "Robert here." Yes, he was a general. He was driving on the I-90 thruway in New York. I explained that Mark Peterson had recommended him, and I was interested in him for a position at CDS. We scheduled an interview, and by the end of it we reached an agreement. He would serve as the new leader of Unistel as its general manager. This timing was providential.

By early 2011, a review of Unistel's finances showed that it was losing money every month, forecasting a loss of at least half a million dollars by the end of the year. The issue was a serious mismatch between the actual cost of spices and the prices that the Defense Logistics Agency (DLA) Troop Support—the arm of the US military responsible for procuring and distributing food supplies all over the world—paid us for the spices. The operation was no longer viable for Unistel, so we contacted SourceAmerica (formerly known as National Industries for the Severely Handicapped, or NISH), which had helped Unistel secure the spice contract years ago. We pleaded with them to attract DLA Troop Support's attention to the matter. Like us, they were not successful. Without an intervention, Unistel continued to bleed financially, and it seemed inevitable that the spice business would have to shut down. Undeterred, I was determined to fix the problem. Failure was not an option.

I had a flashback to the Kodak disposable camera contract, which Unistel lost to Mexico years before. *Not again*, I resolved. One morning, after a fitful night of sleep, the light bulb came on. I arrived at my office and requested that General Mixon (by then he insisted I call him Robert) come to speak with me. *Would my idea work*? It had to. He soon joined me, and we sat across from each other at my small table to review Unistel's dismal numbers. He agreed we were in trouble.

"We're bleeding and facing a shutdown," I said. He nodded at me and frowned. I leaned across the table and said, "Robert, you can help prevent it. We desperately need an intervention at DLA Troop Support."

He slowly nodded, indicating he was carefully listening to me. I watched his body language. He shifted in his seat, yet kept his arms relaxed in an open posture. He surely knew I was about to ask him to use his influence in the military to get the job done.

I said, "Please listen to me. You had a distinguished career in the military. You're a retired general. You can bring attention to this matter and obtain a resolution. I have no doubt." Then I paused.

He was silent, and his expression was unchanged, which I saw as a good sign because it wasn't a clear "No."

"We can't let this happen," I continued. "So I ask you to please reach out to DLA Troop Support's leadership and explain that our spice pricing is upside down. Get a meeting with them if you can. We need to deal directly with their office to solve this problem."

"I'll think about it," he said. I knew it was the right call. I was totally convinced that Robert could help us find the way forward.

The next morning Robert came to my office and seemed very upbeat. He said he had reached out to the office of the commander of DLA Troop Support, Navy Rear Admiral David Baucom, who was not available, but he was directed to Admiral Baucom's chief of staff. I was surprised and yet very pleased. He proceeded to share how he explained Unistel's situation to the chief of staff, who assured Robert he would follow up. Then Robert said, "Sankar, I feel good about this. We should remain positive and hopeful." I was very grateful that he had acted so quickly, and I was cautiously optimistic. Hope sprung up in me.

Within a few days the chief of staff kept his word and reported to Robert that DLA Troop Support had investigated the matter and expected it to be resolved within the next couple of weeks. True to form, two weeks later we received approval of price increases just as we proposed. The increased revenue returned Unistel to self-sufficiency. Thank God our spice business didn't end up the way our Kodak story did. More importantly, we protected the jobs of 50 people with IDD.

Robert's quick results to save Unistel showed me that he had more to give the organization in an advisory role to me as CEO. With his large Rolodex of contacts, he was uniquely suited to expand Unistel's presence in the military space. I promoted him to vice president of strategic initiatives. In business development, he was better positioned to explore new opportunities with the military and he was a fierce protector of our spice business. In my estimation, no one in the military food space could mess with us—not anymore.

36
WARRIOR SALUTE VETERANS SERVICES COMES TO CDS

For unto whomsoever much is given, of him shall be much required.
— Luke 12:48

AS RETIRED GENERAL Robert Mixon and I became closer, I initiated conversations about the care our veterans received when they returned from active duty in Afghanistan and Iraq. I was watching men and women return from the wars with PTSD, traumatic brain injuries, and physical injuries—even sexual trauma. In many cases, they returned home and had nowhere to turn. The Veterans Administration (VA) was overwhelmed during those years and had difficulty accommodating the volume of veterans returning with visible and invisible injuries. I saw the effects firsthand. Homeless veterans walked the streets, slept under bridges, and congregated in makeshift tent communities. I wondered if CDS Monarch could intervene and make a meaningful difference in their lives.

My affection for the military ran deep. From the time I arrived in the United States, its history and politics intrigued me, particularly its key personalities. I read many of the memoirs of the founding fathers: George Washington, Alexander Hamilton, John Adams, Benjamin Franklin, Thomas Jefferson, and others, gleaning their intent for this new republic. I was in awe of how they had led the effort to hold the colonies together during the American Revolution and how eventually the colonies came together to constitute the United States of America. These men sacrificed so much of their lives to defend the homeland. Their final masterpiece—the creation of the three branches of the federal government, and bestowing powers to the states with their own constitutions—was the product of genius. There were many checks and balances in the American political, military, and civil structures that made its citizens feel safe and secure from abuses of government power. This was quite unlike the government that existed in Guyana, where its British parliamentary system, a legacy of British imperialism, was ignored and abused at every turn.

I faithfully watched the news on C-SPAN every night, where I learned even more of how the federal legislative process worked. Then I got hooked on listening to the views of renowned scholars and pundits on PBS shows like *The McLaughlin Group* and *Frontline*. I was evolving into one of America's informed and grateful immigrant citizens.

One evening I was sitting in my recliner watching a news story about veterans returning from Iraq and Afghanistan struggling to find resources, and I could not escape the feeling which had been with me for months that I needed to do my part to help them. They had sacrificed their lives for us, and I wanted to honor their service by helping them in their hour of need. I felt compelled to do my very best as a citizen and show that their sacrifices were not unrecognized.

And at CDS Monarch we had the ability to help. I thought: *CDS must jump in and do our part.* I believed we could improve the lives of our veterans, as an extension of the opportunities I had in the United States. Reflecting on all my accomplishments up to that point, I knew that if I took the initiative, I could make a difference.

In this democracy we call "America," I believe we all have a part to play. I was proud of my brother, Devo, who had joined the US

Navy, where he would spend 20 years in military service. His two sons followed in his footsteps. I admired and respected our volunteer armed forces; their presence all over the world protected free societies and all of us back home. Now I would contribute.

I enlisted Robert's help. He and I studied programs supporting veterans in earnest. The Wounded Warrior Project was the preeminent veteran's service program. It was the most recognized, and carried distinction, but I wanted CDS to find its own unique way to serve veterans. The name "Wounded Warrior" did not appeal to me. The organization did great work, but the thought of referring to veterans that needed our help as wounded warriors didn't tell the whole story. It aroused images of their handicaps and disabilities. It directed the spotlight on the wounds and tended to engender sympathy; "wounded" came before "warrior," both in title and in context. Instead, we needed to show gratitude and honor to our veterans. I thought of how we often greet our veterans with a gesture of great respect, with a salute. Then the name suddenly appeared to me: "Warrior Salute Veterans Services." The title contained everything: they were veterans, they were warriors, and we would salute them. Nothing in the name suggested handicap or disability, visible or invisible.

Next, we mapped out how many veterans we could serve at a given time and how many could be served in a calendar year. With the project scope in mind, we developed a budget. The clinical program was designed to be intensive, where veterans were expected to engage in a structured therapy program daily for as long as they resided in our facility.

After the plan was developed, with Robert by my side, I pitched our noble idea to the CDS Monarch Board of Directors. I was nervous. On the surface, it seemed like I was departing from our core mission to serve people with IDD. In my presentation I was careful to balance the pragmatic with the patriotic. I felt that everyone in the room needed to examine their views on patriotism and their level of commitment to our veterans. I emphasized Unistel's close relationship with the military providing spices and highlighted that if we did this, CDS would indeed be giving back in a meaningful way to the military and our communities. In the for-profit industry, they have a catchy phrase for it: "corporate social responsibility."

I entered the meeting expecting some skepticism. CDS was a charitable organization on the *receiving end* of charitable giving. But I was prepared, and addressed that paradox emphatically. "I want to turn the charity giving model on its head," I said. "We've had a lot of success. Our businesses are thriving. Now we have a chance to impact veterans and help them regain their lives. Even as a nonprofit we have an obligation to give back."

Not a single objection was raised by the board of directors, and they granted their full support. Dennis Buchan, a board member and confidante, spoke up. "Sankar, build it the way *you* want," he said. "If you do it the government's way you'll likely get nothing done." That was all I needed to hear.

I expressed gratitude for the board's support and committed to raising all the necessary funds to operate the program. Like Dennis said, I had to do it my way; there was no funding stream available to us through any government entities.

Robert and I visited many VA-sponsored rehabilitation facilities across the country to gather best practices and new ideas. We found that these world-class facilities primarily dealt with physical trauma. Psychological trauma care was underrepresented; even though progress had been made in research and treatment, a stigma remained stubbornly attached to a diagnosis of PTSD in the military. Few people outside of health care professionals wanted to talk about it or hear about it. Many veterans even blamed themselves for this affliction. When they returned home, many felt their only choice was to isolate themselves. They turned to alcohol abuse and drugs to numb the loneliness and suffering. Addiction, loss of jobs, social and family disruption, homelessness, and incarceration were common results. It was a vicious cycle. We became resolved to help break this cycle.

Robert introduced me to his close friend, General John Batiste, who resided in Rochester and who had a close relationship with Dan DiMicco, CEO of the Nucor Steel Corporation. This company has a national presence, operating many steel factories across the country. One of Nucor's steel mills was in the town of Auburn, only an hour away from our headquarters in Webster. Dan had a personal interest in caring for veterans because his close friend's son was in the VA system and was receiving care for PTSD. He gave his full support for Warrior Salute Veterans Services, and Nucor Steel made a substantial six-figure commitment to its startup.

To begin the program, we rented several apartments in a local complex near our headquarters. Each veteran would have his or her own apartment. In Penfield, we obtained a lease at a strip mall and converted the space into offices and conference rooms. This location would provide clinical care, specifically behavioral health care. We had a very limited budget, so we hired contract clinicians and a manager to oversee the operations. We accepted veterans of all backgrounds.

The first days of Warrior Salute were calm, but this calm was only cosmetic. Staff began to report disturbing stories. The veterans were using alcohol and drugs in and around their apartments. Independent community apartments invited temptation and turned out to be a poor and unsafe environment for veterans suffering from a history of alcohol and drug addiction. Soon enough, the staff and I realized a drastically different approach would be necessary. The only solution was to create a new environment: our veterans needed a group residence that could be monitored.

In 2012, DePaul, a local mental health organization, put a residence in Penfield up for sale. The two-story house was designed for 14 people with mental health needs. I contacted Mark Fuller, DePaul's CEO, telling him that I was interested in the Penfield property. I invited him to lunch at Pomodoro's, an Italian restaurant in the city. They made the best pizzas in town. During lunch, I broached the subject, saying to Mark, "So you're selling one of your residences in Penfield. Is that right?"

"Yes, Sankar," he said. "We're closing that program and selling the house."

I chewed a slice of pepperoni pizza thoughtfully. I didn't want to appear eager for a deal. So I changed the subject, and we enjoyed our meals. As we finished off our meals, I broached the subject again, eager to know the price. I asked Mark how much he wanted for the house.

"We'll be happy with the amount remaining on the mortgage," he said. "About $500,000 to $550,000." Immediately, I knew we would purchase that house but at what price?

There was no way in 2012 we could build a house with fourteen bedrooms for just $550,000 in an upscale neighborhood in our community. To test how serious he was, and not wanting to drop the subject, I asked him if he would take $450,000 for the house. My offer aroused laughter, and I joined in. Then he became more earnest when he realized I wasn't joking. "Really?" he asked. "Are you serious?"

I told him I was absolutely serious.

He furrowed his brow and looked at me; my face remained impassive. "You have a deal," he said. I extended my hand to him, and we shook on it. It was a great moment for Warrior Salute Veterans Services.

Just recently, while at lunch, Mark and I reflected on the deal. I told him it was a godsend for the Veterans program. He responded, "Sankar, you negotiated a hell of a deal." I smiled. *Yes, I did.*

With a location secured, we informed the Penfield town officials of our intent to operate at the residence a rehabilitation program for veterans returning from the wars in Iraq and Afghanistan. We were in the process of purchasing it from DePaul. We had to complete the town's approval process before we could do anything with the residence. The house sat on what can best be described as an "island," carved out by three streets converging around the property, like three rivers. These three streets formed a metaphorical "moat" that isolated the DePaul people with mental health issues from the surrounding community. Across from the residence was a Christian school for children. We didn't anticipate any pushbacks, and expected our project to be welcomed.

Within days, we were invited to a town meeting. News of the house had clearly spread throughout the neighborhood because I arrived to find the venue full. Veterans who were attending our program were also present. I had naïvely expected the town board to quickly approve our request, especially since they already had approved a home for people with mental health needs at the site. A queue had formed, and one by one, townspeople stepped to the podium, each expressing their opposition. My heart sank.

One woman stood up and claimed, "Veterans with PTSD present a risk to my children attending school across the street. Our children can be harmed." There was, of course, no basis for this.

Many didn't want to be perceived as unpatriotic; they were contrite and prefaced their remarks by stating they had relatives who served in the military. But these words were then followed by "but I can't support this project because . . ." followed by a litany of objections.

The prevailing objection was the perception that the veterans could hurt the small children who lived in the neighborhood or attended the nearby school. I was surprised and very disappointed to hear this, and felt uncomfortable for those veterans in attendance who were already in the program at Warrior Salute. As someone who had spent time learning about veterans' issues, I knew that a veteran would sooner commit suicide than hurt anyone else; and harm against children was virtually unheard of. However, facts didn't matter to these townspeople. All that mattered was their irrational fear. Their understanding about PTSD came from movies like *Taxi Driver*.

The principal of the school drove the final nail in the coffin. She stood at the microphone and vehemently opposed the opening of the residence. It was political posturing. Because of the degree of opposition, yet not wanting to appear unappreciative to our veterans, the town supervisor and the board members wisely decided to table the vote. On the drive home I lamented about not being prepared for this reception. Yet I was not discouraged. I never once doubted that we would succeed. The postponement of the vote provided us with an opportunity to educate the broader community.

The next morning, I was surprised to receive a call from the president of the school board. He contacted my office to express that he had nothing to do with the principal's opinion. He promised we would have no further problems from the school staff. He was right. We never heard from that principal again. My confidence swelled as I planned a response to expose our neighbor's lack of compassion for our veterans. I planned to shine an unflattering spotlight on the Penfield community.

What followed was nothing short of a media campaign in our favor. Brother Wease, a veteran himself, invited me to his popular morning radio show, where I decried the lack of patriotism on display at the town meeting. I also shared my journey as an immigrant to the United States and my "American Dream" life in Rochester. I expressed unwavering support to the military and thanked Brother Wease for his service as a Vietnam veteran. He never wanted to be thanked. To the thousands of people who were listening, he expressed outrage about the lack of patriotism displayed at Penfield's board meeting. He committed to me that he would bring this topic up to the community on his radio show *every day* until there was a favorable resolution. I knew I could count on Brother Wease.

In addition, my staff contacted the television stations about what had transpired at the town meeting. I was daring people to go on the record saying that they didn't support veterans. Brother Wease continued to rail against the Penfield community. The television stations featured stories on the town's opposition to the residence; reporters went house to house to record the views of the neighborhood. Town residents didn't like the spotlight shining on them.

Three weeks after the Penfield town board meeting, a follow-up meeting was convened. The board was prepared to render a decision on the residence for veterans. Brother Wease and his team were in attendance. So were all the television stations. The television crews set microphones at the table where the town board members deliberated. We filled the room with veterans and advocates. Some neighbors attended, but it was a much lighter representation than before.

We expected another debate. However, to our surprise, after the town supervisor called the meeting to order, the first topic was a motion to approve CDS's residence for veterans. There was no debate. The board unanimously approved the motion. Democracy had worked. I felt a warm rush of victory.

Nucor Steel made another major contribution to help us purchase the residence. Then the team at Nucor Steel's Auburn plant held a charity golf tournament, raising $35,000 to help with refurbishing the residence. The Auburn team continues to visit the home at least once per year and assist in securing needed items on an ongoing basis; and they continue to hold annual golf tournaments with all proceeds going to the Nucor House. I love seeing this national corporation spending time with a little-known program in Rochester that helps veterans. I will remain forever grateful to Dan DiMicco and Nucor Steel, whose leadership team continues to support the program.

Following Nucor's example, the Rochester community banded together to support renovating the house. Lowe's and Home Depot led the charge, and nearly every business in Rochester assisted. One company contributed the flooring. Another company donated equipment for the kitchen. Another contributed labor. The entire renovation cost $300,000 and was completed in three months. This included new fixtures in the kitchen, new floors throughout the house, and a huge repair around the basement to stop water from leaking into the basement every time it rained. The entire house was repainted inside. The exterior was fully upgraded, from the deck and gazebo to the lawn and landscaping. Finally, every bedroom was furnished. I was determined that this house would look the best in the entire neighborhood—and show the neighbors that CDS did everything first-class.

Even during retirement, I take time to drive by the Nucor House, and I smile with pride every time, noticing the perfectly manicured lawn and well-maintained structure. The CDS leadership continues the tradition.

After its rocky beginning, today our Warrior Salute Veteran Services program and CDS attract a constant outpouring of goodwill from the community. This was an unexpected benefit of providing services to veterans. For example, Oak Hill Country Club, where the PGA golf tournament was held for many years, and again as recently as 2023, invited CDS to hold its annual fundraising tournament there. Bringing the tournament to Oak Hill raised the visibility of Warrior Salute Veterans Services and the golf tournament. By the time I retired from CDS, the tournament was consistently raising more than $600,000 at each event, with all the proceeds supporting the program. How remarkable it was that a nonprofit organization serving people with intellectual disabilities would give back to its community by supporting veterans through charitable donations.

Another good fortune and sign of success is that graduates of the program return to give back, such as Kyle Sill, the very first participant in Warrior Salute. He served in the Iraq War from 2004-08. One day an improvised explosive device (IED) exploded near him. He was thrown into the air and landed, suffering a traumatic brain injury as well as minor injuries. Some of his brothers-in-arms fared worse. He saw many of his fellow soldiers killed and injured. Witnessing the horrors of war and the explosion of the IED, Kyle suffered from PTSD and had difficulties reintegrating into society.

When Kyle came to visit the new Warrior Salute program, he brought his wife and mother with him. Both were worried and wanted him to get better. For six months, Kyle committed himself to healing and recovery. He attended all the sessions with his therapists. With his dedication and commitment to improving himself, Kyle graduated from the program and joined his family back home in upstate New York.

Throughout the years, he's remained in contact with the Warrior Salute program, and from time to time returns to speak at our fundraising events. Kyle represents the CDS Monarch ideal: he was cocooned, transformed himself, and broke free to live a new life. Now he inspires others.

Kyle represents one of many success stories at Warrior Salute. After 12 years in operation, more than 500 veterans have participated in the Warrior Salute Veteran Services program, and more than 90 percent have graduated. On average, we work with 40 veterans a year at a cost of $15,000 per person. The board of directors and staff pride themselves on not charging the veterans anything to attend the program. We want them to focus on themselves, improve their mental and physical health, and return home. Everyone at CDS takes pride in what Warrior Salute Veterans Services provides to our community. In the land of plenty, there is plenty of which we can be proud.

The Nucor House for veterans

37
SPICE BUSINESS PIVOTS TO ASIA

IN 2013, TWO years after DLA Troop Support adjusted their spice payments, Unistel staff reported that spice prices were rising again. I'd always understood that our biggest cost, after labor, was the cost of the spices. Now I wondered if we could strengthen our margins by lowering raw material costs. Unistel was buying spices from brokers in the United States. Most of these spices, however, were imported from other countries. The main growers and processors were in Vietnam, China, and India.

I suggested to Robert that we learn how the brokers procured these spices from other countries. This was a delicate topic to bring up with our brokers because it would expose their actual costs and their own inflated profit margins. They probably wouldn't give us accurate numbers if asked.

Still, we decided to engage our broker on the subject. I asked the Unistel salesman to contact him, pretending that we wished to educate ourselves on supply chain logistics. That conversation went just as we expected. I was reminded of Indiana Jones's assistant, Sallah, as he gravely stared into a pit of snakes. "Asps," he said. "Very dangerous."

The broker suspected our duplicity and deflected. "My process is very complicated," he said somberly. "The business of sourcing and importing spices isn't to be taken lightly. There are many risks." He insisted red tape was very difficult to deal with. Often, getting shipments to the US was a challenge. The overwhelming advice was that we should avoid dealing with overseas suppliers at all costs. Our salesperson delivered the injunction, perhaps as the broker intended, with gravity that expected us to call off the hunt.

Unbeknownst to our broker, when someone tells me I can't do something, those words have the opposite effect. They act like an incantation telling me to do just that. I didn't heed the broker's words for a moment. "No one's going to tell us what to do," I quipped. "How complicated can it be to purchase spices from a primary producer?" A sense of adventure occupied my imagination. I determined we would take the necessary steps and be in the position to purchase spices directly from foreign suppliers—with better quality control and better prices.

My plan was a surprise to no one, and next thing we knew, Robert and I were discussing a plan to go to Asia. We compiled a list of products we needed and the prices we were willing to pay. The success hinged on securing the proper pricing. The Alibaba website turned out to be a go-to marketplace for spice suppliers. All the suppliers were listed with links to their websites. I asked Robert to reach out to suppliers and select the top prospects. We would then map out an itinerary to hit those targets, our own "spice road" so to speak. Robert's efforts identified a short list of top suppliers in China, Vietnam, Thailand, and India. We reached out to these suppliers and, within a couple of weeks, we were on a 17-hour flight to China.

Our first flight landed in Beijing where we picked up a commuter flight to Qingdao, a province in the northern region. Qingdao was the main hub for all spice activity. Even though we arrived in Qingdao about 9:00 a.m., we were greeted by dark skies. It was disorienting. We suspected that we had stepped off the plane into one of China's unconventional time zones, but we soon learned the absence of sunlight was due to a perpetual dense smog that hung over Qingdao and kept out the sun. The smog imparted in the air an unfamiliar metallic and burnt-rubber smell, like we had landed next to a landfill fire. It surprised us that few people wore masks. The smell and smog were our companions for the entire visit to Qingdao.

Chinese envoys picked us up from the airport and stayed close to us. This was not our hosts being solicitous; likely they were appointed by the Communist government to monitor our activities while we were guests in China. It didn't bother us.

If our first impression felt modestly third world, our reception was nothing but first-class. Our contact in Qingdao was named Sabrina from D&B Foods, a garlic supplier. She met us at the airport and had a driver ready to take us to D&B Foods' headquarters. When we drove to the building, my name and Robert's name were flashing on an electronic billboard in front of the building. People were lined up to receive their American guests. They were fluent in English and introduced themselves with American names. We were greeted like foreign ambassadors.

We toured D&B's spice farm, production plant, and cold storage facility. They took us to the laboratory where they demonstrated their quality control processes. The production plant was world class, their processes were refined, and they kept meticulous records. After the tour, we were guided to a conference room where we negotiated our first contract for granulated and powdered garlic at a price considerably below what our broker charged us in the US.

To celebrate, we were chauffeured to a restaurant and ushered into an elegantly decorated private dining room. We were seated around a large, round table about 12 feet in diameter. At the center of the table sat a circular, glass "lazy Susan," where serving dishes would be placed and rotated in front of each guest.

The appetizers arrived. Our business contract completed, the social contract with our hosts dictated that we were expected to try *everything*; to pass up a dish was considered a direct insult. In this spirit, I sampled the pickled cucumber, a delicacy. I found it devoid of flavor and difficult to chew; it had a rubbery consistency and texture. Yet to refuse was out of the question. I quietly told Robert, "*General, you and I are eating the cucumber.*" Certainly, General Mixon was more accustomed to giving commands than receiving them, but he understood the gravity of the situation and did as I asked.

The meal seemed to look up when a server opened a white porcelain bottle of "mao-tai," China's national drink. At first the colorless liquid seemed more like an industrial solvent than a beverage, but I found the flavor enjoyable. Henry Kissinger once said of mao-tai, during a visit with Deng Xiaoping in 1979, "If we drink enough of this, we can solve anything." Our mission, of course, was much more narrowly focused than that, so I anticipated a single shot would be enough to conclude our garlic exploits and satisfy our hosts. I quickly tossed back my shot—only to have my glass promptly refilled. Concern showed on my face: like the pickled cucumber, drinking mao-tai was part of the social contract.

A few more shots into fulfilling our social contract, I began to be aware—if I was aware of anything by that point—that the Chinese were far more accomplished drinkers than Robert and I. They were determined to show these "laowai" that they were amateurs, and I had previously been cautioned that this was all part of the game. Fortunately, we were rescued by the main meal, and for the rest of the evening, the focus shifted from mao-tai to authentic Chinese cuisine and good conversation.

The next day, the effects of the mao-tai dissipated, and we visited a supplier that specialized in ground ginger in a village outside Qingdao. Next to the ginger plant was a row of houses where the workers' families lived. Their ginger had a rich flavor and the price was right. So we decided to do business with them too. In appreciation of our business relationship and a new contract, the owner invited us to dinner at a nearby restaurant. We said goodbye to the workers at the plant; even the workers' spouses came out of the homes to wave at us as we drove away.

I was perplexed when we arrived and were ushered into a dining room, only to encounter the same families we had just left behind at the factory welcoming us to the meal. We couldn't comprehend how they had arrived at the restaurant before us when they had left well after us. It was like they were performing some type of magic trick where the whole plant was complicit. The same curious phenomenon occurred several more times during our trip to China. We finally realized that it must have been the custom for drivers to take guests on a different, longer route, to allow the hosts to arrive before us. But we never did learn the true reason this was done.

During this trip, we also visited Linyi, a remote, rural village where some spice businesses were located. We must have looked hungry, because the willingness to feed us was again on display. Our host in Linyi was very excited to take us to lunch at a local restaurant. Once we arrived, he clapped his hands theatrically as the servers appeared. "We're having a very specially prepared dish," he said. Our mouths watered with anticipation.

"Special" was an understatement. A platter piled with the heads of rabbits that had been simmered in some sort of stew was placed in front of us. Robert and I grimaced at each other and swallowed hard. Was this some sort of test? Did the servers, by accident, bring us the discarded heads? Was the rest of the rabbit soon to follow? The pride on our host's face told us otherwise. This was a small village, and we didn't want to show disrespect to the locals. They had done everything they could to make us feel welcome. We each placed a rabbit head onto our plates, privately lamenting the rabbits that had been sacrificed for our benefit. We began timidly picking meat from the cheek bones. It seemed like a lot of unnecessary effort. I believe our host expected us to crack open the head, like Florida stone crab, and eat the brains, but we somehow escaped this stage of our culinary misadventure.

Another unexpected, but more pleasant, thing happened in Linyi that evening. After completing business, we stopped in our hotel bar for a drink. Tiredness had started to creep in, and we needed to just take some time to relax. Next to the bar was a lounge and stage. At some point during the evening a young woman made her way to the stage and set up a microphone and amplifier. I didn't pay much attention to her until she started to sing. Her voice had a beautiful quality, and all the songs she sang were American. Lionel Ritchie's "Three Times a Lady" was one. Nat King Cole's "Unforgettable" was another. I loved her performance and felt homesick. But China was only the first leg of our journey.

From China we flew to Bangkok, Thailand, to meet with a supplier. Thailand promised to be exotic: ancient temples hidden in dark forests, elephant parks, white sand beaches, and modern Bangkok. Exploring its spices should also prove to be exotic.

We found Bangkok to be overcrowded and busy. Multilane highways were buzzing with trucks, cars, scooters, and bicycles that sped by tire to tire. A train system connected the city's major arteries; still, traffic was congested, unlike anything I'd seen in the US. Sightseeing began midmorning to avoid the early morning rush, but that afternoon we ran into gridlock. Traffic came to a virtual standstill. At one point, as the Marriott Hotel where we were staying came into view, we asked our driver if he would let us out so we could walk. He insisted we remain in the vehicle. The way he told us this was as if he wanted to say, "What, are you crazy?" behind his Thai accent, so we concluded it was best to comply. What should have been a 10-minute drive turned into one hour.

Fortunately, our next contact agreed to come to us, and made it unnecessary to leave the hotel. The broker's representative arrived late by almost half an hour. Given the traffic situation, we would have understood. But he didn't even call to tell us or attempt to apologize, and we took this as a bad sign.

We asked him basic questions about their spices and production. He avoided direct answers or eye contact, and instead spoke in vague generalities. Then he pulled out a container of black *peppercorns* from his suitcase; prior to the meeting we had emphasized we didn't have a way to process peppercorns and were interested in ground black pepper. The packaging looked like it came from a grocery store. Alarm bells started to go off. Nevertheless, we invited him to the conference room we had reserved at the Marriott for the meeting. He unabashedly availed himself of our hospitality, eagerly helping himself to the coffee and snacks. More alarm bells went off: the hospitality was "upside down." We were supposed to be *his* guests, hoping to do business with *him*. It was in stark contrast to the cordiality and accommodation of our Chinese partners, who early on set a high hospitality standard.

It became clear this representative was at the level of a used car lot salesman. Sensing our growing irritation, he quickly offered to take us to his boss. He led us outside the hotel where we anticipated his vehicle would be waiting, or at least a taxi. Instead, we followed him down a sidewalk and up a staircase to a train kiosk, where we were instructed to purchase our own tokens. Robert glanced at me and mouthed, "This isn't good." The gentleman was oblivious to our concerns. I felt sorry for him and gave him one of the tokens, which he did not refuse. Robert and I began to suspect there was little interest in our business, and the company had sent out a low-level employee to deal with us. In the end our attitude toward his boss was irreconcilably spoiled. The meeting didn't go well, as expected. We never did do business with that company. We turned our attention to learning more about Bangkok.

One day, I walked out of the hotel and made my way up the street to grab a taxi to explore downtown Bangkok. A woman standing at the corner approached me and asked if I was a foreigner. She seemed very welcoming and gave me many recommendations for entertainment and food. Then she said if I was looking for jewelry, she would take me to a "special jeweler." At first I was reluctant, but I was interested in bringing back something special for Yvonne. I knew that Bangkok was known for jewelry, so I suspended any suspicions and followed her to the jewelry store where I was introduced to some very high-pressure salespeople. To effect release from my captors, I purchased a couple of broaches and a necklace that I didn't want. Robert and I left Bangkok and resolved never to return to Thailand.

From Bangkok we flew to Ho Chi Minh City (formerly Saigon) in the south of Vietnam. Like Bangkok, the streets bustled with cars and motorcycles day and night. The number of motorcycles passing through every intersection was striking; they moved together in synchronicity like swarms of birds.

Our visit focused on securing a contract to buy black pepper directly from Petrolimex, a highly recommended supplier. We were driven to Petrolimex's plant, which was about an hour and a half outside of Ho Chi Minh City, and there we sat with one of the managers to negotiate a contract. As we asked him about the grinding process for pepper, he mentioned that Petrolimex also ground cinnamon, a product Unistel also supplied the military. I couldn't believe our luck. We settled on a contract, helping Unistel to significantly reduce our costs for the two products.

During our visit to Ho Chi Minh City, someone told us about a flea market near our hotel where we could purchase clothes, perfume, cologne, belts, and any other items to bring back to the United States. Counterfeit Michael Kors, Dolce & Gabbana, and Coach handbags were sold cheaply. The vendors had become experts in duplicating name brands, including the insignias. I bought some men's cologne, only to discover it watered down once I got home, and had to use half a bottle before I could detect a fragrance that remained. I am sure I was not the only tourist to fall prey to purchasing bootlegged cologne. But I admired the effort they made to operate their business.

The Vietnamese were wonderful and warm people, but I stopped purchasing "brand" gifts to bring home. When we returned home, at one of my visits to the ophthalmologist, who was of Vietnamese descent, I asked about the watered-down cologne. He and I shared a good laugh as he explained how the Vietnamese people looked at business; they did whatever was needed to make a buck, even if they had to cheat a little.

From Ho Chi Minh City we flew to Delhi. Surprisingly, we found ground travel even more tedious and difficult than in China, Thailand, and Vietnam. Whole "parking lots" of vehicles and noise moved together in unison at a glacial pace. Accompanying this glacier was a cacophony of horns. Cars and motorcycles navigated the sea of vehicles like mechanical bats. Rules of the road didn't seem to exist, or matter. I felt every kilometer put our lives in danger, but surprisingly we never got into an accident for the duration of our trip.

We found the people of India to be very warm, welcoming, and helpful. One time, in a rush to get to the airline terminal to catch my flight, I tripped and momentarily went airborne before landing face down and sprawled out on the ground. Under my momentum, my suitcase continued traveling in a different direction. I am certain there are airports in the US where I would have been ignored. In India, people rushed to my assistance, helped me up, and asked if I was OK. Then they retrieved my suitcase. The people were gracious, and fortunately I only suffered some bruises and a sprained elbow. Unfortunately, the incident was a foreshadowing of our spice negotiations.

At first, our meetings in India seemed to go smoothly, far better than in Thailand. The local brokers arrived, prepared with prices and other information. They were gracious and, like in China, insisted on hosting meals. The authentic Indian cuisine was rich in flavors, and I couldn't get enough. The dishes were different, but equally good. They were much spicier than the Chinese food, and the variety of flavors was more complex. Fortunately, either through heritage, genetics, or conditioning, I found even the spiciest food manageable. I was not quite as confident about Robert, who avoided any spicy dishes during these meals. If there was any discomfort, he didn't divulge this, and always complimented the meal and our hosts.

Our hosts took us to tour their spice plants where, after the customary haggling back and forth, we settled on purchasing a variety of spices. To my surprise, their follow-up communication was not forthright. They couldn't commit to agreed-upon prices, citing daily fluctuations in the commodities market. I was not convinced. This was a different experience compared to China and Vietnam. I was disillusioned because, on account of my heritage, I expected smooth business relations. It took a while to develop an approach to negotiations with the Indian suppliers that worked for both parties. In the end, we established a very close relationship with a broker that has made doing business in India better, with less heartburn.

Regardless of the minor failures, the Asia trip was overwhelmingly a success, and we saved the company hundreds of thousands of dollars in costs. We returned to Asia year after year to renegotiate old contracts and establish new ones, and the savings to Unistel have continued. Our US brokers had been wrong; they were trying to protect their own interests and profits, and greatly underestimated our resolve and resourcefulness.

Procuring our own spices was a game changer for Unistel. We were able to reinvest some of the profits in the mission of CDS, and feed some into the foundation. Within the next five years, the Unistel spice business grew from a $100,000 a year operation to $10 million a year. During our peak year we generated $13 million. That was worth enduring the 17-hour flights to China and the 24-hour flights back home from India. And, yes, Unistel has continued to employ 50 people with IDD. That's what it was all about.

38
HAVING FUN: WANTING A FAIR DEAL

IT WASN'T ALL business. Robert and I wanted to enjoy some of the sights while traveling in Asia. During every trip to India, we made sure to visit the Taj Mahal, truly one of the Seven Wonders of the World. This magnificent structure, made of white stone and marble, is inlaid with intricate designs of colored marble. Entering the complex, we were greeted by elegant courtyards that partially concealed the magnificent structure until it came into full view. It was breathtaking. Every time we visited, it was a different, almost spiritual experience. And of course, every time we visited China, we took the time to visit the Great Wall.

On one of our trips to India, we traveled to see a 2,000-year-old temple along the coast of India in a city, Chennai. As we learned at the Taj Mahal and other tourist attractions, entrance fees varied. Indians charged tourists 10 times more than what they charged local Indian residents. I thought this was preposterous and decided to have some fun with it. So this time I cooked up a scheme. Since I was of Indian heritage and had dark skin, I could always pass as a native and avail myself of the cheaper price. I wondered if I could present myself at the ticket counter and get away with purchasing two tickets—one for me and one for Robert—at the "discounted" price. Robert stayed out of view. I casually asked for two tickets, but as soon as I spoke, my cover was blown. My accent gave me away. I didn't speak Hindi.

"Where are you from?" the clerk asked suspiciously in perfect English.

I wanted to say, "None of your business," but said, "Chennai." It wasn't a lie: we had arrived at the temple from our hotel in Chennai. He was caught off guard and became flustered. "Fifty rupees," he finally said, indicating 25 rupees for each ticket. I almost got away with it when a group of young Indian hoodlums standing near Robert began chanting "Gringo! Gringo!" as they pointed to Robert. He gave a cursory wave of his hand.

"Gotcha," the clerk said as he grinned, surprisingly using an American idiom. "Twenty-five rupees for you, and 250 rupees for the gringo."

In the end, we were only talking about a difference of less than two dollars. It was simply the principle that tourists paid 10 times the price of locals, whatever that amount was. I returned to Robert with the tickets. I was content with the "mixed result" of my con. In actuality, the clerk could have charged us both the full amount, since we were both gringos. But he must have appreciated my effort and given me the local discount. In a way, it was the way that I approached pricing at Unistel. I wanted fair prices, even if it meant using unconventional tactics to get them.

I was equally charmed by India and China. Every year when we returned to China, I was awed by the way buildings had been erected between our visits. The cities experienced a large migration of people from the villages and rural areas, and high-rise apartments arose every six months to accommodate them. The masses came to work in factories that made products to ship to the United States and everywhere else in the world. Year after year we witnessed a remarkable transformation.

China is run by the Communist party but, owing to Chairman Mao in the 1980s, has embraced capitalism as the key to economic growth. Like many countries experiencing rapid industrial growth, Beijing and Qingdao generated their share of pollution and sat under a blanket of smog. Furthermore, China relied on coal-fired plants to provide much of its energy. Well-meaning but poorly informed climate activists need to look at these realities every time they blame the US for not doing enough. Each time we were transported from one meeting to another, I knew when we were approaching another city because the sky would take on an eerie, grey-brown veil. As a result, Robert suffered mild respiratory issues on these trips.

Robert and I were delighted to experience authentic Chinese food. It had little resemblance to the deep-fried and sweet-and-sour covered Chinese food in the United States. There was an unmistakable natural and fresh flavor in the food we ate. I believe the best meal we had was hosted by a paprika supplier, Qingdao Fuxin Kang Company. After our meeting ended, they invited us into a building where someone had prepared fresh grilled flounder accompanied by a large variety of green vegetables and plenty of cold Chinese beer. It was a memorable meal.

Now that I have retired, I reminisce with family and friends about the wonderful people I met along the way. Regardless of my different heritage and culture, I was able to develop and nurture close and mutually beneficial relationships so that people with IDD could achieve their American dreams.

39
IN AND OUT OF CONSOLIDATION

BY THE YEAR 2012, CDS Monarch was running on "all cylinders." Its affordable housing division continued to expand, CDS Monarch's delivery on mission to the people with IDD was strong, Warrior Salute was thriving, iCircle was moving ahead on managed care, and Unistel's spice business was growing.

During one of the annual strategic planning sessions, I presented to the Unistel team the opportunity to expand its offerings beyond spices. The idea came to me when I attended a meeting of the Research and Development Associates (R&DA) trade association, representing companies in the military food business. This is a regular gathering among prime vendors supplying food to the military, their contractors, and representatives from the Defense Logistics Agency (DLA) troop support. There, I was having a conversation about Unistel's spices with the representatives of Supreme Foods, a partner for whom we were packaging and shipping spices to US troops in Iraq. They suggested that, since Unistel packaged spices, we might be interested in consolidating a wide variety of foods—already packaged by major US manufacturers—and ship them to the Middle East. This was fascinating. I was interested, but cautious.

Unistel had the Department of Labor issue regarding IDD employee wages in its rearview mirror. Now was the time to further grow and diversify, but I needed to fully understand the upsides, downsides, and risks before pulling the trigger. On the plus side, my eyes shined as I described my vision to Robert. I explained to him how this new consolidation activity could provide work for our individuals with IDD at Unistel. After we consolidated products, we could coordinate with DLA Troop Support for shipping companies to pick up the products from us. We would provide them with complete manifests, substantiating the contents and meeting the Middle East countries' requirements. We had been doing this for the spices, shipping them all over the world to US military installations. To become a consolidator handling large volumes of products would require us to understand the shipping requirements. Without it, we were "shooting in the dark." Also, we did not know if the unit price was enough. Yet, as an entrepreneur, I wanted to take the risk. Robert was on board.

The CDS Board of Directors approved the venture. To be successful, though, we needed someone on the inside to help. Robert reached out to a friend and former colleague of his, retired Lieutenant General Robert Dail (Bob, as he liked to be called), who held the CEO position at Supreme Foods, a prime vendor operating in the Middle East. At one point in his illustrious 30-year military career, Bob was the commander of DLA Troop Support. He was a logistics expert through and through, and I was gratified that he had agreed to introduce us to Supreme Foods.

Soon after, Supreme Foods sent their procurement officer, who visited Unistel, toured the plant, and met with our staff. He liked what he saw, and shortly after, Supreme Foods placed orders. The arrangement was that Unistel would purchase the food products on behalf of Supreme Foods, ship them, and then be reimbursed for the purchases. This entailed some risk because we were paying to procure the products before being paid. But the opportunity outweighed the risk.

In a whirlwind, Robert and I traveled to Washington, DC, to meet Bob and his team. The highly decorated general had a very engaging personality and sympathized with our mission to provide employment opportunities to individuals with IDD. The unemployment rate among people with IDD was 60 percent. As we talked, Bob came to appreciate my deep patriotism and Unistel's commitment to supporting the US military during war time. He and I instantly clicked, and in a short time, the generals and I flew to Dubai to meet with Supreme Foods' leadership. There, we reached an agreement to consolidate a wide range of food products.

Part of the consolidation requirements included that we meet with the major food manufacturers—Kraft, Nabisco, and Nestle. I admired the military for sparing no expense to provide to our troops the best foods. Seeing the close relationship between the military and these major manufacturers was an education. Each had a senior staff position dedicated to handling military procurement. Every American should be proud of this partnership on behalf of our brave men and women in uniform. I felt much pride in saying that Unistel did its part to help the military while our country was fighting wars overseas.

Soon Unistel began packaging products and shipping them out, doing just one or two containers a week. This low volume allowed staff time to learn the consolidation business on the job. The Supreme Foods staff worked closely with us to get the shipping requirements for the Middle East right. We slowly and carefully grew the team, hiring staff that knew how to purchase products, who oversaw the consolidation process and, most importantly, who knew the shipping process to ensure our shipments would pass through the ports of Dubai. Having complete and accurate information on the shipping manifests was critically important. Unistel was on the hook to pay any penalties resulting from delayed shipments.

At the height of the Iraq war, in one year Unistel consolidated and shipped approximately $30 million worth of food products on behalf of the US military. On average, we were shipping six to eight containers of food products per week. The consolidation business with Supreme Foods was quite profitable—with the right volume and the right unit price.

As the US began pulling out of the Middle East, our contracts with Supreme Food came to an end, and we explored how our consolidation business could continue beyond the conflict. I hated losing the competency we had meticulously built. Since we had already established Unistel as a consolidator and built the infrastructure, we looked for a new partner. With the wars winding down and the troops returning home, the military was readjusting its forces around the world, increasing its presence in Europe. So we looked to another prime vendor we could consolidate products for, Theodor Wille Intertrade (TWI) based in Germany. It had a $35 million contract to provide food for US forces in northern Europe.

TWI was of particular interest because they were in the process of being acquired by Atlantic Diving Supplies (ADS), a company with a nearly $1 billion business with DLA troop support, providing a wide range of products that were shipped worldwide. More importantly, Bob sat on the board of ADS, which was poised to acquire TWI. He felt Unistel was well positioned to do consolidation with TWI. This was a very exciting proposition.

As the purchase of TWI transpired over the next year, Bob introduced my senior staff and me to the gentleman who would be running the business, who had served on Bob's team at Supreme Foods. He was an expert in the military food business and was poised to head TWI business as part of ADS. He intimated to me that he was interested in moving away from the current TWI consolidator. He was open to Unistel being the new consolidator, and over time we reached an agreement; we reviewed and came to an understanding of each party's responsibilities. Yet we couldn't pin down the shipping requirements for the European countries, and the unit price was 25 percent lower than what we got with Supreme Foods.

A few months into Unistel's consolidation business with TWI, our business office staff reported troubling numbers on the monthly financials. We were consistently losing money. We scrubbed the numbers and saw that the consolidation rate we received from TWI was inadequate to cover our costs. We made staffing efficiencies, but for as much as we did, those changes weren't enough to take the consolidation business out of the red.

To make matters worse, TWI administration demanded that Unistel take responsibility for shipments that were held at European ports due to deficient manifests. Every day that a shipment was delayed, a penalty subscribed to Unistel accrued. Penalties were piling up. Yet we struggled to obtain clear instructions for the manifests. TWI accepted no responsibility. Unistel eventually worked out the manifest issue, and staff achieved some ease with their work. Yet the finances didn't improve. I proposed a rate increase to TWI and was initially advised that my request was reasonable. I felt confident going into a meeting with the TWI leadership. I laid out our case and presented our documentation. As I passed around the copies, I noticed the two TWI leaders exchanging glances. *Should I be worried?* I wondered for the first time.

"Sankar, we're not convinced you need more money," the CFO said. There it was. What we thought was reasonable was not.

"We feel something must be wrong in these calculations," he continued.

I felt indignant. My staff in the business office were the best, including several talented accountants who knew very well how to make a sound financial statement. There was no escaping that the consolidation business was losing money. The fault wasn't in the math, but in the projected costs versus the actual costs of doing business.

We also had challenges with the expansion of consolidating frozen products. We needed dedicated cold storage, an expensive infrastructure Unistel lacked. We had worked with a contractor in Rochester, but after a short time they put us on notice that they were ending the contract. Since we couldn't build cold storage ourselves, we were at a dead end and began looking for a new provider.

Cold storage was one of many subcontractor costs that bit into the revenue and detracted from our mission to employ individuals with IDD. Eventually, subcontractors handled nearly all the consolidation work. Still, when my staff suggested we pull Unistel out of the TWI contract, I balked. I was emotionally invested in the relationships I'd formed in the process of growing the business—and invested in the patriotic feeling that we helped feed our troops. But these weren't my deciding factors. I dug my heels into consolidation because I could not accept failure.

Several consultations with the staff and board of directors convinced me the bigger failure than leaving consolidation was staying in and continuing to bleed CDS's resources. That made pulling out of consolidation more palatable. I was responsible for the organization and couldn't allow one department to drag down the others.

Even as Unistel exited the consolidation business, I admired Bob Dail and valued my relationship with him. I most appreciated that he became a believer in the CDS mission, especially our Warrior Salute Veterans Services program. For as long as I was CEO, he remained at my side as a trusted advisor with whom I could exchange ideas and call upon to support the mission of the organization. He and his wife, Anne, made visiting CDS in Rochester an annual trip, and they became good friends.

Always looking for the positive, I'm grateful Unistel's venture into consolidation led Bob Dail into the CDS family. And my staff and I took the time to learn why that business venture was unsuccessful—we should've had a concrete understanding of how to do business in European countries from TWI, upfront. *Lessons learned.*

From left: General Mixon, me, David Bellavia, General Dail, and Richard Ferrari

40
AN EDUCATION IN BUSINESS DEALINGS

DURING ITS FIRST two years, iCircle's membership grew to more than 4,000 members and revenues of $150 million. The next year, membership increased to 5,000 members with revenue of $175 million. iCircle had become a behemoth compared to CDS's other businesses. It required everyone's attention and focus. Within a short time, iCircle's members were complaining about the lack of response from the care management team. Throwing money at it was not the solution. Independent Living Systems (ILS), a company based in Florida but with a presence in New York, entered into a contract with iCircle to provide the care management function. This required ILS to build a care management team, but the team did not meet its obligations. They hired a few people, and a visit to their office in NYC confirmed what we suspected: offices were vacant that should have been occupied. Members were complaining daily about ILS's lack of responsiveness. I asked the ILS leadership about this, reminding them of the commitments they had made. But without any action to remediate the problem, month after month, members and the iCircle management were disillusioned and concerned.

Jose Planta, ILS's CEO, and his assistant, Mary Ferman, travelled to Rochester to attend our golf tournament, but the event was rained out. Taking advantage of their presence, I asked for a meeting at the golf course's clubhouse. They seemed upbeat as they took their seats.

I wasted no time laying out the problem. The ILS care managers were taking too long to respond to the members, which caused great concern. I could not understand why that was happening. We needed an explanation. None came.

We pressed the issue, showing the phone logs. No one could argue that we had a problem. iCircle was creating pain for people by putting them off and not providing what they needed—the very fear people expressed repeatedly about managed care. The situation was unacceptable.

Mary tried to suggest our numbers could be off, but I was having none of it. I said, "One thing needs to happen. You must hire more staff and improve your services or else there will be consequences."

They promised to investigate the matter, but service never improved, so we were forced to terminate that contract. But we weren't through with ILS entirely. Just when we thought we had room to build a new track record, in 2018, three years into operating the MLTC plan, the Office of the Medicaid Inspector General (OMIG) audited iCircle and discovered the past deficiencies, resulting in a high seven-figure penalty. For the next three years OMIG reviewed the matter. Our attorney was in constant communication with the auditors and ILS leadership. iCircle was responsible for the care management function that was under review. The penalty hung over our heads like a ton of bricks.

We were all relieved when, in 2021, all parties came to an understanding and the matter was settled. That was a wake-up call. We were getting an education in business dealings unlike anything our management team had experienced before.

On the positive side, iCircle had quietly done the hard work, and in the process gained the confidence of its members and state officials, who regarded iCircle as a vital support system for people with chronic illnesses in upstate New York. One amazing data point was that 250 people with IDD who lived independently in their communities signed on with iCircle; thereafter, they exited the OPWDD system and elected to be supported by iCircle. The numbers showed that we were doing something right. We felt we were getting a handle on operating a managed care company and we were feeling good about the future.

As the iCircle plan grew, there was a need for a full-time chief medical officer (CMO). There were demands on authorizing services, monitoring the services delivered, and keeping track of the plan's performance against the quality metrics. It was a full-time job. Finding a doctor to do it was a tougher task than anticipated. By this time, I had developed a close network of friends and associates at the Oak Hill Country Club, where I was a member. Oak Hill's membership comprised the upper echelon of the Rochester community. There I met Dr. Max Chung, a very successful dentist. He and I were at lunch one day when I mentioned that iCircle was in need of a CMO. I was surprised when he showed interest, indicating that a physician, who was a close friend, had retired recently but might be reconsidering. With some undue pressure on Dr. Chung (People say I can be pushy), I was able to have a meeting with the retired physician, Dr. Joel Haas.

Dr. Haas reminded me of Mark Peterson, coming into the meeting simply as a favor to Max, just as Mark had met with me as a favor to our director of development years ago. At the meeting, I shared my vision for iCircle and the role, and introduced Dr. Haas to the staff. I wasn't sure if he'd join us, but was so happy when he did. He performed his duties at iCircle with such ease that, of course, I roped him into helping in other areas. He represented the best in class in the medical field, demonstrating care, compassion, competence, and dedication to his job. I am proud to call him my friend, even after retirement. Having Dr. Haas in the CMO role ensured that iCircle delivered its services reliably and with high quality. From agreeing to spend just one year at iCircle, he dedicated five years to the staff and the people we served, and remains connected to the organization. What a find! Providential, I say.

41
A GREAT OPPORTUNITY

ONE MORNING IN 2018, I was at my desk when my phone rang. The caller was Mike Mascari, a close colleague in New York City. He and I had served as members of the New York State OPWDD task force on managed care for people with IDD. Mike had served in several senior staff positions at the state level before retiring. He informed me he was coming out of retirement to help with the state's transition of the IDD service system to managed care. Yes, eight years after the managed care initiative was announced, New York still hadn't rolled it out. I congratulated Mike on coming out of retirement to help with this important initiative.

He stated the reason for his call, saying, "Sankar, you and your organization have done a great job of building the infrastructure to operate an IDD managed care company in upstate New York. The next transition, as you know, is the development of care coordination organizations [CCOs]. It's a great opportunity for you to help with the next phase. I'd like you to serve on the taskforce and I urge you to begin putting together a coalition of providers to operate a care coordination organization." I needed no convincing.

I affirmed my commitment, telling Mike that I would do whatever was needed to help establish a CCO. At that time, there was a renewed sense that managed care was coming to New York; the task force's work shifted to the start-up of the CCOs. Up to this point, organizations serving the IDD community had their own in-house service coordination departments that coordinated services and helped individuals and families access government resources. The CCO initiative proposed to eliminate the in-house service coordination departments and establish independent for-profit entities to do care management, the precursory step to managed care.

I was excited. We had done the hard work to be prepared for this moment. iCircle was well on its way to being a managed long term care (MLTC) plan. We were poised to bring about the new CCO initiative to fruition.

I made appointments with my fellow nonprofit CEOs. My initial excitement was dampened when they expressed concern that the state-managed care initiative had stalled. It took a lot of convincing to get providers to join our new CCO, which would be one of similar organizations across the state. Finally, we brought together a group of 17 providers, forming our new CCO, Prime Care Coordination (PCC). Across all the members, PCC covered 7,500 lives and more than 300 employees. With our stakeholders in place, things moved at a fast pace.

CDS Life Transitions Board Chair Greg Gribben, a partner at the Woods Oviatt Gilman law firm, worked with us to set up PCC as a legal for-profit entity. We established the board of directors and convened a meeting to elect its leaders. The board chair would be Ed Hayes, president and CEO of Cayuga Centers, and a good friend. I would serve as vice chair. With the board in place, we approved the by-laws. With the PCC governance all set, we moved to establish a memorandum of understanding between iCircle (the managed care company) and PCC (the care coordination company), outlining an agreement to work collaboratively to establish an IDD-managed care company. *What an effort.* With all the preparations completed, we exhaled with the knowledge that we were ready for what the future had in store.

42
GOING OFF COURSE

WE MOVED AHEAD to building the PCC staffing infrastructure. The leadership onboarded all service coordinators from the 17 owner organizations onto the PCC payroll. Soon we had assembled more than 300 new employees into one workforce. These employees came from different organizations with unique cultures, different compensation packages, and varying performance expectations. PCC's challenge was to create new and consistent expectations across the board. We developed competitive benefit packages, and clearly defined roles and responsibilities, and in the process brought the team together.

Wanting to build a unified work culture, we introduced CDS's performance management system. CDS paid people well, gave them great benefits, and provided opportunities for them to earn more money through a performance incentive plan, issuing bonuses twice per year. PCC employees would be treated the same. They welcomed the changes.

PCC Board Chair Ed Hayes and I always had good communication; we were very supportive of each other. A few months into PCC's operations, during one of our conversations he requested that CDS provide PCC's back-office functions.

I was surprised, but welcomed the opportunity to help. We had a robust HR system and a strong Quality Assurance Department.

Our IT team was deep. Our business office, run by Judy Consadine, had an envied financial reporting system. She had worked her way up the corporate ladder at CDS for her entire career, demonstrating a strong work ethic, always. She kept her head down and let her work speak for itself. Now it was speaking volumes.

We developed an administrative services organization (ASO) proposal, which the PCC Board approved. CDS began delivering ASO services, but the organization continued to struggle. There was a lack of discipline and defined process; the management remained unfocused.

In PCC's first year of operation, it was audited by OPWDD and received a Statement of Deficiencies (SOD). Due to the seriousness of the issues identified, PCC was placed on "enhanced oversight," which meant that its activities would be monitored by OPWDD until it made improvements. This level of sanction was something none of us were prepared for. I shuddered to remember the time CDS was in trouble.

This status was of deep concern to PCC, and brought back nightmares of the time CDS was experiencing similar troubles.

Shortly after the audit results, the PCC Board of Directors set up a special committee to work with management to address every item of the SOD and provide a thorough response. As part of this, we had to create improvement plans. We were effectively on "probation" with OPWDD, which had the power to shut off our lights.

My biggest concern, beyond the future of PCC, was the SOD's impact on PCC's partnership with iCircle, which continued to make plans to become a managed care company for individuals with IDD. It was imperative that we resolve the enhanced oversight situation. And even if PCC was able to do so, and come off of probation, could it still deliver on its promises to CDS Life Transitions and iCircle? We were making investments to prepare for a future that was unknown.

PART IV

COLLATERAL ARTERIES

Part IV reveals a final series of improbable events that happened in my personal and business life. Chapter 45 begins in early 2019 as I contemplate the job offer of a lifetime—and the opportunity to manage an $8 billion annual budget. Urgent neck surgery for severe cervical spinal stenosis occurs amidst troubling news about PCC's 2020 budget. While solving the largest crisis CDS has faced, new symptoms of coronary arterial blockages send me back to the hospital. In Chapter 47, I initiate a bold plan to restore PCC to solvency and service excellence. My last accomplishment as CEO occurs in Chapter 50 when iCircle is hit by a financial meteor that leaves a $33.5 million crater, but which we are able to fill within 18 months, without external help or outside cash infusions. The book closes with a retrospective from retirement with thoughts on civil institutions, religion, and never giving up.

43
HOW I TURNED DOWN A ONCE-IN-A-LIFETIME OFFER—OVERSEEING AN $8 BILLION BUDGET

IN 2019, I received a surprising call from an intermediary connected to the New York State governor's office asking me to consider taking the commissioner of OPWDD position, which had become vacant. This was a surprise.

I had to reflect on how improbable this opportunity really was. When I emigrated from the third world to the United States of America in 1977, my first job was at the Dame Belt Factory in a decaying building in Manhattan. The workforce consisted of Puerto Ricans and West Indians, predominantly from Guyana. Everybody brought their lunch, usually rice and curried fish. We carefully wrapped our food at home in aluminum foil, and as soon as we arrived at work, we placed it on the plant's antiquated steam heating vents, bringing our food to the proper temperature by lunch time. Having lunch alongside my coworkers, doing the same thing day after day, made me realize that I wanted more for my life.

From the dusty floors of Dame Belt, I worked my way up to become the CEO of one of the largest nonprofit organizations in upstate New York. I was the only Indian, and the only Guyanese, in the boardroom.

Now I felt great honor that people in the governor's office had recognized me and my accomplishments, and had confidence that I had the knowledge and talents to successfully manage a high-level government position. I would be managing an $8 billion budget and serving more than 120,000 people with IDD across New York State. I would also be leading a system with many challenges that needed to be transformed.

But the person who nominated me for the commissioner role didn't know that I had recently been faced with a new and serious health concern. The problem surfaced while suffering from a respiratory infection that inflicted me with a relentless cough. One night I couldn't sleep, coughing nonstop. During one episode I felt a razor-sharp pain shooting down my left arm, and into my hands and fingers. Afterward, I realized that *both* hands felt quite numb. I suspected something was seriously wrong.

After consulting with my primary care physician, I was referred to the neurosurgeon who had operated on my lower back years before for spinal stenosis. Dr. Pierre Girgis had also, by this time, become a dear friend. He reviewed the MRI and noted that the vertebrae in my neck had degenerated and shifted, causing severe pressure on my spinal cord. If this pressure was not relieved, the pain and numbness in my hands would progress. What's more, I faced permanent neurological damage that could leave me unable to walk within the year. Surgery was strongly advised, but it would be a long and involved operation, with a long recovery that would certainly stress my heart. I was at a dilemma; my heart bypass surgery in 2002 put me at a much higher risk. I believed there was a high probability I would not survive the surgery. I panicked. I put off surgery and simply worked through the pain for the next eight months.

As anticipated, the pain and numbness in my hands became more pronounced. Then I began to experience symptoms that involved my legs: I had difficulty going up and down stairs, and my legs began to lose coordination. Dr. Girgis was frank. He told me I could no longer postpone surgery, that some of the damage was likely permanent, and that to prevent further damage and possibly losing the ability to walk, I needed surgery *soon*.

I was conflicted. The recommendation for the commissioner's job couldn't have come at a worse time. I was told the recovery after neck fusion, if it was successful, would take six months to a year. The role of commissioner would require me to move to Albany, or suffer a four-hour, punishing commute each way, putting strain on a freshly fused neck. This meant the governor would have to delay hiring me for perhaps a year. The overwhelming concerns were that my heart bypasses were aging and approaching their shelf life, and my role as CEO demanded long hours and brought considerable stress. In fact, my primary care physician had, on multiple occasions, recommended that I take a medical retirement.

My main concern, though, was the neck fusion surgery; it was unreasonable for me to request that the governor hold off on filling the position for a year as I recovered from it. Still, out of respect and honor to be nominated, I sent in my resume and attended interviews in Albany and New York City. I confidently gave my perspective on the OPWDD system, its future, and what I would bring to the job. The governor's staff was very complimentary.

As commissioner of OPWDD, my main objective would have been to ensure sustainability. For example, the costs for the traditional residential and day programs that OPWDD supported could not continue. My vision was to force the reengineering of those programs and provide opportunities for people with IDD to live in much more independent affordable communities, with a strong support system, while significantly reducing Medicaid costs through managed care. I believed I could work with local communities across New York State to transform the system.

While I awaited the governor's decision, resigned to the risks of my neck surgery, I wanted to spend as much time with my family as possible. We had scheduled a cruise to the Caribbean, which I cautiously still planned to take. A few days before the trip, I received a call from the governor's office offering me the position. I felt dizzy; I had gone from lowly immigrant belt factory worker to New York State commissioner of OPWDD—the pinnacle of my career. It was like a siren song, seducing me, pulling me to Albany. Yet too many roads were intersecting in my life at the same time, and I told the governor I needed some time to think.

For the first time in my life, I was completely at a loss of what to do. I looked to everyone I knew for advice. Many raised the expected medical concerns; and my family did not want to move to Albany. The CDS Life Transitions Board of Directors didn't want me to go, and dropped anchors, encouraging me to stay. A common theme was the tremendous opposition people believed I would face introducing my bold initiatives that would lead to frustration. People on the "inside" also cautioned that little would be accomplished because of the agonizingly slow pace of the bureaucracy. Jim Introne said it sagely: "In government a person has wide authority to say no, but very little authority to say yes."

I came to my decision against the undulating blue scrim of the Caribbean. I was on the ship's top deck watching the Island of St. Thomas, its beach growing larger as we approached the dock. While I desperately wanted the commissioner job, the realization that I could put my health in jeopardy overshadowed the opportunity. I'd rather be at the beach.

By the time we returned home, my mind was made up. I called the governor's office and respectfully declined the offer. I experienced both a feeling of relief and sadness when I hung up the phone. Then I made arrangements for my absence for the neck surgery and recovery. The surgery was successful, owing to the skill of my neurosurgeon, Pierre Girgis, and I thankfully suffered no cardiac complications. My postoperative recovery, on the other hand, was quite difficult; it was the most painful period I had endured in my life, far greater in fact than my cardiac surgery. In retrospect, as difficult as that period was, I am glad I had the surgery. Years later I still have residual pain in my arm and weakness in my legs, but I cannot imagine the debility I would have eventually suffered if I had not proceeded.

The mixed feelings of providence and lost opportunity that followed my decision to turn down the commissioner position and remain at CDS have never left me. On the one hand, I believed I missed a unique opportunity to make big and lasting changes at OPWDD that would benefit the state financially, and the people we served personally. I admit it would have been a thrilling responsibility to oversee an $8 billion budget that touched hundreds of thousands of people in New York State. On the other hand, I believe I made the correct decision. Jim Introne was likely right with what he told me about the powerlessness people feel in government positions. And the board and people I have worked with at CDS have constantly reminded me of the incredible value I brought, growing the organization in an unprecedented way and leading the organization through crisis. My ability to impact lives at CDS has far outweighed the limited opportunities I would have had as OPWDD commissioner. Finally, my health status was a large, unknown variable in this picture.

Later that year, I would discover my old bypass arteries had become occluded, and once again faced my mortality. My tenure as commissioner would have been short-lived, releasing feelings of failure and regret. I was hit with the realities of my health, but at the same time had dodged a bullet. In my mind, providence had guided me once again.

44
DETERMINATION

AFTER A TURBULENT first year, I became concerned that PCC might not survive. Enrollment grew, but much more slowly than had been projected. Expenses were out of control. As a result, expenses outpaced revenues. The 2020 budget predicted a significant loss. My goal, despite anemic finances, was to keep PCC in good graces with OPWDD. For guidance, I reached out to Jeffrey Sachs, who headed the Sachs Policy Group. Jeffrey invited me to New York City to meet with him and discuss possibilities. I was grateful for his support, hoping that the wisdom he shared would help me and the PCC team figure out next steps; but as it turned out, I narrowly made the flight out of Rochester.

The day I was to fly to New York City and meet with Jeffrey, my assistant regularly monitored my schedule and checked the status of the flight. My meeting with him was at 4:00 p.m., and I was scheduled on a JetBlue flight that would get me there in time. However, just before noon, as I was meeting with the M&T Bank Board of Directors, I received a text from my assistant notifying me my flight was delayed. The good news was that she had found an alternative Delta flight; the bad news was that it was scheduled to lift off from the runway at 1:00 p.m. That meant I had about one hour to make it to the airport, park my car, purchase a ticket, make it through security, and make it to the gate to board the plane. A good athlete might have considered this an acceptable challenge. But I was still recovering from neck surgery and barely able to lift my legs from the ground without stumbling, so any "sprint to the gate" was out of the picture. Nevertheless, I recalled once improbably making a flight out of Guyana, so I excused myself from the M&T Board, grabbed my briefcase, and left.

I arrived at the Delta counter at 12:25 p.m., grateful I didn't get a speeding ticket. I explained to the attendant that I would like to get on the 1:00 p.m. flight to New York City. She looked at the time and said, "Sir, I don't think we can get you on that flight. It's too late."

I pleaded with her, bringing up my meeting, implying it was critical for me to get to New York ("If not for me, do it for the children" type of stuff). Whatever I said must have worked.

While the attendant typed away furiously, my attention was pulled to the check-in counter next to me. Another customer seemed to be in a heated argument with his increasingly flustered counter agent. His voice was getting louder, his face red. "But Mr. Goodman..." she kept trying to interject, unsuccessfully. Evidently "Mr. Goodman" was also trying to get on a flight, although his tactics differed somewhat from mine. I simply turned to my agent and smiled understandingly.

My agent was able to get into the system, but it wouldn't accept my credit card. The agent said, apologetically, that due to the time, the system had closed transactions for the flight. Then a supervisor suddenly appeared as if from nowhere and provided her with a code that allowed the transaction to be completed. She told me she would notify the gate that I was coming. I had my ticket and was on my way to the TSA security checkpoint.

My heart sank when I reached the checkpoint. It looked like lines the day before Thanksgiving. It was now 12:45 p.m. and the terminal door would close in five minutes. Once again, I recalled a distressed, 19-year-old boy in Guyana trying to make it to the airport, confronting a massive bus driver at a bar finishing his lunch. I channeled this young man and yelled out, "Hi everyone. I'm sorry but I have five minutes to make a flight. I hope you're not upset with me, but I must make my way to the head of this line." No one said anything, so I interpreted their silence as assent. More likely it was shock. I worked my way to the front of the line, excusing myself as I passed each passenger.

I placed my bag onto the conveyor belt for screening and passed through the metal detector. I waited. My bag didn't appear. Looking past the TSA agents, I saw my bag was being held up by a "log jam" of other bags, waiting to go through the baggage screen. I boldly stepped *back through* the detector and pushed other bags aside so mine could pass. Passengers just stared at me. Once again through the metal detector, with bag in hand, I waddled to the gate like a baby duck.

When I arrived, the gate was deserted, except for an attendant squinting at her computer. I approached the attendant who looked at me, surprised. I gave her my ticket, holding my breath. To my relief she assured me that the flight hadn't departed yet, but then said, in a somewhat panicked way, "Oh my!" She instructed me to wait as she disappeared down the gangway at a sprint.

I was bewildered until a few minutes later when I heard an angry voice get louder as they came up the gangway and reentered the gate area. The attendant was escorting a furious Mr. Goodman off the plane and back into the airport! As he passed me, he stabbed a finger in my direction and shouted, "He got here *after* me! And you're putting *him* on the plane?"

The attendant said to him flatly, "Sir, all I can tell you is he has a valid ticket and you don't; he's getting on the flight and you're not."

I hurried down the gangway, stepped on board and showed my ticket to the flight attendant. She noticed that I wasn't assigned a seat. After consulting with another flight attendant, she told me there was a seat in first class I could have.

During that entire incident, I had remained focused on one goal: to make it to my meeting with Jeffrey Sachs that afternoon. Failure was not an option. I remained determined and didn't give up, willing at times to take nontraditional steps. But at no time did I become angry or disrespectful—which I suspect may have been one of the reasons I made it onto the flight and Mr. Goodman didn't.

At my meeting with Jeffery, he advised that we focus on two things: preserving PCC's financial health, and working our way out of the state's "enhanced oversight" status. In practice, keeping PCC financially solvent and out of trouble seemed as challenging as catching that Delta flight to New York City. I returned to Rochester committed to helping PCC get out of trouble.

The PCC Board of Directors was concerned and set up a committee to oversee the management's response to the SOD. My confidence in the management was shaken. In my mind, the biggest concern for PCC was how it would work with iCircle when New York rolled out managed care, but it was not the time to address this. PCC had to make improvements in short order; it would either sink or swim.

45
COLLATERAL ARTERIES

PLEASE ALLOW ME to return to where the beginning of my story left off in 2019, lying on the operating table at Rochester General Hospital, with Dr. Ong attempting unsuccessfully to place stents in my blocked arteries.

"Why are you here?" Dr. Ong, again, asked.

"What do you mean, 'Why am I here?'" I asked, puzzled.

He said, "Well, from what we can see, your heart is functioning just fine. I can't see that your heart is in any trouble. I don't understand why you're in my operating room." Evidently this is what he meant by asking, "Why are you here?" As he began wrapping up, he recommended I go back and speak to my cardiologist.

Yvonne and I discussed Dr. Ong's remarks as we returned home from the hospital. We tried to read into them to give us hope. Surely Dr. Ong wouldn't have hesitated to recommend bypass surgery if he felt it was necessary. I contacted my cardiologist's office and spoke to his nurse practitioner, Terri, who said they were reviewing the angiogram and would soon have recommendations.

I returned to work and immediately consulted with Dr. Joel Haas. Joel had been with the organization for about a year and a half and was always willing to discuss my health concerns and interface with my personal doctors, including when I underwent neck surgery. In this way he had become a close confidante. He listened carefully as I explained the events leading up to my angiogram with Dr. Ong.

Joel conducted his own review of my case, including a review of my heart bypass surgery, contributing medical conditions, and recent history. His approach was objective and clinical, but he talked to me like a friend, in language that was easy to follow. Despite the anatomy of my blood vessels, he agreed my heart seemed to be functioning surprisingly well, and not the way a heart would behave that was being gradually starved of oxygen. In my favor, he said one of the feeding vessels was a left internal mammary artery, or LIMA, which was a pipeline bringing blood to my heart. He was impressed by the way I had aggressively managed risk factors like blood pressure, cholesterol, and blood sugar, and that I religiously indulged in exercise. Perhaps my symptoms were unrelated to my heart. He recommended I consult with the surgeon, Dr. Cheerin, who had done my bypass surgery, instead of the cardiologist. The heart surgeon was the true "civil engineer" who could say what was possible. Joel even offered to prepare questions for me to ask the surgeon. I left my meeting with Joel with hope, thinking everything was going to work out OK.

That Sunday morning, Yvonne and I attended Browncroft Community Church in Penfield, as we had done for 15 years. At the end of his sermon, Pastor Robert Cattalani made an "altar call," or summons to the altar, for people needing special prayer. People began filing out of the pews and heading to the altar. At the urging of Yvonne, I took my place in the line that was forming.

At the altar, Ryan, a young man serving on the church's elder board, asked me what was going on. I told him. He placed both hands on my shoulders and offered a prayer. The effect of the prayer was instantaneous. I felt as if all the worries, the concerns, and the preoccupations about mortality evaporated. The sensation was intensely spiritual. I returned to my place beside Yvonne, a changed person.

A few days later Yvonne and I were driving to my appointment with Dr. Cheerin at Rochester General Hospital and my phone rang. Joel called me to share a few more thoughts. He told me the consideration would be the condition of my heart, and whether it could still function and give me adequate quality of life, without surgery. He reviewed the questions he gave me for Dr. Cheerin. Finally, Joel said, "Don't necessarily assume that Dr. Cheerin will recommend open-heart surgery." His words gave me more hope.

As Yvonne and I sat in a conference room waiting for Dr. Cheerin, I felt like I was waiting for a jury to return with a verdict, yet I grabbed on to my experience in church the day before and kept focused on it for dear life. I wanted the sense of peace at the Sunday service to stay and it did. I was no longer worried and afraid. Then the door opened.

Dr. Cheerin entered and sat across from Yvonne and I. He immediately got down to business. He explained that he had carefully reviewed my angiogram and acknowledged that my case was not straightforward. He explained further that four of the five bypass arteries had occluded. But the verdict was not unanimous: the fifth bypass—the one supplied by the LIMA—was "working like a champ." Then he added, "And many new collateral arteries have formed over the last 17 years." He went on to share that my heart had opened new pathways to feed it with blood and oxygen. In his words, my heart "revascularized." There was no urgent need for bypass surgery. Furthermore, surgery would be high-risk. So he advised against surgery.

I was in disbelief, yet very relieved. I still wanted a question answered. "What quality of life can I expect?" I asked.

"Sankar, you're in good health. Since 2002, you've made lifestyle changes that have kept you healthy. Go ahead and live your life." he replied.

Three months later, we went to Spain on a delegation with the American Association on Intellectual and Developmental Disabilities. The trip's purpose was to study how services for people with intellectual disabilities were organized in Spain. We visited Madrid, Bilbao, and Barcelona, and walked extensively. Spain can be quite hilly, and walking uphill, I felt at times as though I was pushing myself and irritating my neck surgery. But I never felt chest pain. My confidence in my health was returning. I was humbled by the fragility of the human body, but I marveled at the body's ability to heal.

When I shared with Dr. Momot, my primary care physician, what Dr. Cheerin had told me about the four arteries that had occluded, and the collateral arteries that had opened, I asked how this had happened.

"The four arteries that closed up," he said, "that was going to happen anyway. They were just thin-walled veins that came from your leg. They are not made to hold up to the pressure in the arteries or last forever. That is why bypass surgery has a shelf life of about 15 years. At that point, most people have to have another bypass, or die from their disease. But the collaterals—*that was all you*. The lifestyle changes you made after your surgery allowed the collaterals to open, fed by the LIMA, even as the other arteries slowly closed up. You have taken care of yourself. You have watched your diet. You exercise every day. You have managed your stress. You did it."

I said a prayer as soon as I left Dr. Momot's office.

The most profound lesson I've learned in my life is that there is so much opportunity for each of us to avail ourselves of God's bounty. We live in the richest country in the world, the United States of America. Life moves at a fast and sometimes furious pace. We are better off if we join in and enjoy the ride. After a life full of drama, challenges, obstacles, and yet so many accomplishments, I can say I have enjoyed the ride and I look forward to staying on the path, even at a slower pace.

46
CDS INTERVENES

THE NEWS FROM my doctors about my heart had affected my outlook on my own future. I turned in earnest to the future of PCC. I advised the CDS Life Transitions Board of Directors to stay fully engaged with the PCC leadership. Since CDS had helped spearhead the launch of PCC, there was general agreement that CDS would provide support if needed. Furthermore, iCircle, an affiliate of CDS, was an established managed care company. Along with iCircle, PCC was the key to bringing managed care to people with IDD.

I surmised that CDS could have control and influence on PCC operations, and turn it around, if it purchased the other owners' financial interests in PCC. I approached CDS Board Chair, Greg Gribben, who had great expertise in such transactions, to explore this possibility. I then worked with Ed Hayes to convene a meeting of the PCC executive committee including Dr. Andy Lopez, a neuropsychologist who ran an organization called Quest in Utica, New York, and had personal experience in the valuation of companies. He recommended that PCC, if it was open to a purchase of its owners' interests, that it engage a valuation firm to place a value on it, and use that information to consider CDS's offer. The CDS Board of Directors held multiple meetings, and spent time on the finances, since the purchase would involve millions of dollars. In my arguments for the purchase, I warned that if PCC continued its downward trajectory, OPWDD had the authority to step in, take control, and assign the membership to other CCOs, which would be a disaster. For reassurance, I reminded them that a group of executives who served on the iCircle Board also served on the PCC Board. Everyone was committed to PCC. Hopefully, we would work collaboratively and agree on a path forward.

Without PCC, I continued my argument to the CDS Board, iCircle would not have enough covered lives (members) to operate a managed care plan for individuals with IDD. If we didn't shore up PCC, we might as well shut down iCircle. There was not one word of disagreement. The CDS Life Transitions Board agreed to purchase the financial interests of the 17 owners of PCC, including CDS Monarch.

But getting CDS Life Transitions to agree to a purchase was just the first step. I had to convince the rest of the PCC organizations to sell their interests. I floated the idea of a buyout to Ed Hayes. He conceded that the finances of PCC were fragile, and was receptive to the proposal. I explained that CDS Life Transitions was prepared to pay a substantial amount to the owners. Furthermore, the sale to CDS Life Transitions was necessary to prevent PCC from financial ruin and eventual demise.

"And to be honest, I'm busy enough with my own job," Ed added, suggesting the problems at PCC were creating a burden. I reassured him that PCC would maintain independent governance, which was a State requirement.

At a PCC Board meeting in November of 2019, I delivered a presentation on how CDS Life Transitions proposed to purchase the financial interests of the owners. I captured the history of our efforts in the Finger Lakes region—coming together to prevent a monopoly in the managed care system for people with IDD, which was attempted by the group in Buffalo. Sixteen private nonprofit organizations had banded together with CDS to create our own path, providing leadership and financial resources. Together, we established iCircle, a nonprofit managed care company, which continued to grow day by day, and gain experience in the managed care insurance arena. Establishing PCC as a CCO put us in the best position to be an IDD managed care company. As I scanned the room, I reassured all the PCC owners that the CDS proposal to purchase the financial interests of the owners was mainly to protect PCC's and iCircle's future. Further, I reassured everyone that PCC would retain its independent governance structure—the people in that very room.

After months of negotiation, a small group of PCC Board members assigned to negotiate with CDS Life Transitions came to me with their offer. They said, "Here's our price. If you give us this price, the PCC Board of Directors will approve it." Their number was almost twice what CDS Life Transition had been ready to offer. I was shocked. Nevertheless, I knew I had to find a way to make the sale go through.

Finally, I devised a solution to the impasse. With the approval of the CDS Board of Directors, I reached out to the PCC negotiating group and through intensive discussions we came up with a viable proposal. A portion of the sale price would be put in escrow for four years in the event there was a payback to New York State. If no payback materialized, the funds would be released to the owners. At the last minute, one of the owners tried to cut a side deal with me but that was quickly shot down. The purchase of the financial interests proceeded when the PCC Board approved the transaction.

47
THE RIGHT PLACE AT THE RIGHT TIME

WITH ALL THE due diligence done, the legal teams representing both parties simply needed to collect signatures from all the owners, each of whom had already voted for the transaction. On the day set for the transaction to be completed, I was in the office trying to work as if it was a normal day, but I had difficulty focusing. I was startled each time the phone rang.

Around 11:00 in the morning, one of the calls that came through was from Greg Gribben. "We have one holdout on the purchase," he said.

"Well, who is it?" I asked, puzzled.

"The call was strange," Greg said. "The lawyer for PCC gave no explanations. He only said that the executive director of one of the IDD organizations told their attorney that she was uncomfortable selling their interest to CDS Life Transitions."

I was concerned. It was the 11th hour, and everyone wanted the process to be over. "Who's the attorney?" I asked.

"An attorney at the Barclay Damon law firm. Through its Rochester office," Greg said. He gave me the lawyer's name and we ended the call. I was in a state of agitation, and thankful my collateral coronary arteries were working. *We've worked tirelessly on this project. Come hell or high water, this transaction is going through*, I thought.

About six months prior, a good friend of mine, Glenn Pezzulo, who was on the CDS Life Transitions Board, had joined the Barclay Damon law firm. I immediately called him and asked if he knew the attorney that Greg told me about.

Glenn replied, "I do. His office is just down the hall from mine—why?"

"CDS needs your help," I said, and explained the predicament. Glenn agreed to meet with his colleague and convince him to advise his client, the hold-out executive director, to sign the documents. After I ended my conversation with Glenn, an agonizing hour passed before he called me back.

"I talked to the attorney, Sankar, and unfortunately he was noncommittal," Glenn said. Then he continued, "I must admit, the whole conversation felt odd. Even though I took the time to explain how, as a board member, I was proud of the great work CDS Life Transitions did, and that the sale of PCC would preserve their place in the future of managed care for individuals with IDD, he just kept looking out the window. He wouldn't even look me in the eye."

I thanked Glenn for his advocacy. There was nothing else to do. I remained optimistic that something good would happen. After another hour passed, Greg Gribben called back. "Great news," he said cheerfully. "I don't know what happened, but I just heard that the executive director who was holding out signed the document."

I exhaled. Once again, I felt as if providence had a hand. Fortunately, Glenn had moved to Barclay Damon only six months before. Had Glenn not been on the board, and moved to Barclay Damon, the transaction would have been dead in the water.

Then came a new wrinkle from M&T Bank, which had approved the loan. Evidently, the relationship manager handling the loan transaction hadn't secured clearance to move ahead. Although the underwriters at the bank received the documents, no one had bothered to look at them. I was dumbfounded. This loan was a no-brainer for the bank because the CDS Wolf Foundation agreed to serve as a guarantor. If we forfeited, the bank would get the money, regardless. They had zero exposure.

I reached out to a senior officer at the bank, Dan Burns, a friend and fellow member at Oak Hill Country Club, and asked him to do whatever he could to expedite the transaction. He told me he would do what he could, but could not make promises. I was disheartened to think that months of planning and negotiations could be sucked down the proverbial drain because of a simple bureaucratic oversight.

At 4:15 p.m., clearance for the purchase came through under the wire. Dan had done it.

For the first time in months, I felt optimistic about PCC's future. It had become personal. I fully believed that iCircle and PCC were poised to come together for the benefit of individuals with IDD.

I am reminded of a young man, Matthew Gabello, whose story makes my efforts seem small in comparison. He came to my attention when he was selected to participate in the 2024 Special Olympics Italia Winter Games in Italy as an ambassador of the United States. CDS was buzzing with the news.

Many of the staff knew him as an early participant in PCC. Along with Matthew's disability diagnosis, he was given limits, but he simply ignored them—and so did his mother. Over the years, PCC staff had helped him and his mother navigate all the agencies and access resources, sometimes finding support they didn't know existed. When he took an interest in ice skating at age 17, he decided to take professional lessons. What is more, his care coordinator, Erica, helped him receive reimbursement for all his skating classes.

I suspect that no one could tell Matthew that he couldn't do something. If they did, he would say, "Watch this," and prove them wrong. And he was proving it—from the small skating rinks in Rochester, New York, to the world stage in Italy.

If he could do it, so can I and you. Never give up because you think something is impossible.

48
COVID RESPONSE

IN EARLY FEBRUARY of 2020, Yvonne and I traveled to Los Cabos, Mexico, to a conference sponsored by our workers' compensation insurance captive, Raffles. On that trip I read the unraveling story about a novel respiratory virus that had originated in China in late December 2019 and was spreading to other parts of the world. Originally the World Health Organization (WHO) tried to put the world at ease, claiming it had "no evidence of human-to-human spread." By the end of January, however, this assessment proved to be wrong, and WHO had declared a global health emergency. The virus had been identified as a coronavirus and given a name: COVID-19; it was already in the United States, but hadn't yet reached New York State. COVID-19 was preparing to become a global pandemic, and early data suggested it carried a mortality rate 10 times greater than the influenza virus.

I forwarded the article to Dr. Haas to get his opinion and his assessment of the potential risk to our organization—not only our employees, but the elderly, frail individuals we served in their homes who could be especially vulnerable to a novel virus. I would come to realize how provident it was to have Dr. Haas in our organization as the virus spread to the United States and New York State, and eventually to our doorstep.

The national and local news was updated multiple times a day as the virus spread exponentially. Then on March 1, 2020, it happened: the first case of COVID-19 was reported in New York State and within two weeks it had breached our shores into Monroe County. We moved into action. Bulletins from the New York State Department of Health began regularly filling the inbox of our email. One week later, the country shut down. New terms entered our collective lexicon, like "social distancing" and "flattening the curve."

To do my part as CEO, I talked regularly with Dr. Haas as we developed a robust COVID Pandemic Preparedness Plan that incorporated recommendations from local and national health organizations and held daily video conferences with the executive team for status updates. Our priority was the safety of the individuals we served and our staff. The meetings were very helpful in managing the demands placed on the staff across our multiservice organization. From our residences for people with intellectual disabilities to the day programs, the Unistel spice packaging plant, the iCircle MLTC care management services, Prime Care Coordination and Warrior Salute, we sought out and provided information to the employees constantly to maintain the confidence of the staff on the frontlines.

After my executive team conferences, I advised the board members of what was going on, providing any news and obtaining their guidance. One of our concerns was that the frontline staff in our CDS residences and caregivers in the iCircle MLTC Program might not show up to work, either because they were ill, or they had concerns for themselves and their families. Remarkably, everyone chose to come to work every day, knowing full well that every time they were placing themselves at risk for exposure to COVID. I was most grateful for their service at that critical time.

Like most Americans, although we needed to stay safe and avoid becoming ill, our lives couldn't come to a complete halt. At the height of COVID in 2020, my family began to feel cloistered and restless, so we decided to accept some risk and travel to Universal Studios in Florida. With my health issues, I was mindful that I was in a "high-risk" category. This had to be balanced with my strong desire to be with my family. Universal had done a remarkable job of handling the pandemic. All safety protocols had been implemented, and were being enforced, for all the guests. Seating was spaced out on park buses that limited capacity to 25 percent. Social distancing was in place everywhere. Hand sanitizer stations were set up at every turn. Masks were required at all times when in public. Temperature check stations were set up at the entrances of every hotel. The efforts worked: I returned home from that trip without catching COVID.

Like at Universal Studios, we set up strict protocols—including quarantine protocols for exposed and ill individuals—at our headquarters and our residences. In cooperation with the local Department of Health, a testing station was set up at our headquarters, and Dr. Haas traveled to the residences to test individuals who were suspected of having COVID. Eventually, when the COVID vaccines were released, Dr. Haas educated the staff on the benefits and risks of the vaccine, and even arranged COVID vaccine clinics for all our staff.

But, eventually, I was unable to wait out the pandemic without catching COVID. My responsibilities as CEO put me in potential contact with many people. Despite my efforts, I became ill. I developed some head congestion and a headache. I wasn't too concerned because I had been vaccinated. Out of caution I stayed home for two days, and seemed to recover. Feeling much better, I went to work on the third day. Out of an abundance of caution, I asked Dr. Haas to come to my office and administer the COVID test. I was surprised when it showed that I was positive for COVID. I left headquarters and isolated myself in my home office.

My quarantine was actually not all that bad. It was a "mixed blessing." It forced me to decompress from the stress of my work and responsibilities, and I could enjoy reading my books without a sense of guilt. My grandchildren came to visit every day to give me support, making sure to maintain a safe distance. Looking back, I believe those were some of my most enjoyable days.

Now that we can look back and reflect on how our country, and the world, responded to COVID, we can see that many did their best under the circumstances, and we can admit that mistakes were made. Of course, we were dealing with an unknown virus, with an unknown behavior, and when this happens, fear overrides rationality. Furthermore, our health leaders had to apply what they knew, borrowing from experiences with previous pandemics. And there were big gaps in knowledge that needed to be filled. But analyzing some of the decisions that were made, I realized that these decisions are never made independent of politics and power. We think of science—and medical science—as being objective and free of political influence. But it never is. Hopefully, for all the people who died and those who suffered physically and mentally during this pandemic, their suffering has not been in vain, and we will be able to deal with the next pandemic—there will always be another pandemic—much more effectively and wisely.

49
HARD DECISIONS

ONE DAY IN June of 2020, I learned that the iCircle providers serving our members weren't being paid on time, and some were not getting paid at all. I didn't see how this was possible. We were obligated to pay providers within 45 days of receiving an invoice, and iCircle had a reputation for paying its vendors on time; so this news represented a disturbing deviation from our practice. Even more confusing, iCircle's financial auditors had reported that its finances were in order. *What was I missing?*

As I laid in bed at night, unable to sleep, inner alarms were telling me this was just a symptom of a much more serious problem. My sixth sense was telling me iCircle was in deep financial trouble.

The following day, after sleeping very little, I was able to confirm in a meeting with my staff that iCircle wasn't paying providers on time, and the line of credit was fully tapped. I consulted with the board of directors, and they agreed to bring in an external accounting firm to perform a forensic audit. Since iCircle MLTC was contracted by New York State Medicaid, we were legally required to report financial irregularities and troubles to the Department of Health. A meeting was arranged. An audit was called for.

The board of directors hired Fust Charles and Chambers and its subsidiary, Microscope, LLC, based in Syracuse, to perform the audit. Within a month, they provided new and adjusted financial statements. These showed that in the prior two years, instead of running profits as had been reported by iCircle's CFO, iCircle ran *deep losses*. In fact, iCircle was standing over a significant multimillion-dollar hole.

The next step was the most difficult. I notified the Department of Health about the problem we uncovered. Donna Frescatore, the New York State Medicaid director, requested a phone conference. Before the call, I sought advice from Jim Introne. We decided full transparency was the best course of action. I decided it would be best for me to "fall on my sword" and apologize to the Medicaid director for the situation. It was the correct posture to take. By the time the call ended, the conversation shifted from assigning blame to deciding how to fix the problem. It was certainly within the Department of Health's authority to withdraw iCircle's MLTC license. But instead, the Medicaid director graciously chose to work with iCircle and give it time to fix the problem.

Similarly, we notified the Centers for Medicaid and Medicare Service (CMS) of the financial issues. They were not as understanding, and responded by promptly withdrawing their conditional approval for our Dual Special Needs Plan license that we had been working on for over a year. That license would have allowed us to expand benefits and assist individuals with IDD, and members of the iCircle MLTC who qualified for both Medicare and Medicaid, to bring all their health care needs under one plan. Losing CMS approval was a huge blow to iCircle and our organization.

Next we had to begin to work on making payment arrangements with providers. iCircle needed its provider network to operate, and failure to pay risked losing those providers. All this had to be done under strictest confidentiality while protecting our staff from uncertainty. I was always of the view that leadership needed to carry the burden of such decisions and not spread it through the ranks, including frontline staff. Since they fielded the provider complaints, leadership gave full support and reassurances. Telling the hardworking staff that the company was insolvent would have had devastating effects. Staff would have left iCircle like a burning ship. The best way they could help was to continue doing their work while we resolved the finances.

I was committed not to let stress impact my health or my ability to do my job. I was a demanding boss, setting high expectations of everyone, and I believe it was because of this that the staff performed magnificently during the crisis. To ensure morale stayed high, I avoided being pulled into a vortex of panic and doom, and I kept the message simple: *Do your job, and everything will be OK.*

But crisis after crisis was taking its toll. My doctor finally convinced me that I was still human and not invincible, and I needed to retire. The problem with my heart, while it resolved favorably, was still a warning. Behind the scenes, I was mapping out a two-year path for me to hand over the reins to a new CEO, and had conversations with the board.

In early 2022, I announced my retirement, setting a target for 2023. But since the iCircle financial crisis had happened on my watch, I was determined to resolve it before my exit and not leave it as a legacy for the future CEO. Consequently, I continued to work tirelessly with the board of directors to perform a forensic analysis of the iCircle problem and design a solution. To this end, Greg Gribben, Rich Yarmel and Rich Ferrari, all committed leaders of the CDS Life Transitions Board, spent countless hours on the phone with me, providing their wisdom and unique perspectives.

Committed to a solution, I reached out to close friends who understood the health insurance business. One day, I called Jim Introne to explore our options.

"Sankar, you guys don't have any money," Jim told me matter-of-factly. "Why do you feel you must pay the providers at their full rates?"

This never occurred to me. We had signed contracts with these providers, who provided services for iCircle in good faith with the understanding they would be paid. Our reputation was predicated on this principle, and no less. We had a legal obligation to honor our contract.

"That doesn't mean you can't renegotiate rates with these providers," he continued. "They already know fully well that your finances are upside down. They might be reassured that you are trying to pay them *something*, rather than nothing at all."

This wasn't the solution I was expecting. We had given these providers our word, and I considered reneging on our word the first step on a slippery slope that led to the slow demise of iCircle.

Jim continued, "By what you have told me, it is doubtful that you will be able to get out of this unless you drastically cut rates to your providers." He expressed resentment that the providers were constantly expecting to be made whole at iCircle's expense. He added, "Now you can invite them to be part of the solution—if they want this work in the long term."

He left me to make a hard decision, but I knew Jim was right. In consultation with the iCircle CFO, we announced a 20 percent rate reduction, on average, for the providers. Not all providers were handled the same; we had preferred providers who had worked with us in the past on reasonable rates, or who had provided critical services. Nevertheless, everyone was going to get a haircut. We prepared for the tidal wave of complaints, but we had to keep ourselves anchored. Our survival depended on it.

This worked. Remarkably, reducing our provider payments lowered our expenses by over $15 million on an annualized basis. Then we reduced staffing costs by about $1 million. To all this we added retroactive payments we received from New York State. Working together, the combination of these measures allowed iCircle to effect *a complete financial turnaround within 18 months*. We were in a deep hole, millions of dollars in the red, and ended up above water in a year and a half. It was miraculous. And we accomplished this with no cash infusions from New York State, or elsewhere.

Now that our finances were restored, another issue remained: the Dual Special Needs Plan license that CMS had retracted. I reached out to the new New York State Medicaid Director and requested that he support our reapplication, considering iCircle's fast financial turnaround. He was happy to help—provided we could provide proof of current and future solvency.

I understood the only proof of our financial turnaround that would satisfy the New York State Department of Health and the Department of Financial Services would have to come from an independent audit of iCircle's 2021 financial statements. I incentivized Fust Charles Chambers to expedite their annual audit, and by February of 2022 we obtained a complete audit of iCircle's financial statements, an accomplishment which was unprecedented. Standard audits were typically completed over four months. This was nothing close to "standard," and we got it done in half the time.

The Fust Charles Chambers audit team's numbers aligned perfectly with the numbers provided by iCircle's staff; we promptly provided the audited statements to the Department of Health and they approved us to proceed with the DSNP reapplication.

We accomplished the improbable. To prevent a similar recurrence, we completely overhauled the policies and procedures and reorganized staff. Some were asked to leave. We did the hard work, and my staff deserved all the credit. Above all, a special extension of extreme gratitude must be given to iCircle Chief Operating Officer, Sharon Marble, who did all she could to maintain staff stability, motivating them to work beyond their comfort zones to get the job done.

Taking responsibility for what transpired never escaped me. I answered to the iCircle Board of Directors and the CDS Life Transitions Board of Directors, both of which stood by me every step of the way, as did Greg Gribben, the board chair. I'm forever grateful for their loyalty to the organization, their commitment, and their patience and generosity to me during this difficult time.

The transition from one CEO to another can be disruptive and turbulent, as happened at CDS in the late 1990s. Sometimes several trials are needed to find the right executive. Thankfully, we didn't have to repeat the trials of the late 1990s with my departure. We planned the succession, and executed it, over a two-year period. A lot of credit goes to the board of directors that ultimately made all the key decisions for the transition, including choosing my successor—my son, Andrew.

In March of 2023, I retired from CDS Life Transitions, an organization touching and improving over 15,000 lives in upstate New York. From its humble beginnings, the organization remains vibrant with more than 1,200 highly skilled and dedicated staff, and an annual budget of over $300 million.

What an improbable journey!

CONCLUSION

Coming to America as a legal immigrant from the third world to becoming the CEO of CDS, helping it become a 300 million dollar company and achieving my American Dream has been a most fulfilling, rewarding and wonderful journey. I have been truly blessed to enjoy a thirty three year career at CDS of which twenty five were as its CEO. Then, I decided to retire not fully appreciating what it entailed. Retiring from a job that I lived 24 hours a day has been an adjustment- easier said than done. I can't help that my mind is always busy. Though, after two years, I am finally settling into a routine that allows me to relax and enjoy myself.

I've found that you can make all the plans you want and envision all the great things you'll do during retirement—only to find that for a period you are stuck in the past, and effort is required to move forward. As with any major life change, you must forge a way forward to find new meaning, and that usually requires an excavation of what's come before. Writing this book has been an exercise in that process.

Reflecting on my journey at CDS Life Transitions—what the company does for our citizens and where it's headed with my son, Andrew, its CEO—I remain uplifted and excited. CDS opened one residence for 10 people with intellectual disabilities in 1977, and 47 years later it touches more than 15,000 lives in upstate New York. It has under its umbrella distinct and diversified mission based businesses that will endure. The future is bright.

I hope that CDS continues its march forward with the confidence placed in it by the good citizens of our community. I hope the organization continues its tradition of serving people without regard for their families' socioeconomic status. CDS clearly has a leadership role in how services are delivered in upstate New York. As it moves its footprints to other states, it has an opportunity to build more innovative and inspiring businesses, which are desperately needed.

Retirement has given me more time to consider religion, which has always had a huge influence on me. While my father remained a Hindu until he died, my mother, my siblings, and I attended church and came to believe in Christ's teachings. Later, at Uncle Isaac's church in New Amsterdam, a large city in Berbice right along the Berbice river, I accepted Christ into my life and was baptized.

I'm 68 years old now, and while I have an abiding faith in Christ and believe in him, I still don't have answers to questions that arise in my mind from time to time: *Why do bad things happen to good people? How does a caring God allow a little child to suffer and die, and yet let a murderer live? Why does God allow humans to commit the most heinous crimes? How is it that a murderer can accept Christ on his dying bed and be forgiven? Will I see my father in heaven, a man who lived a life worshipping his God? How can a God who created human beings stand by and watch suffering all over the world? Is God so distant that He does not see what is going on?* When I look up at the stars at night and wonder about the universe and our planet's place in it, I can't help but think that our constructs of God, our creator, is quite limited, and there is much we cannot and do not understand.

I accept Christ as my savior by faith. His abiding presence helps me to embrace every day with strength, courage and a deep sense of peace.

I believe that we're born with a conscience, and we innately know right from wrong. I have made my share of mistakes and have learned from every one of them. I had to find ways to get over deep rooted pain and hurt. It was up to me to make peace and forge a new path forward. This led me to experiencing the power of forgiveness and the healing it brings.

Many improbable things have happened to me as I chronicled in this book. I remain confident that with God's help and his purpose for me on this earth, I can continue to be of value wherever He leads me.

The most rewarding part of retirement is spending more time with my grandchildren. Yvonne and I are truly blessed to have these special human beings in our lives. When they are with us, they have our total attention and their love sustains us in more ways than they will ever know. A special thank you to Andrew and his wife, Emy, for allowing us to be with our most favorite people; David, Caleb, Lily and Hayley.

As for my health, by all accounts, I should have died a long time ago, yet I am still here. With severe medical issues, my body was "carved up like a Thanksgiving turkey". Yet, I feel blessed. My neck is doing extremely well, considering that *five vertebrae are fused together*. Surgery on my lower back has helped me to remain active. I live with daily physical pain, which reminds me that I'm alive and doing well. My heart, which suffered two attacks, reorganized itself, creating new collateral arteries when the bypass arteries were no longer viable. As the Bible chorus I sang as a child in Sunday school says: "This little heart of mine, I'm gonna let it shine." And I have. It keeps me going every day. In closing, I'd like to share with you a few verses of one of my favorite songs by Bethel Music and Jenn Johnson. It's called the Goodness of God:

> **I love you, Lord, Oh, your mercy never fails me**
> **All my days, I've been held in Your hands**
> From the moment that I wake up, Until I lay my head
> Oh, I will sing of the goodness of God

And all my life you have been faithful,
And all my life you have been so, so good
With every breath that I am able
 I will sing of the goodness of God

I love your voice, You have led me through the fire
And in the darkness night, You are close like no other
I've known you as a father, I've known you as a friend
And I've lived in the goodness of God, Yeah

It is my sincere wish that you find this book helpful. May God bless you.

From left: Caleb, Lily, Emy, Andrew, me, Yvonne, Abigayle, David, and Hayley

Emy and Andrew with their children, from left: David, Caleb, Hayley, and Lily

REVIEW INQUIRY

Hey, it's Sankar here.

I hope you've enjoyed the book, finding it both useful and fun. I have a favor to ask you.

Would you consider giving it a rating wherever you bought the book? Online book stores are more likely to promote a book when they feel good about its content, and reader reviews are a great barometer for a book's quality.

So please go to the website of wherever you bought the book, search for my name and the book title, and leave a review. If able, perhaps consider adding a picture of you holding the book. That increases the likelihood your review will be accepted!

Many thanks in advance,

Sankar Sewnauth

WILL YOU SHARE THE LOVE?

Get this book for a friend, associate, or family member!

If you have found this book valuable and know others who would find it useful, consider buying them a copy as a gift. Special bulk discounts are available if you would like your whole team or organization to benefit from reading this book. Just contact sankarsewnauth@gmail.com.

WOULD YOU LIKE SANKAR SEWNAUTH TO SPEAK TO YOUR ORGANIZATION?

Book Sankar Now!

Sankar Sewnauth accepts a limited number of speaking/coaching/training engagements each year. To learn how you can bring his message to your organization, visit sdsconsultingservices.com. You may also contact him at either http://sdsmgmtllc.com or by email at sankarsewnauth@gmail.com.

ACKNOWLEDGMENTS

My journey from the third world to becoming the CEO of a major nonprofit organization in upstate New York wouldn't have been possible without the people who helped me along the way. Many are mentioned in the book. It's worth repeating that my family's support has meant the world to me: My beautiful wife of 43 years, Yvonne, is a wonderful partner and mother. She has made my life worth living every day. Without her, I don't know where I would be. She has stood by me every step of the way. I'm sure she would say that I took the part of the wedding vow, "in sickness and in health," to its extreme. Having someone with whom I can enjoy the twilight of my life is wonderful.

My children, Abigayle and Andrew, are living meaningful and God-fearing lives that make us proud. We love them dearly. They are good citizens. My grandchildren, David, Caleb, Lily, and Hayley, are wonderful human beings growing and developing with the guidance of their wonderful mother, Emy, and their father, Andrew. They fill our lives with immense joy and richness because of who they are.

Looking back at our parents, Sewnauth and Shiela, I'm filled with gratitude for their sacrifices bringing up five children while dealing with their personal difficulties. My siblings, Sabita, Indro (deceased), Devo, Jankie, and I have grown close over the years. The struggles of our emotion-packed lives, coupled with our individual accomplishments, have hopefully established an enduring family legacy. We all have children and grandchildren.

Yvonne's family has contributed so much to our lives. Yvonne's father, Basil, and her mother, Jean, together with Yvonne's sisters, Rebecca (Shivon) and Ramona (Shelly), have treated me like family from day one. Since my brothers-in-law, Rohan and Dron (Rick), joined the family, we established a bond that has remained strong these many years.

This project wouldn't have been complete without me telling the CDS journey. Along the way, I met remarkable people who dedicated themselves to their children and others with special needs at CDS. Their vision to create an organization that cared for their loved ones, providing opportunities for them to live fulfilling lives, became my vision. My life was forever changed when I first met them as a young and inexperienced direct care employee. Your trust and love have made my life journey every bit rewarding and fulfilling. As we look back at my journey, I hope I made you all proud.

Lew and Phyllis Wolf, CDS's key founders, sacrificed on behalf of their son, Daryl, and others to build CDS into a resilient and transformative organization. The faith, unwavering love, and loyalty they placed in me will never be forgotten. Every day, as I walked up the stairs at the CDS headquarters and passed by their elegant photograph, I reminded myself of their love and sacrifice.

Board members who stood by me along the way include: Mark Peterson, Kevin LeGrett, Jim Zimmer, Bob McFadden, Dr. Norm Allentoff, Daniel Crozet, Greg Gribben, Doug Gosnell, General Robert Dail, General Robert Mixon, Jen Carlson, Rich Yarmel, Bill Woodard, Pat Manuel, Edward Hayes, Warren Hern, Doug Usiak, Scott Benjamin, Dr. Andy Lopez, Dr. Pierre Girgis, Ann Marie Cook, Rene Snyder, Mary Boatfield, Hilda Escher, Ron Thomas, Maria Dibble, Susan Travis, and so many more. I couldn't have done the job without their steadfast support.

Staff members who helped me on the CDS journey and some who continue to dedicate themselves to CDS are: Sy Zielinski, Deb Bean, Sharon Marble, Judy Consadine, Kate Wagner, Dr. Joel Haas, Damian Marinaccio, Rich Staggert, Patty Arcese, Brian Stephenson,

ACKNOWLEDGMENTS

Laura Southern, Deb Haskins, Rebecca Henderson, Melissa Brown, Sandy Brown, Chris Ryan, Terria Thompson, Mark Curletta, Tom DeRoller, Justin Mirando, Steve Singley, Bruce Schulze, Eddie Favro, Carlos Morales, Beth Grier-Leva, Jeff Sanderson, Michelle Schwartz, Kim Albert, Rene Chichester, Carrie Carra, and so many more.

To the friends outside CDS who stood by my side during some trying times, I say thank you. They are: Cenette Burdine, Jim Introne, Jeffrey Sachs, Bruce Feig, and Justin McCarthy, CDS's lobbyist and a dear friend, who passed away in 2023.

To the doctors who continue to provide the support to me that has kept me going, I am very grateful. They are: Deniz Pirincci, Christopher Momot, Joel Haas, Pierre Girgis, Al Lanni, and Bipul Baibhav. I've given them enough opportunity to know every inch of me. They have provided indispensable advice. Thank you.

To Pastor Rob Cattalani and his staff at Browncroft Community Church (BCC), thank you. Being part of the BCC church family means a lot to me and my family, whether we attend in person or online.

To the individuals with special needs whom I considered friends, you are in my heart forever. Some that come to mind are: David, Don, Kelly, Krissy, Hubert, Anne, Dudley, Gary, Bobby, and Jay. Thank you for the honor to serve you.

To the frontline, direct care, and clinical staff, you are the backbone of the organization. I am grateful to you for your dedication to the people we serve. To the frontline and mid-level managers, you juggle priorities every day and do it so well. Keep up the good work.

As I look back at the writing process, I can say it takes a willingness to confront one's vulnerabilities. To help me with this and so much more was my editor, Cindy Childress, whose steadfastness kept us on point. She helped me organize my thoughts while skillfully taking everything I wrote and making it better. I could not have done this project without her.

When I was advised to have a second-tier edit of the book, I could think of no one else to help but Dr. Joel Haas. We all know him to be a first-rate physician, but what people may not know is that he is also a first-rate writer. He readily agreed and dedicated many hours to scrutinizing every line, improving the book beyond words.

I also wish to thank Everett O'Keefe, founder and president of Ignite Press, who encouraged me along the way, and who provided insights into the publishing process. I appreciate him taking on this project.

I've mentioned providence throughout the book—that without God's presence in my life, I would have been long gone from this earth. I am reminded every day of his love and abiding presence.

CODA: NEVER GIVE UP

Recently, I visited General Bob Dail in Myrtle Beach, South Carolina, traveling on American Airlines. To go there and back to Rochester, New York, I had one stop in Charlotte, North Carolina. Everything was fine on the way to Myrtle Beach, but not on the route home. I was leaving Myrtle Beach on a Friday, and that's just not a good day to fly. Sure enough, my departing flight from Myrtle Beach was delayed by an hour. The flight landed in Charlotte right about the time my flight from Charlotte to Rochester was scheduled to take off. As the plane taxied, I looked at my phone. American Airlines had sent an email notification that they had already rebooked me on a flight to Rochester to depart *five hours later* that night. I was tired and just wanted to get home. Sitting in the airport for that long did not appeal to me. I decided not to accept the rebooking, convinced that if I tried I could get home earlier.

After exiting the plane, I went to my originally scheduled gate. Perhaps the flight was delayed, as many were that Friday. The airport was *very* crowded. Travelers were congregated in droves at every gate, such that there was barely room as I made my way along the wide walkway. I glanced at an American Airlines schedule monitor, scanning for my flight to Rochester. The departure time was delayed 12 minutes with only 5 minutes left, but I wasn't dissuaded. When I arrived at the gate, the area was mostly empty, with a short line of passengers going through the boarding process. So I stepped in line. Hope arose even though I wasn't out of the woods yet. Since the airline had rebooked me onto another flight, they had likely assigned my seat to someone else.

My turn arrived, and I handed the gate agent my phone. He scanned my boarding pass. His computer beeped, and instead of a green light, I saw a red beam reflecting on his uniform. *Of course, American Airlines gave up my seat,* I thought, but I said nothing to the agent. He scanned the boarding pass again with the same result. I remained stoic. He asked for my identification and handed it to his associate who began entering information on another computer. This went on for about five minutes. The flight was possibly full, with no seat left for me. I held my breath, hoping there was one empty seat.

Then the printer behind the counter whirred. The agent reached for the boarding pass, scanned it, and handed it to me. I didn't even look at my seat assignment; I just entered the jetway. My new seat was in the middle of three seats. I always prefer an aisle seat, but that was no time to get picky. At least I was on my regularly scheduled flight and didn't have to endure an avoidable five-hour layover. That's not the end of the story.

As my flight lifted off, I realized my golf bag was very likely not on that flight. I hoped the airline would sort it out. You see, I was scheduled to play a round of golf at 9:00 the next morning with my buddies at Oak Hill Country Club. I didn't want to disappoint them.

To my pleasant surprise, I landed in Rochester and read an email from American Airlines notifying me that my golf bag would be arriving in Rochester on the late flight that night. To retrieve my clubs I would have to return to the airport when that flight arrived around midnight. Or I could see if American Airlines would deliver my golf bag early the next morning.

I went to the American Airlines office by the arrivals area and the young woman at the counter wanted to help. I explained my predicament. Upon finding my information on her computer, she informed me that the golf bag would be arriving in Rochester late that night, something I already knew. I told her about the scheduled golf outing the following morning and pleaded with her to find a way for the clubs to be delivered first thing the next day. She said it was possible they could be delivered early, but she wasn't confident because someone on the overnight shift would make that decision. She agreed to impress upon that person that the golf clubs had to be delivered to our home early the next morning. We agreed she would call my cell phone with an update after speaking with the overnight personnel. I left the airport thinking that there was a 50/50 chance my golf clubs would make it to our home early the next morning.

By bedtime, I hadn't received a call from the young lady in the AA office. I wished I'd asked what time the next shift started. I usually left my cell phone on a charger downstairs overnight, but that night I kept the phone on the nightstand by my bed. No call awakened me during the night.

I got up at 7:00 a.m. and checked my phone. No missed calls. No email with an update. I used the AA app to track my bag. It confirmed that my bag was still at the airport. Through the app I called AA's toll-free number, but reached the call center serving the entire United States; they had no additional information and couldn't give me a local number to call. I noticed that AA also communicated via a texting service on their app. I decided to try it. Soon a live agent replied. I provided all the necessary information and waited. Maybe I would hear good news.

After a few minutes, I received a text back from the agent saying that my golf bag was delivered at 6:15 a.m. I rushed to my front door, opened it, and saw nothing directly ahead of me. However, as I glanced to the left, the edge of my black golf bag came into view. I started laughing. I never thought of checking the front door for the golf bag because I was told not to expect a delivery until after the AA office opened at 7:30 a.m.

American Airlines came through for me. The young lady and the overnight staff at their Rochester airport office were magnificent. They exceeded my expectations. I made sure to give everyone the highest rating when I took the airline's survey. I had plenty of time to prepare for my round of golf. I poured myself a cup of coffee, feeling pleased with myself for not giving up and enlisting others to help me achieve my goal. Everything that transpired from Charlotte to Rochester was so improbable; it reaffirmed my feeling that these things happen to me for a reason: *I never give up.*

ABOUT THE AUTHOR

Sankar Sewnauth is the retired president and CEO of CDS Life Transitions Inc., where he transformed a struggling nonprofit into a $300 million enterprise over 25 years. An immigrant from Guyana, Sankar embodies the American Dream, rising from delivering direct care to pioneering innovative solutions for individuals with disabilities, veterans, and families. A graduate of Eastern Nazarene College (BA) and SUNY Brockport (MPA), he now shares his expertise through SDS Management Consulting Services, helping businesses achieve growth and impact. Sankar's story is one of perseverance, resilience, and purpose, offering inspiration to anyone pursuing their dreams. He lives in Penfield, New York, with his wife, Yvonne, and their family. Sankar can be reached at: sdsconsultingservices.com

Made in the USA
Middletown, DE
25 May 2025